Women in Twentieth-Century Literature: A Jungian View

WOMEN IN TWENTIETH-CENTURY LITERATURE: A Jungian View

BETTINA L. KNAPP

The Pennsylvania State University Press
University Park and London

To Estelle and Stephen with love and admiration

With my deepest gratitude and thanks to Alba Amoia for her editorial assistance and her friendship.

Library of Congress Cataloging-in-Publication Data

Knapp, Bettina Liebowitz, 1926–
Women in twentieth-century literature.

Bibliography: p.
Includes index.
1. Women in literature. 2. Literature, Modern—20th century—History and criticism. 3. Psychoanalysis and literature. 4. Jung, C.G. (Carl Gustav), 1875–1961. I. Title.
PN56.5.W64K57 1987 809′.93352042 86-43033
ISBN 0-271-00493-2

Printed in the United States of America

Contents

Introduction

Dr. Jung: The unconscious begins at the boundary line of the field of vision, and back of that is invisibility, where the demon is supposed to be. So the poison comes naturally from that region and not from the region of argument. But the man protests and says: Oh no, their back is pure and sacred. What does that refer to?

Answer: To the idealization of women.

Dr. Jung: Exactly. That is typical, not only of individual women but of whole nations, beginning with sacred motherhood, and the purity and chastity of women, and all that. It is a typical healthy-minded mistake. It is an optimism, but a most destructive kind of optimism.[1]

For centuries women have been idealized or reviled in religions, works of art, and empirical relationships. To have projected such idealization or revilement onto the feminine principle must have answered—and still does—some unknown need within individuals, societies, and nations. The very word *projection* implies an act of thrusting or throwing forward—a "process whereby an unconscious quality or content of one's own is perceived and reacted to in an outer object."[2] To project, then, is to attribute or assign characteristics we love or hate onto others. While we believe the qualities we ascribe to an individual or to a group belong to others, they are, in fact, our own. Because we are unaware of their existence within us, since they live inchoate in our subliminal sphere, they need conscious development to be understood, and then integrated into the psyche, so we can use them in a positive manner.

Only by becoming aware of this kind of archaic and primitive contents within the unconscious can persons or societies come to terms with their projections. Analysis, explications, probings, discussions may all help clarify aspects of what lies embedded within the depths of the psyche, unredeemed, repressed, and latent. To understand some aspects of the heavily charged psychic energy within a person's unconscious would help direct it into positive and constructive channels. To hate or love, to admire or denigrate groups or individuals—conditions that have reached harrowing proportions in modern times—is to allow oneself to succumb to the dominion of an autonomous unconscious force within the psyche. Thoughts and emotions then are considered uncontrollable passions, divesting the ego (the center of consciousness) of its independence.

To recognize contents emerging from the unconscious is, therefore, of crucial importance to all people, particularly for women, who have been victimized for so many centuries by man's projections. Particularly today, when society is changing so rapidly, a woman may have a difficult time—knowing what and who she is. Only by clarifying conditions and situations, and by distinguishing between subject and object, can a person begin to face and deal with reality. The greater the light shed on subliminal spheres within the psyche, the better equipped are individuals to discriminate and understand the meaning and impact of those powers which inundate and blind them, robbing them of their psychological independence. Clarification is difficult and frequently painful. It may lead to *confrontation*, but this may encourage people to come to grips with their projections—those troublesome powers they project unknowingly onto others because they either long to possess them or because they are plagued and hurt by them.

To study and analyze fictional works allows both critic and reader to gain insights into the unconscious of creative authors, the better to comprehend, cope with, and perhaps assess certain conflicting, vulnerable, and—yes—joyous forces inherent in the psyches of people today. We are limiting our explorations in *Women in Twentieth-Century Literature: A Jungian View* to an examination of some of the feminine characters in the works of eight women and two men in order better to penetrate some of the mysteries of the *eternal feminine*. We hope that, through the analysis of fictional beings, some of our readers will better see themselves not merely as projections of someone else's negative or positive characteristics, but as entities unto themselves—as living, evolving, creative beings whose options and destinies are theirs.

We will be using C. G. Jung's basic analytical technique and vocabulary in our exploration of the various feminine types encountered in the course of our study, but we also will reevaluate and revise some of these concepts when the need arises. Thus we hope to keep pace with changing times and different customs, and avoid a single-minded inquiry. As Heraclitus stated in 500 B.C., everything in the cosmos is in a state of flux. So, too, do ideas, beliefs, and concepts change continuously. To be enslaved by any psychological, religious, or political ideology, or by a single approach to literary criticism, is to destroy the freedom of creativity which brought it into being. It also divests one of the capacity to think and feel for oneself and to develop one's potential. Our Jungian interpretation of the feminine types analyzed in this volume is only one among many other valid explorations of their behavior.

Indeed, *stasis* goes counter to Jung's own beliefs, which are based on modification, alteration, and transformation of preceding knowledge. What may be valid for one person, at one period in time and in one culture, may not be so for another. What is crucial is to maintain an open mind when broaching delicate, volatile, and controversial subjects.

Jung's basic terminology will be defined here, but only very briefly, since it will be discussed when applicable in the chapters to follow. The concept of the *collective unconscious* (or *objective psyche*) is one of Jung's great contributions. It "takes the theory and practice of psychotherapy out of the exclusive realm of psychopathology and relates it to the whole history of the evolution of the psyche in all its cultural manifestations." Its contents, which are suprapersonal and non-individual, and, for the most part, inaccessible to conscious awareness, are manifested in *archetypal images*.[3]

Archetypal images (from the Greek *archi*, beginning, and *typos*, stamp or original form in a series of variations) are implicit in dreams, visions, myths, legends, fairy tales, and cultural manifestations of all types. The *archetype* has been compared by Dr. Edward Edinger to the instinct. He writes:

> An instinct is a pattern of behavior which is inborn and characteristic for a certain species. Instincts are discovered by observing the behavior patterns of individual organisms and, from this data, reaching the generalization that certain patterns of behavior are the common instinctual equipment of a given species. The instincts are the unknown motivating dynamisms that determine an animal's behavior on the biological level. An archetype is to the psyche what an instinct is to the body. The existence of archetypes is inferred by the same process as that by which we infer the existence of instincts. Just as instincts common to a species are postulated by observing the uniformities in biological behavior, so archetypes are inferred by observing the uniformities in psychic phenomena. Just as instincts are unknown motivating dynamisms of biological behavior, archetypes are unknown motivating dynamisms of the psyche. Archetypes are the psychic instincts of the human species.

> Although biological instincts and psychic archetypes have a very close connection, exactly what this connection is we do not know anymore than we understand just how the mind and body are connected.[4]

Archetypes are contained in the collective unconscious. They are made manifest in archetypal (primordial) images: experienced in such universal motifs as the *great mother*, the *spiritual father*, *transformation*, the *Self*, and others. Because archetypal images are endowed with *libido* (psychic energy), they arouse strong emotional reactions in the individual experiencing them, frequently evoking the *numinosum*, a sense of the divine or transpersonal power which transcends the ego.

Images, symbols, and motifs will, therefore, be examined throughout *Women in Twentieth-Century Literature: A Jungian View*, in order to try to better understand their meaning, their impact on the protagonists, and the light they shed on their cultures. The variety of intents and designs, both on a personal and collective level, of such symbols and images as water, cave, earth, sky, clouds, mountains, mandalas, and more, will also be explored. Some may even play a part in the death/rebirth mysteries, in sacrifice, redemption, and salvation. As such, a religious and philosophical dimension comes into focus, and with it an understanding of the psychological development or regression of the various protagonists.

The *personal unconscious* (also called the *shadow*), as distinguished from the collective unconscious, is derived from an individual's personal experience, and its contents are subject to awareness and may be integrated into the ego. (The *ego* is that part of the psyche which "stands between the inner world and the outer world, and its task is to adapt to both."[5]) An exploration of the shadow, viewed frequently as those factors within the personality that the ego considers unacceptable and therefore represses, rejects, or projects, may be transformed into positive factors within the personality. If allowed to remain unconscious, however, shadow characteristics may lurk in dark and dangerous areas, leading eventually to destructive and vicious behavioral patterns.

According to Jung, a contrasexual and autonomous psychic content exists within the female as *animus*, and is described as an inner man; it is also present in the male as *anima*. Anima and animus have been delineated in creative works, symbolically, and since time immemorial: feminine images ranging from harlot to the hyperdulian virgin; and male forces, encompassing Don Juans to divinities. When experienced unconsciously, both anima and animus can wreak havoc; when sentient, they can not only be a source of inspiration, but can lead to a greater understanding in human relationships by opening the door onto the deeper layers of the psyche—the collective unconscious.

The *persona* (the word comes from the Latin term meaning the actor's mask or "public face") mediates between inner and outer worlds. The persona includes some personal characteristics of the individual, and aspects emanating from the family's or society's expectations of her or him. The mask both hides and protects the individual seeking to adapt to the workaday world. Difficulties arise when an unconscious over-identification with the persona takes place: Under such conditions, *inflation* (*hubris*) or *alienation* may come into being.[6] The persona may also mask a weakened ego, thereby leading to its eclipse.

Jung's theory of the four functions (*thinking*, which is rational; *feeling*, which regulates values, especially in relationships; *sensation*, which promotes adaptation to reality; *intuition*, the faculty which perceives via the unconscious) will also be explored in our probing of fictional female characters.

The notion of *individuation*, or the process of "psychic differentiation" that distinguishes each individual as unique and separate from the collective, is developed in terms of the personalities, actions, and events surrounding the lives of the fictional characters focused upon. The inner life of the characters may then be experienced by the reader as a living entity, provoking reflection as well as a desire to assess the literary masterpiece in terms of the protagonist's own existential condition.

That we have chosen to explore certain female types in the writings of authors from diverse lands, multiple socioeconomic levels and religious faiths, helps us better understand the psychological patternings of the people involved. It also illustrates the diversity and universality of Jungian analysis and criticism. Such probing takes the literary work out of its individual and conventional context and relates it to humankind in general. This unique approach lifts readers out of their specific and perhaps isolated worlds and allows them to expand their vision, and thus relate more easily to issues whose reality is part of an ongoing and cyclical world.

Women in Twentieth-Century Literature: A Jungian View is not theoretical in nature. Rather, its approach is practical. Each chapter deals with but a single work, attempting in this way to flesh out a variety of psychological types so as to simplify our analysis of the women involved. Although, as stated before, we have used Jung's vocabulary and his archetypal techniques as a tool to probe the psyches of the fictional characters under scrutiny, we do not always accept, for example, what has recently been termed Jung's "benevolent patriarchal" views concerning the feminine psyche.

Broadly speaking, Jung believes the woman's psyche to be the adverse and reverse of the man's—complementary to his. He has remarked time and time again that *Eros*, or the principle of relatedness and feeling, is dominant in the female; that *Logos*, the analytical way, the power to discriminate and judge, is supreme in the male. Such categorizing is no longer valid in today's world. There is the woman who thinks first, then feels. There is the man who feels first, then thinks.[7] Jung's Eros/Logos dichotomy serves to limit and obscure certain factors within the personality that might otherwise evolve as a unit—and become integrated into the whole being. Because Jung associated man with thought and woman with feeling, he fostered the continuation of the *gender stereotype*: man as sentient, and woman as a caring and sustaining figure. Sharper and clearer boundary lines having been set between the two, a derogatory image frequently results. The woman is endowed with a primitive and undifferentiated psyche, while the male is spiritually and intellectually superior. According to this same anima/animus duality, woman is deprived of a *soul*, weakening still further the feminine image, while also suggesting that her animus, envisaged for the most part as a negative and destructive quantity, leads to the astonishing assumptions and fantasies that women make about men and produces thereby "an inexhaustible supply of illogical arguments and false explanations."[8] Such attitudes may impede the development of a person's potential, resulting in the opposite of Jung's productive and positive views. When not restricted to gender, Jung's anima/animus archetypes depict a basic androgyny which reveals new and dynamic modes of behavior—multiple sides of the mystery which is personality.

That differences exist between male and female psychology is a moot consideration, open to continuous investigation. By maintaining a fluid system whereby personalities pursue the process of self-realization, and in which feminine and masculine images and forms are constantly modified, one goes beyond the biases of one's time, transcends gender typology and stereotypical thinking, and probes the infinite riches of the human psyche so as to find some semblance of equilibrium and fulfillment.

Psychology is theory. Theories—as all else—are subject to change. What may seem significant at one period or in one society or culture may prove to be unsound or not applicable at another. Extremes, or any set of specifically defined views, may in time lead to simplistic thinking, pitfalls, and errors, arresting development, perpetuating established categories, disregarding sociocultural relativity, maintaining sex roles, and robbing individuals of their capacity for self-determination. To be intransigent is to divest a person of his or her essential birthright. The freedom to probe, to discover new and vital information which might be helpful to the individual and to society, leads, on the other hand, to increased experience and consciousness.

We have tried in this book to understand better the feminine nature through an analysis of fictional characters—a course which may be disorienting and even fearsome and chaotic, since probing into abysses leads us to the brink of the unknown. It may also add another dimension to woman's uniqueness, since we will no longer see her only as a vessel, a funnel, or a receptacle for procreation; nor as a male surrogate, counterpart, or opposite; nor simply as an androgynous compilation. We will see her as a functioning person in her own right: a multifaceted being living in a culturally pluralistic society. Conceding, relating, creating when she deems it appropriate to do so, woman makes her own way in this world with or without a partner—independently, understanding of herself as individual.

In *Women in Twentieth-Century Literature: A Jungian View* the reader will view all types of women, young and old, beautiful and ugly, good and bad, not only as they affect the male primarily (though this is also explored) but as they live out their own lives as women. A chronological order is maintained in an attempt to understand the coeval problems facing the fictional characters—both Occidental and Oriental—who come under scrutiny. Each chapter focuses on a single work by the following writers: Federico García Lorca, Elizabeth Bowen, Isak Dinesen, Natalia Ginzburg, Flannery O'Connor, Jean Rhys, Nathalie Sarraute, Pa Chin, Fumiko Enchi, and Anita Desai. The psychological, spiritual, physical, and sociological views of the fictional characters investigated may allow the reader to analyze with the depths of her or his being. Such a confrontation, identification, or projection may—through analysis of the personality involved—help harmonize or unify what has been severely cut, divided, polarized, and compartmentalized. Or it may not. Probings of, and encounters with, creatures of fantasy, as will be undertaken in the chapters to come, may serve to flesh out certain unconscious and conscious needs within readers of disparate cultures, inviting them to sound out their own souls, minds, senses, intuitive faculties, and bodies in more universal, analogical, and syncretistic ways.

The opening chapter explores Federico García Lorca's *Yerma* (1934). A modern reworking of an ancient mystery, this play might have been enacted at Eleusis, Samothrace, Lourdes, or any other sacred shrine. It probes the problem of woman's barrenness, the resulting pain and feelings of alienation, and the numinous happenings which lead to murder.

Elizabeth Bowen's *Death of the Heart* (1938) explores the teenage archetype, with its patterns of behavior or inherited modes of psychic functioning. The theme of exile is focused upon in Bowen's novel, dissecting the inner world of a sixteen-year-old girl bereft of parents, security, and, most importantly, love.

Isak Dinesen's "Peter and Rosa" centers on death, not life, spirit, or earth. The psyches of the fifteen-year-old protagonists living in northern Denmark, near Elsinore, are scrutinized from an alchemical point of view, as a transfiguration from *fixatio*, a stagnant psychological and spiritual condition, to *solutio*, or the dissolution of these problems through the water ritual.

Natalia Ginzburg's novel *All Our Yesterdays* (1952) fleshes out the drama of children growing up in Mussolini's Italy. The narrative pace of her novel, with its cumulative energy and suspense, concentrates not on grandiose deeds, but rather on the minute feelings and thoughts of young people who try, each in his and her own way, to find some meaning for their absurd existences. The psyches of two young girls are singled out for analysis: one, considered a cocotte; the other, given the appellation of insect. Why are their attitudes psychologically arresting? their ways different? their associations absorbing?

Flannery O'Connor's short story "Everything That Rises Must Converge" (1956) may be looked upon as a religious ritual which discloses the dark side of the human experience. Sacrifice is its core; a parasitic/castrating relationship between mother and son, its essence.

Jean Rhys's *Wide Sargasso Sea* (1967) features the problems confronting two embryonic psyches in a mother/daughter identification and alienation situation. The action, which takes place in Jamaica in the 1830s, tells of life in a world where the imposition of the white man's patriarchal law deprived women of most of their rights. Its protagonist is Antoinette, Edward Rochester's West Indian wife, whom Charlotte Brontë depicted in her state of madness in *Jane Eyre*.

Nathalie Sarraute's *Between Life and Death* (1968) deals with the concept of androgyny and the creative process, from the amorphous uncreated work of art, to its completion in the book. Sarraute's protagonist, the Writer/Androgyne, takes the reader through the multiple stages of the literary trajectory: from the blank sheet of paper with its unlimited possibilities, to the manifestation of the first glyph and the birth of the novel as "thing" or "object."

Pa Chin's *Family* (1931) invites us to plumb the secret worlds of three female characters in China, under a decadent, feudal regime in the process of disintegration. The poetic interludes, the pictorial qualities, and the transpersonal approach to nature as experienced by the protagonists in *Family* add a new dimension to the study. Discussions of Confucian morality and Taoism will help the reader understand the fate of the deeply introverted women existing in an ultra-patriarchal system. One of them suffers from anorexia nervosa; another is suicidal; while a third is healthy and able to cope with the atmosphere of extreme repression that palls on them all.

Fumiko Enchi's *Masks* (1958) lures us into the heart of the feminine world in Japan—its mysteries, its sacred and profane rituals, its exorcisms and initiatory rites—interwoven with Buddhism and Shintoism and the role of the mask in No theatre (performances which women, excluded, could view only from the outside). Some readers may find *Masks* shocking; others, satisfying. All will be fascinated by the highly charged *meta-events* depicted.

The novel of the Indian writer Anita Desai, *Fire on the Mountain* (1977), dramatizes the ordeals which a great-grandmother must experience as she prepares for the *rite* to exit from life. The disciplines which alter and amplify her existential and religious outlook when her great-granddaughter visits her high on her mountain retreat are explored, as are the meanings and affects upon the protagonists of such androgynous Hindu deities as Shiva/Parvati, and such images as fire—that vital energy that moves through nature eternally.

Jung had suggested time and time again that psychic life is a dynamic, uninterrupted permutation between the conscious and the unconscious. Such an interchange can, if properly realized, lead toward the integration of conflicting elements within the personality and toward wholeness of the Self—a process he termed *individuation*. To develop one's potential, to become increasingly conscious of one's attributes and deficiencies, to remain open to new enrichment, enables an individual to reach some kind of psychological equilibrium and fulfillment.

Ours is an inquiry and not a statement, a probing and not a determination. Questions are posited, conjectures set forward, comparisons and analogies suggested. Answers may be forthcoming, but are at best only temporary, serving to stabilize for the moment and to offer some kind of transient footing in the individual journey which is life. As the Japanese haiku poet Soin wrote:

> How fragile, how ephemeral in flight
> This life—for instance: butterfly, alight![9]

1 Federico García Lorca's *Yerma*: A Woman's Mystery

Federico García Lorca's *Yerma* (1934)[1] is a modern reworking of an ancient mystery which might have been enacted at Eleusis, Samothrace, Lourdes, Venusberg, or any other sacred shrine. It is the dramatization of secret doctrines and initiation rituals, and of verbal and gestural symbols.

Since *Yerma*, a three-act tragedy, deals with a woman's barrenness, the numinous happenings focus on fertility. Originally part of agrarian family cults, fertility rituals include protective or entombing ceremonies (I, i; II, ii), purification rituals (II, i), and a lysis (III, i, ii), which are sacred sequences in which the mystai thrash out the religious experience directly. Because such exteriorizations of primordial encounters have lived in the cultures and psyches of peoples throughout history, they can be said to be of mythic proportions. Because *Yerma* is a myth (from the word *mythos*, meaning "fable"), the happenings in the play transcend linear time; they live in a kind of eternity. Nor are the events dramatized to be considered necessarily personal; they are also collective. They are not invented simply for the sake of entertainment—though they may also be that—but are rather a living and burning reality of the Spanish culture and psyche as a whole and of Lorca's own vision.

Born in Guentevaqueros, not far from Granada, Lorca displayed his love both for theatre and musical composition early in life. He frequently incorporated musical forms into his plays, poems, and ballads, even collaborating instrumentally with such composers as Manuel de Falla. Lorca's dramas are said to have been influenced by the social satires and comedies of Jacinto Benavente, and most specifically by *The Passion Flower*, which is similar in theme to Lorca's own *Blood Wedding* (1933). There are other playwrights who may also have influenced Lorca's development as a dramatist: Ramón Valle-Inclán, who used his surrealistic vision to scorn and deride what he felt to be aesthetically and socially unacceptable; and Jacinto Grau and Antonio and Manuel Machado, whose plays frequently dealt with themes from ancient Spanish folklore and mythology. Nevertheless, Lorca's dramas are uniquely his own, with the stark restraint of their lyricism, the simplicity of their plots and settings, and the bone-hardness of their archetypal characters.[2]

Yerma is to be approached as both an individual and a collective happening, with emphasis focused on woman; on Mariolatry in particular, and its inherent polarities (saint/sinner); and on the victimization of son/husband by a would-be Mother. In that *Yerma* is a mystery and mythic in quality, its protagonists are not to be looked upon as flesh-and-blood human beings, but rather as archetypes.

Archetypes exist preconsciously and "form the structural dominants of the psyche in general." They may be considered "inherited modes of psychic functioning," corresponding to the "inborn way in which the chick emerges from the egg, the bird builds its nest." The archetype "is to the psyche what an instinct is to the body. . . . Just as instincts common to a species are postulated by observing the uniformities in biological behavior, archetypes are unknown motivating dynamisms of the psyche."[3]

The archetypes peopling Lorca's stage live on the most primitive of levels and act in keeping with their own inherited and biological patterns of behavior. Yerma, the protagonist of Lorca's tragedy, makes us privy to the agony of the barren woman: She has been married for two years when the play begins, and seven years pass between Act I and II; still she remains sterile. The archetype of the infertile woman is not unique, as attested to in the Bible. Not only did some women, long past the childbearing age, give birth, but several of them were even visited by angels before the birth: Sarah had Isaac, Rebecca had twins Esau and Jacob, and Hannah had Samuel; Manoah's wife bore Samson after the event was announced to her by an angel; and the same was true for Elisabeth, John's mother, and for Mary, who was told that she was "highly favoured" and "blessed" among women before giving birth to Jesus.[4] Nor are births requiring the help of divine intervention unknown in ancient times: Isis bore Horus through the intercession of the Holy Spirit Kamutef.[5]

That Yerma's desire for a child is her sole raison d'être is understandable. Though it is intimated that Victor, the shepherd, had been the object of her desire, as an obedient daughter she agreed to a loveless marriage to Juan. Nor does her wanting to become a mother violate the dictates of her culture. On the contrary, it would have enhanced her stature in the community: She would have been exactly like the others. Unable to become pregnant, she is set apart, and she suffers the excoriating torments of one who is not like the others—a pariah of sorts. Yerma's personality also distinguishes her from the typical young, jovial, lovable, and natural girl. She is a woman corroded by religious and sexual problems. She is psychologically empty. Her attitude toward her husband is cold, distant, and perfunctory. He is there to fertilize her: to function as a stud. Such a relationship can yield no fruit since no feeling or fire exists between them. Because the dichotomy between the two is unbreachable, Yerma's fantasy world takes over. It alone, at least at the outset, allows her a modicum of happiness.

The play opens with a dream vision—or a *visitation*—which is not surprising, since we are dealing here with a mystery. It is early in the morning of a spring day; she and her husband are asleep. The stage is bathed in a strange light—that of atemporal happenings: "A Shepherd enters on tiptoe looking fixedly at Yerma. He leads by the hand a Child dressed in white." Not only do the dream figures reveal a compensatory image for the void Yerma experiences in her life, but they also lend an eerie and irrational quality to the developments.

Who is this shepherd about whom Yerma is dreaming? He is certainly a reference to the strong and powerful Victor, the keeper of the flock—Lorca's mythical Abel—while Juan, thin and pale, is a tiller of the soil, like Cain. Juan works so hard inseminating the earth that he has no time to do the same for Yerma. That Victor leads a child dressed in white suggests the arrival of the "Son of Man": the pure, resplendent hope of her future—that element that gives her life purpose and love. If the child archetype is considered as a conjunction of opposites, it indicates a fluid relationship between the unconscious and consciousness. It is a condition able to pave the way for a spiritual and psychological change in the individual dreaming about such an image.

The shock of reality intrudes when Yerma awakens. The disparity between her dream (an unconscious compensatory urge) and the actual situation takes shape and arouses anger. She projects her trauma onto her husband and castigates him for his wanness and feebleness. Still hopeful of remedying the situation, she offers him a glass of milk. It will make him more robust: "Your body is not strong enough for it," she says, referring to the sexual act.

That she offers him milk is in keeping both with her desire to strengthen him and the mystery revolving around the Virgin Mary. Lactation was the only biological function the Virgin was allowed outside of the asexual act of weeping.[6] Yerma's gift of milk to Juan, then, is to be identified with the joy of a nursing mother: It is she who passes on her nourishing power to her newborn. Images such as Mary nursing Christ, or Hera, her son Hercules, or Isis, Horus, are all implicit in fertility rituals.

Yerma's emphasis on Juan's frailty is her way of castigating (castrating) him. He is to blame, then, for her failure to conceive. His attention to Mother Earth, and his continuous insemination of this unquenchable collective power, leave him little energy to perform the sexual act. Even more important is the fact that Juan has no understanding of his wife's anguish. Not having any progeny seems not to bother him. His concern centers upon his crops and the money these will yield, and the maintaining of his honor. What others say and think about him and his wife dominates his thoughts. Since Juan's world is centered outside of the home and not within it, he is uninvolved in what is brewing in this inner sphere. The opposite is true of Yerma.

Yerma's only means of assuaging the void within her—her sexual and spiritual emptiness—is to make Juan her scapegoat: her *shadow* figure. The shadow, defined as that part of the unconscious that contains aspects of a personality of which the individual is unaware, may contain "inferior characteristics and weaknesses which the ego's self-esteem will not permit it to recognize."[7] Let us mention that in ancient times the collective shadow, viewed as the evils of a community, was projected or heaped onto a goat by a priest; the animal was then sent out into the wilderness, and the clan was purged of its sins. The evil of the community supposedly disappeared along with the animal. By blaming Juan for a failure that might have been hers—or of both parties—Yerma is not facing her problem authentically. Unable to come to terms with it and to rectify it, she avoids it.

What increases her turmoil is Juan's insistence that she remain within her home. "You know well enough I don't like you to be going out," Juan tells her. "I never go out," she responds. The home, viewed psychologically, encourages a condition of introversion; it fosters dream and reverie—the irrational sphere. It may also be looked upon as a uterus, feeding and nurturing the creative factor within an individual—those aspects that develop one's potential. When mystery religions flourished in Egypt, at the time of Imhotep (2980–50 B.C.), and in Greece when Aesculapius (c. 600 B.C.) was worshipped, the ill would enter temples or were hoisted feetfirst into deep, dark, and narrow grottoes inhabited by snakes and venomous creatures, there to remain until such time as a healing dream came to them. After they explained their dream to the priest, it was interpreted, and if considered positive, the patient was declared to be in good health and was released.

Unlike such incubation dreams, however, Yerma's periods of withdrawal into her home yield not healing, but rather entombment or incarceration. The forced seclusion foisted upon her by Juan—in keeping with the customs of the day and therefore crucial to the maintenance of his honor—encourages periods of deep introversion on her part. More and more she feels cut off from the world outside and from herself. She cannot share her pain and sorrow with others; her solitude deepens, as does her fantasy world. A concomitant split between reality and compensatory imaginary conditions grows wider.

A woman who concentrates only on the home and her husband's welfare rarely, if ever, experiences a sense of identity outside of the home, as an individual in her own right. Wedded to the family, particularly in rural areas and in Lorca's time, a woman never evolved, never experienced a sense of personal purpose in life. She was a funnel, a servant, a mediatrix; she served as a procreative force in society, seeing to the physical and moral welfare of others and herself.

Remaining enclosed within four walls, Yerma, unable to express her problems with the hope of solving them, compounds them. Her thoughts revolve exclusively around the *child archetype*. This archetype, like any severe complex, is endowed with what one may call a type of electric current composed of affective charges and feeling tones. The affects given off by complexes are sometimes so great as to be capable of acting physically upon the person experiencing the complex. Rather than surrendering to this energetic force inhabiting her unconscious and thereby working with it openly, Yerma is shattered by it. Her ego (the center of her conscious personality) is dominated by this single image, which generates in its wake continuous frustrations and perpetual obstacles, preventing her from reaching her goal. The greater her imprisonment in her house (her unconscious), the more powerful is the domination of her idée fixe. Chaos inhabits her subliminal realm; rigidity, her conscious sphere. As if in a hermetically sealed jar, Yerma's inner pulsations grow increasingly cataclysmic. The situation becomes explosive.

As Yerma's shadow figure, Juan represents all that is negative, impotent, and uncreative in her life. As an aspect of the patriarchal collective sphere, he stands for systematization, morality, and feminine incarceration. A fixed, unyielding, unbending, and sterile force, then, has proclaimed dominion over her. She, who must remain obedient and subservient to him, is in no way emotionally involved. Since she is cut off from her feelings, no growth, no evolution, no warmth can be hoped for in her arid and sterile world. Increasing resentment on her part paves the way for a heightening of her aggressivity. Only destruction or dismemberment can come to pass, leading perhaps to a *renovatio*, or at least to an end of the repressive status quo she is compelled to endure.

Other factors are also present. Yerma's barrenness may be seen symbolically, as a sign of the time. Not only is it a paradigm of the disharmony between husband and wife, but it is also a basic antagonism existing in the very foundations of Spanish culture and its dominant religion, Roman

Catholicism. Under the patriarchal system of the time, the feminine principle was not only demeaned, but violated. A woman was a man's appendage; she served one function: to bear children. In keeping with the practice of Mariolatry, she was either a saint, and therefore to be worshipped, or a sinner, to be reviled. In either case, she was an object. Because she was nothing in her own right, if she differed in any way from either of these extremes, she became an outcast and stagnated, or regressed to an insalubrious world. In that Yerma has thus far been unable to fulfill the "saintly" task of motherhood, she lives alienated from her fellow beings and from herself. Yet, she keeps trying to rectify her condition.

Once Juan leaves to perform the daily chores in the fields, Yerma begins sewing, then "passes her hand over her belly, [and] lifts her arms in a beautiful sigh," as if cradling, nursing, loving, and warming her newborn. She sings out her lyrical verses about the baby she hopes to have. Lorca's choice of song—music—to express the wonderment of motherhood allows him to convey the tenderness of the mood: Yerma's words caress the ear; their smooth intonations touch, as if gently stroking the velvety smoothness of an infant's skin. She is *Mother* now, bathing in the beatific and passionate love of one so dependent upon her. The stillness of the home, no longer an entombment, has been transfigured. A *temenos*, a sacred space, exists for her, filled with the beauty and power of the archetypal image representing mother and child.

Sewing, like weaving, also replicates the mystery of creation. As Yerma commands her thread, her colors, and her network of designs, she is visually organizing her destiny: She is fashioning and building a way of life for herself. Let us recall that the Greek Fates were women and that they made, wove, and cut the thread of life. So, too, does Yerma hope to be the artificer of her future.

Maria, married only four months, walks into Yerma's home carrying fabric, laces, tassels, and ribbons. She tells Yerma that, when her husband learned she had become pregnant, he gave her money to buy these things and she did not even have to ask him for it. How did it all happen? Yerma asks. How does it feel to be with child? Her husband pressed his mouth against her cheek, Maria answers, and "it seems to me my child is a dove of fire he made slip in through my ear."

Such symbols are implicit in the mystery of the Annunciation. The Holy Ghost, it is said, flew down in the form of a dove, fecundating the Virgin Mary through the ear. That the ear was chosen for the conception indicates Mary's obedience to the divine word. By having heard and accepted the announcement, she freely conceived Jesus.[8] The ear, which hears the word, is not only a symbol for comprehension; it is also a sexual image, along with fire, which refers to the energy needed for the insemination process.

Mother Earth and Father Heaven, then, are necessary for the flame of insemination to fecundate woman. From Maria's statement, we learn that she experiences not only passion, as attested to by the use of the word fire, but spiritual and emotional contentment and involvement.

Yerma cannot even begin to understand the meaning of the mystery of passion in lovemaking. She feels no flame for her husband, either sexual or spiritual. He is an inseminator, a procreating agent, a rainmaker, while she is the funnel and the bridge to the future. Although she longs to open herself up to the mystery of life—the process of pregnancy she seeks to have enacted in her body—she cannot. She has no sense of her flesh or of sexuality, so bound is she by her idée fixe, by the child archetype which saps her instinct, her vitality, and drains her ego. She also knows that if she does not conceive, her blood will turn to poison: Love will turn to hate, health to sickness, peace to war.

A driven woman who is incapable of relating to her husband sexually, or in any other way, tries—as initiates have since ancient times—to enact rituals that she thinks might help her achieve her goal. At night, for example, she walks on the ground outside of her home; during the day she brings her husband his food in the fields. As she puts her feet down and touches Mother Earth, she hopes to be secretly impregnated by the contact with this nurturing force. Her husband is inseminating symbolically each time he breaks ground to plant his seeds, and also when he waters them, making the area moist and receptive to the germinating process—rituals he carries out with love and care.

When Victor, on his way home from work, stops at Yerma's home and learns that she is still not pregnant, he encourages her to have Juan "try harder" (II, i). After he leaves, Yerma walks toward the place where Victor had stood and "breathes deeply" as if she were inhaling sheer joy, strength, rapture—the very essence of life denied her by her restrictive and regressive husband. Victor, the shepherd, could have been her inseminator; she could have procreated carnally with him. With Juan, she knows only frigidity.

That Yerma is frigid toward her husband is made evident in her reactions to an old woman (I, ii) who has had fourteen children and two husbands and who lives "with her skirts to the wind" (and that is why "children came like water"). Yerma wants to learn her secret: "Why am I childless?" she questions. The old woman tells her she has always looked upon her body as something beautiful, unlike the Christians, who consider it sinful. Nor does she believe in God: In fact, she despises him. Feelings of guilt, sin, and asceticism do not concern her at all. Passionate and sensual, she has a lust for life. Unlike St. Theresa of Avila, who forever sought to do penance, or the Flagellants, who indulged in a collective *imitatio Christi*, scourging themselves until they drew blood, the old woman enjoys the beauty of nature in all of its forms.[9] "Don't you feel something like a dream when he brings his lips close to yours?" she asks Yerma. No, is the response. Yet, as she thinks back to Victor, there could have been such a time. Now, however, pleasure has been banished from her world.

Two girls appear on the scene: One has left her baby at home and is in a hurry to return; the other is married, has no children, and does not want any. She hates to cook and to wash. Her parents insisted she marry. For what? she wonders: "We did the same things as sweethearts that we do now. It's all just the old folks' silly ideas." Unwilling to conform to what she considers unpleasant, she is determined to tend to her needs and desires as much as possible and not remain "stuck" inside a house doing what she does not like to do. Her life will be a bed of roses, not yet a vale of tears.

Yerma, making her way home, hears Victor's jubilant, earthy, and physical voice singing out in the distance: "Why, shepherd, sleep alone?" They meet and she comments on the vibrancy of his voice: "It's like a stream of water that fills your mouth." Like Abel, he is a man at peace with himself; he knows—he feels—he loves, and happiness overflows. As the two look at each other fixedly, Juan intrudes. Fearful of what neighbors might say if they see Victor and his wife talking together, he orders her to go home. He will remain to water the trees.

Alone and entombed in her coffin/home, Yerma's suffering turns into a virtual martyrdom, a paradigm of the negative and destructive side of Christianity. Like the Penitentials who suffered atonement, who prayed, sacrificed, repented, and humiliated themselves in all ways to earn salvation, Yerma is plunged into the agony of helplessness.

Act II opens with a purification ritual similar to the ceremonies enacted in the ancient mystery religions, as well as in contemporary ones. The village girls are washing their clothes in a flowing mountain stream, singing out their loves and the pleasures of life's rewards. "Joy, joy, joy" is chanted by one whose swollen womb is visible beneath her dress. Gossiping is also the rule of the day. Yerma is their focal point: They are convinced that Victor is her lover because "she carries his picture—in her eyes." As a sinner, therefore, she cannot bear a child.

The scene shifts from this highly active, entertaining, and happy one to Yerma's home at twilight (II, ii). Juan, so intent upon saving his honor, has asked his two maiden sisters to move into his home so that they can supervise his wife. Like elements of a Greek chorus, they are there, present or behind the scenes, following her every move or breath, and even divining her inner thoughts. An area that once had served Yerma as a refuge for her dream world is now transformed into a prison. Her home has become a destructive domain, where rage and pain prevail.

Returning from the fountain with two pitchers of water for the home, Yerma is severely reprimanded by her husband. A sense of shame is instilled in her, as well as feelings of guilt. She is accused of going out too much: "The sheep in the fold and women at home." She replies: "I'll learn to bear my cross as best I can. . . . If I could suddenly turn into an old woman and have a mouth like a withered flower, I could smile and share my life with you. But now—now you leave me alone with my thorns."

Increasingly outspoken, Yerma looks straight at Juan, fixedly, deliberately—with passion. Not the passion of love, but rather of hate. She speaks of her feelings of entombment, of incarceration—"tied tight in my coffin." He has no understanding of her pain or of her needs. Men have many activities that take up their attention: tending to cattle, trees, conversations. Women have only children. Angrily, he responds: "You persist in running your head against a stone." The stone image describes his feelings most exactly: hard, inert, yet a living power. Stones also represent sacred forces: the Kaaba for the Muslim; the Omphalos for the ancient Greek; the Beith-El for the Hebrew; the philosophers' stone for the alchemist; Christ, the cornerstone of the Church; the refined angular stone of the mason. Neither sacred nor enduring forces interest Yerma, who counters Juan's statement by suggesting that he should speak of "a basket of flowers and sweet scents," thereby invoking more feminine, beautiful, and gentle images.

Increasingly ill at ease as Yerma's anger festers, Juan tries to run away from his obligations rather than face them. He speaks about his work in the fields, and his inability to remain with her. "You're not a real woman," he blurts out. Her psychological and sexual ambiguity becomes most overt as she confesses, "I don't know what I am." No identity; faceless. Alienated from her own deepest feminine nature, Yerma's emotional development is increasingly stunted. Neither male nor female, she has become an unworkable appendage of the phallic Mother.

In Act III (i), which takes place in the house of the sorceress Dolores, there is also a mystery ritual. Viewed by a patriarchate as the primitive aspect of the feminine, Dolores, a prognosticator of future events, participates secretly in nature and consequently is a redoubtable and threatening power. Considered by the ancient Egyptians, Greeks, and Romans as part of the life process, priestesses or sibyls were approached with awe and trepidation—not as evil forces. The Christians, on the contrary, looked upon them with dread, as somber and fearful powers which had to be destroyed. As representatives of hidden desires and of unregenerate instincts, priestesses and sorceresses took on the countenance of terrifying energies, incompatible with the prevailing collective ego. As such, they have been most frequently represented as ugly, diabolical manifestations of the irrational, instinctual, undisciplined, and undomesticated world—

the antithesis of the idealized, ordered, peaceful woman as viewed in Mariolatry. But she who is spiritual, sinless, and beautiful is an abstraction and therefore unrealizable.

That Yerma came to consult Dolores indicates the power of her pain and the pathos of her condition. She is not afraid of partaking in the mysteries relating to Mother Earth as represented by Dolores. Two other old women are also present, one of whom advises Yerma to find refuge in her husband's love while she waits "for God's grace." He is a good man, she tells her. No. Yerma feels nothing for Juan. "He goes out with his sheep over his trails, and counts his money at night." And when he is near her, "I feel a waist cold as a corpse's," she confesses. She has changed, she realizes. She who had always despised passionate women wishes she could become "a mountain of fire." This, she understands, is her only salvation.

When Dolores tells Yerma she must recite the "laurel prayer" twice, and St. Anne's prayer as well, she links Christian and "pagan" mysteries and ideologies. Laurel was chewed or burned by the Delphic Oracle before she announced her prognostications. When a favorable answer was forthcoming, she returned with a crown of laurel leaves on top of her head. This same plant, dedicated to Apollo, brought wisdom and victory. Because it remained green in winter, the Romans associated it with immortality, fecundity, and vegetation. As for St. Anne's prayer, it absolved a believer from sin, allowing the penitent to experience the numinosum, opening him or her to divinity through the feminine principle.

Before Yerma leaves this sacred precinct, Juan and his two sisters enter Dolores's hut. Although Juan berates her for sullying his honor, Yerma seems to have been strengthened by her exposure to the realm of the Great Mother, as incarnated in Dolores and the other women present. Through them, she has touched her own deepest feminine roots—that inner force which heightens a woman's might and insight. The added energy enables her to respond in kind to her husband's vilifications; she is unwilling now to accept guilt: "I too would shout, if I could, so that even the dead would rise and see the innocence that covers me." It is Yerma who realizes that she must protect her own honor from being sullied by her husband. The more certain she becomes of her way, the more overt are her actions and demeanor, and the more fearful a force—a *vagina dentata*—does she become in her husband's eyes. Juan is unconsciously terrified of this archetypal figure over which he now knows he has no control. She now appears to him as a deceiver, a corruptor, a demonic potentate. "I'm no match for your cleverness," he says. Yerma's eyes, meanwhile, are like two piercing forces, "two needles" ready to pierce her husband. She is Evil; she is Death for Juan, ready to dissolve the status quo. As she accuses him of sterility and impotence, a transfiguration seems to be taking place, preparing for the play's lysis. Releasing affective charges and feeling tones as she speaks out her powerful lines, Yerma virtually slaughters rational attitudes and thought processes. Two archetypal powers are warring onstage: not merely husband and wife, each pointing to the other as the guilty party, but collective forces, each vying for supremacy.

Nevertheless, Yerma also has her other side. In a deeply moving sequence, she speaks of her need of Juan, of her love for him; and as she moves forward to embrace him, he commands her to "get away." Alone again, she feels like "the moon search[ing] for herself in the sky" and cries out her pain, her martyrdom, and her emptiness. Silence, he commands. The neighbors might hear. But Yerma no longer cares about saving face, nor about life. Freedom, and not constriction, is what she needs. "At least let my voice go free, now that I'm entering the darkest part of the pit." For the first time her body has given birth—to song, to poetry, to rapture, to the beauty of Word. Like the Virgin Mary, who conceived through the ear, she, too, has become a procreative power—be it spiritual or abstract—giving lyrical expression to her innermost soul-state. As Juan has suggested, she lives in her head and not in her physical being. "Cursed be the body!" she cries out, victimized as she is by the asceticism which her culture has forced upon her, cutting off soul from flesh.

That the concluding scene (III, ii) should take place at night in a hermitage high in the mountains is in keeping with the numinosity of the happenings. Some mountains—Faust's Walpurgisnacht, Tannhauser's Venusberg, the Bacchantes' Mt. Cithaeron—are believed to contain the throne of the Great Goddess or the Mountain Woman.[10] It is on the mountain—a sacred area—that men and women allow their pent-up emotions to be unleashed, and their repressed instincts buried deep within their collective unconscious to be acted out. Unchanneled impulses, however, sometimes spell destruction and may lead to a dissociation of the personality. When they have free range, they sometimes overwhelm the ego, thereby obliterating any kind of real relationship with the outside world.

As pagan and Christian rituals fuse in this mountain scene, fertility celebrations are encouraged on one side of the stage, while on the other, Catholic chapel ceremonies unfold. Revellers and a chorus of dancers carrying bells leap about in wild abandon, voicing their erotic needs in songs observing the joys of natural life. Reality is increasingly obliterated, while released energy activates the most obscure primal forces. Juxtaposed to the scene of frenzy is Yerma, who, accompanied by six women, comes to pray in the chapel. Barefoot, she carries decorated candles to honor her patron saint, begging for her intercession in worldly matters.

A male and female personification of the Devil, with all of the paraphernalia, including masks, dances, songs, and gesture, make their way onto the stage, miming the act of sexual intercourse and conception. The Christian prejudice against instincts and earth forces, which were equated with sinful and Satanic powers, compelled the faithful to long for its opposite: the inhuman divine/ideal sphere. Extreme asceticism elicits its opposite. Attempts to repress the spontaneous impulses of an inner spirit by an overly conscious control of the ego only serve to accentuate the imbalance within individuals, leading more urgently to a need for redemption.

The Devil, symbolizing all forces that trouble, weaken, and dispossess a person of grace, is for this same reason Lucifer—the Light Bringer—illuminating what has been buried in darkness and chaos. In keeping with this idea, Lorca wrote in his stage directions: "The beauty of this scene must be overt." As the Devils cavort about, they "are not in any fashion grotesque, but of great beauty and with a feeling of pure earth."

A complex of opposites is lived out on stage: Earth and Heaven, Body and Spirit, Good and Evil, God and the Devil. Two ways of life, which until now had been antipodal one to the other, will merge. An old woman tells Yerma: "Women come here to know new men. And the saint performs the miracle." She understands what troubles Yerma and so invites her to live in her house with her children, to pay no attention to what people will say, to overcome the repressive forces dominating her world. Yerma, however, cannot divest herself of her honor, of her inherited mode of psychic functioning. Caught up in her own masochistic, repressive world, she sums up her psychic condition perfectly: "I'm like a dry field where a thousand pairs of oxen plow, and you offer me a little glass of well water. Mine is a sorrow already beyond the flesh."

Juan, who has been hiding behind a cart, has heard the entire conversation. Unaffected by his wife's sorrow, not caring whether he has children, he is caught up in the atmosphere of instinctuality and is dazzled by its power and beauty. He wants to take his wife, sexually, powerfully, formidably—and only for the pleasure it will yield him. "Kiss me . . . like this," he sings to her triumphantly.

Yerma's rage knows no bounds. Unable to express her feelings of excoriating hurt, she suddenly shrieks out the *word* for the *ear* to hear, seizes Juan by the throat, and chokes him to death.

> "Barren, barren, but sure. Now I really know it for sure. And alone. . . . Now I'll sleep without startling myself awake, anxious to see if I feel in my blood another new blood. My body dry forever! What do you want? Don't come near me, because I've killed my son. I myself have killed my son!"

The entire lysis is reminiscent in its harrowing viscerality of Euripides' *Bacchants*, the priestesses of Dionysus, those "wild women" who also danced their release from a patriarchal, repressive environment, dismembering their prey in the process. Similarly, Yerma symbolically devours the future genitor.

The symbolic dismemberment disrupts previous orientations and values. Confusion reigns; chaos has broken loose. Nothing is clear, nor are values distinct. Yerma is the one who gives birth to a new life force. She emerges victorious from Lorca's tragedy, for it is she who unseats and topples what was, adhering to Nietzsche's premonitory dictum: "We must liberate ourselves from morality in order to be able to live morally."[11]

2 Elizabeth Bowen's *Death of the Heart:* The Teenage Archetype

Elizabeth Bowen's *Death of the Heart* (1938) probes the patterns of behavior or inherited modes of psychic functioning of the teenage archetype. Exiled at sixteen from a world of love and security after the death of her parents, Portia, the protagonist of Bowen's novel, has been assigned to relatives who neither want nor relate to her. In time, she learns through pain and hurt to fight back, irritating adults by her frankness and jarring them by the vigor of her ingenuousness. Not only does she succeed in asserting herself by awakening latent powers within her subliminal world which come to her aid in time of stress, but her intense drive for life shocks her foster parents into a new state of awareness concerning the sterility and aridity of their lives.

Psychologically, *The Death of the Heart* may be described as Portia's fall from Paradise—from the *uroboric* state of innocence. This occurs when she is cut off from her primal world and thrust into a polished and sophisticated London household, where she feels (with reason) like an unwanted stranger. No longer contained in what could be called a sanctuary of love and understanding, Portia realizes that she must struggle to survive the coercive and harsh environment in which she now finds herself. The conflict she experiences helps her to become more objective and detached in evaluating her situation. Gone are the fantasies she had nourished about the beautiful life she would lead in her new home; and with this loss has come "the death of the heart." Because Portia is not given to morbidity, she acts, and reacts to her distress, wryly and pithily, even launching into verbal thrusts when necessary. The give-and-take experience endows her with increased awareness, thereby helping her to develop an understanding of her needs, desires, and potential. Thus she can begin to build her personality and carve out a world for herself. Such a transformation may be described, psychologically, as the coming into being and the growth of the ego out of the Self—leading to independence and maturity. The ego has been defined as "the center of consciousness and the seat of the individual's experience of subjective identity." As for the Self, it is viewed as "the central and comprehensive archetype expressing the totality of the psyche as organized around a dynamic center. . . . The Self is experienced as the objective, transpersonal center of identity which transcends the ego. Empirically it cannot be distinguished from the image of God."[1]

Elizabeth Bowen (1899–1973) was born in Dublin but left this city with her mother when she was seven, after her barrister father had recovered from brain fever. Once her education was completed at the Downe House (Westerham, Kent) in 1916, Elizabeth returned to Dublin, where she worked in a hospital for shell-shocked veterans. At the conclusion of World War I, she returned to London and began her studies at the London Council School of Art. She married Alan Charles Cameron in 1923 and moved to Old Headington, right outside of Oxford, where he was employed in the school system. It was here that Bowen wrote *Encounters* (1923) and *The Hotel* (1928), among other works. In 1935 the Camerons moved to a home near Regent Park in London. Publishing nearly a book a year, Bowen also contributed articles to the *New Statesman* and found time to become an active participant in literary circles, including the Bloomsbury group. During World War II, she wrote for the Ministry of Information and offered her services as an air-raid warden. Upon the death of her husband (1952), she moved to Bowen's Court in County Cork, the family estate which she inherited from her father. From 1960 to her death, she made her home in Old Headington, in England.[2]

The Fall into "The World"

That Bowen entitled the first section of her novel "The World" suggests both a mythological and archetypal context: the universality and eternality of Portia's pattern of behavior. Her fall from Paradise—from the nomadic existence she lived with her parents on the French Riviera until their demise—to earth, and her life at the home of Anna and Thomas Quayne, are the crux of the drama of Part I of Bowen's novel.

When Portia arrives at the Quaynes' we may say, psychologically, that her ego is still unformed; it has not yet taken on consistency, nor has it acquired empirical reality. Bowen's stunning opening image of a cold

January morning in London conveys the sterility of the characters Portia will have to confront in order to grow in strength and consciousness:

> That morning's ice, no more than a brittle film, had cracked and was now floating in segments. These tapped together or, parting, left channels of dark water, down which swans in slow indignation swam. The island stood in frozen woody brown dusk . . . the sky was shut to the sun.[3]

This paradigmatic visualization, which features Anna Quayne strolling along the Regency terraces with one of her writer friends, St. Quentin, may be looked upon as a semiotic rendering of her personality. Unbending and remote, Anna is devoid of warmth and feeling: "Her placid derisive smile, her way of drawing her chin in when she did smile, often made [St. Quentin] think of a sardonic bland white duck" (5). Just as no common denominator links the fragmented slabs of ice in the river, so Anna cannot relate to herself or anyone in her household. Each person in her home—at 2 Windsor Terrace—exists as a separate entity, inhabiting his or her domain and concerned only with his or her well-being. Frigidity dominates the environment.

Portia's entrance into 2 Windsor Terrace is depicted as a "breath of raw air that had come in" to this highly sophisticated home (23). And she is just that: raw, untutored, outspoken, and in need of spiritual guidance, warmth, love, and friendship. Portia seeks a hearth and a homey atmosphere—a contemporary version of the fulfillment provided by the Greek goddess Hestia.

Representative of a psychic state, Hestia keeps the sacred fire of the hearth burning, encouraging members of a family to center on or gravitate toward it, thereby focusing themselves and finding their equilibrium. As guardian of the home, Hestia keeps the domestic flame lit, inviting people to gather together, talk, relate, feel, and seek connecting values with others and with themselves.[4]

In vain does Portia search for the Hestia archetype which would give a solid foundation to her world. Instead, in Anna, she faces a negative Great Mother: a Medusa-like woman who has illusions of being a Circe. Her pattern of behavior, both biological and psychological, centers upon herself. There is nothing spontaneous or warm about Portia's foster mother, just as there is no flame in the Quaynes' home around which the family revolves.

Since Hestia is looked upon, archetypally, as the guardian of the home, her image is architectural. Houses in general, considered as internalized space, are made up of people with drives, defenses, fantasies, and emotions, creating a personal and interpersonal set of dynamics. Thus it is not surprising to find that Bowen, like Balzac and other novelists, personifies houses: They represent psychological and functional conditions. In *The Death of the Heart*, two architectural constructs come into view: 2 Windsor Terrace in London and Waikiki at Seale-on-Sea. These two homes are metaphors that yield a wealth of overt and covert sensations; they are places where the exiled Portia lives, and where she attempts to center herself and organize and assess the changes occurring in her life and her psyche.

It does not take Portia long to realize that the inhabitants at Windsor Terrace act according to their own mode of psychic functioning: Each being is "impaled upon a private obsession" (221); each lives in his or her own secret, silent, saturnine world, marked with unfulfilled potential and undirected possibilities. Portia hears "an unliving echo" reverberate throughout the building, as if banalities, superficialities, hypocrisies are being repeated endlessly (23). Reminiscent of the Greek nymph Echo, who could never initiate a word or sentence, conversations at Windsor Terrace are only repeated, and emotions, tautologized. Nor does real love inhabit Portia's new world—merely self-admiration. The Quaynes and their coterie of guests are regressive and narcissistic, in love with their own images. A deadness marks the atmosphere.

Portia is stunned, at first, by the immobility, stiffness, and inertia reigning within the Quaynes' home. Describing "one of those pauses in the life of a house" when nothing moves, nothing happens, Bowen writes:

> This was a house without any life above-stairs, a house to which nobody had returned yet, which, through the big windows, darkness and silence had naturally stolen in on and begun to inhabit. (23)

Emptiness alone exists at 2 Windsor Terrace. Nothing more.

"So I am with them in London," Portia says to herself, as if dropping into a situation and a group of people unexpectedly, unwillingly, unpremeditatedly. Alienated not merely from her own world and family, but also from any sort of cheerfulness, warmth, and conviviality of life in a happy family, Portia understands in time the meaning of solitude and isolation. The Quaynes' home is the perfect emblem for this psychological state: "There's no past in this house," no memories (99). To walk through its rooms is like strolling about in a wilderness or a desert. Two Windsor Terrace has no roots, no magic, no original form or essence. When no vestigial memory of childhood exists in a building, there is no "linking back" (*religio*); there are no patterns of behavior or motifs of functioning which might help a teenager to compensate for her loss.[5] The Quaynes' home poses a threat to Portia's well-being, since Anna, the negative mother image, who views herself as a kind of dragon lady, a snake, a Gorgon or Medusa, might swallow her up; Anna is ready and waiting to obliterate Portia's still weakly structured ego.

Everything about Anna's world is fixed, ordered, staid, passionless. After marrying Thomas Quayne following an unhappy love affair, she erected a barrier around her world. A husband would support her economically; his presence would give her the proper social status; and a coterie of male admirers would bolster her sense of self. Anything that disturbs this static and vacuous existence that she has created for herself is anathema to her. In no way, therefore, does she consider involving Portia in her world; she simply does not want to be bothered with the teenager. She is willing to fulfill the rudimentary obligations of seeing that Portia is well clothed, fed, and schooled, but nothing more. Hard, sophisticated, and stiff, Anna is a woman who, as the opening image intimates, never thawed out, never came into her own. "She'd let live and let die—so long as she wasn't trespassed upon. And she wasn't trespassed upon," remarks her housekeeper, Matchett (103). Dissatisfied and incomplete, Anna has literally cut herself off from her feeling world; she lives only on the surface, peripherally.

Anna, who fancies herself a vamp, a Circe, a kind of enchantress, has no real relationship with Thomas, her silent, introverted, undemanding husband. Nor can she sympathize with his embarrassment over the adulterous affair his menopausal father had, and which resulted in Portia's birth. That Anna considers Portia's presence in her home with alarm—a virtual threat to her well-being—not only indicates fear of innovation, but indicates her undifferentiated psychological condition. Change is to be avoided—including the new thoughts and burgeoning feelings which are so frequently part and parcel of youth. Only by prolonging what is, can Anna hope to pursue her vacuous life-style, which she believes suits her needs. It is certainly a protection; it is also an incarceration which can lead in the long run to a mephitic psychological condition.

A household made up of a negative mother image and a passive and solipsistic father figure is detrimental to a teenager, and especially to the orphaned Portia. She cannot thrive on mere coexistence; she must in some way participate in the household activities, thus learning to fill the void brought on by the loss of her parents. Portia's personality may be described, symbolically, as made up of fire—that is, emotional, warm, and loving. If she gets near Anna and Thomas in some way, so as to alter their iced, fixed beings, she will be able to melt their rigid psyches, thereby fluidifying and altering their relationships—the very process Anna is intent upon avoiding. To accomplish such an integrative goal is a monumental task for the most adept; certainly, for a teenager like Portia, with so little experience, it is impossible.

So unformed is Portia's ego, so faceless is her personality, that when she first arrives at the Quaynes' there is really nothing distinctive about her, as attested by the dress she wears at tea: "Her dark dress almost blotted her out against a dark lacquer screen." Anna, who subsequently buys all of her frocks, hats, and coats, is in effect molding Portia's taste—as well as her personality. "She need not look like an orphan: it's bad for her," Anna contends. She must fit into the decor, into the landscape of 2 Windsor Terrace. There must be nothing notable, nothing exceptional, about her. Only then would Portia not cause trouble.

Unformed as Portia is, she nevertheless has a strong drive for self-development, which was not made to echo the desires of others or to follow the dictates of someone who she realizes instinctively has no feeling for her. Intense charges of libido (psychic energy) bombard Portia whenever she feels threatened. Her unconscious cannot simply remain passive in the face of danger. It always reacts, catalyzing heretofore unsuspected contents within her subliminal sphere. The longer she remains at the Quaynes' home, the more her resentment toward them and their life-style grows. Action, and not torpor, is Portia's way.[6]

Relationships grow even more difficult after Anna discovers Portia's diary hidden among some papers in her room. She reads it without a pang of conscience, and it corroborates feelings she has already had about Portia's need to achieve and to grow. It reveals to Anna an aggressive quality on the part of the teenager, which increases Anna's fear of her and which she will attempt to dilute and to delete. That Portia spells trouble is obvious to Anna from certain statements included in the diary, as well as from the teenager's extraordinary perception. She has an incisive eye and misses nothing; her way of observing others ever so scrupulously and her capacity to see beyond people's masks, straight into the heart of the matter, are unusual. Nor, Anna remarks, does Portia "misconstruct."

Anna is right to consider Portia's presence a threat, an intrusion, an irritant to her way of life. Anna, who has never wanted to commit herself to anything or anybody, is the antithesis of Portia. She is a dilettante who "posed as being more indolent than she felt, for fear of finding herself less able than she could wish" (44). Nevertheless, Anna is gifted. She draws well and also plays the piano, but "she did nothing she did not happen to do casually and well" (44). To pursue a course, to probe, to improve, to deepen herself—to delve into human relationships—are simply not part of her personality.

Portia's first attempt to be loved and involve herself in family affairs is her effort to please the Quaynes as best she can. At teatime, Anna, who is entertaining one of her men friends, suggests that Portia go and talk with Thomas in his study. The teenager, shy and uncomfortable with her present company and believing that her half brother really wants to be with her, is delighted to comply. (Little does she know that Anna's real motivation is to get rid of the bothersome intruder. As it turns out, Thomas is not even aware that Portia has returned from school.) Portia's agitation, her feelings of inferiority and embarrassment as she makes her way out of the dining room to go to the study, are conveyed most extraordinarily in Bowen's very special gestural language:

> Then holding herself so erect that she quivered, taking long soft steps on the balls of her feet, and at the same time with an orphaned unostentation, she started making towards the door. She moved crabwise, as though the others were royalty, never quite turning her back on them—and they, waiting for her to be quite gone, watched. She wore a dark wool dress, in Anna's excellent taste, buttoned from throat to hem and belted with heavy leather. The belt slid down her thin hips, and she nervously gripped at it, pulling it up. Short sleeves showed her very thin arms and big delicate elbow joints. Her body was all concave and jerkily fluid lines; it moved with sensitive looseness, loosely threaded together: each movement had a touch of exaggeration, as though some secret power kept springing out. At the same time she looked cautious, aware of the world in which she had to live. . . . the ordeal of getting out of the drawing room tightened her mouth up and made her fingers curl—her wrists were pressed to her thighs. She got to the door, threw it ceremoniously open, then turned with one hand on it, proudly ready to show she could speak again. (32)

The above image depicts a naive, fearful, and awkward Portia, a teenager afraid of facing strangers, particularly those whose natures are so unresponsive and hard. Portia's unformed body parallels her embryonic ego. Both are thin; neither is filled out. That her dress does not fit her suggests that Portia has not yet found her niche in the Quaynes' scheme of things—in their "world." Her "concave" body and its "jerkily fluid" lines indicate a lack of certainty as to how she should behave and how she can best learn to relate to strangers. Semiotically, the *cave* of *concave* is dark and secretive. In Portia's case, however, such a structure may not be strong enough to contain her needs, and it could, if too great stress were placed upon it, *cave in* under adult pressure. Nor is Portia psychologically integrated: Rather, she is fragmented, disconnected, loosely bound, as if only "threaded together." There is nothing sure, smooth, or cohesive in her personality. She has neither center nor focus as yet; she is still groping, trying to find her way. Unconsciously, she is desperately searching for a household where the Hestian hearth exists in all of its warmth and understanding. Still, Portia is cautious. Unwilling to divulge her feelings and her innocence, she is intent upon hiding what she feels might not be acceptable to this social group which she must now call her own. To lay her feelings bare might make her more vulnerable to pain.

To enter Thomas's study is, for the teenager, "an act of intimacy" requiring considerable strength, which she has not yet developed. Rather than walking into her half brother's room with aplomb, she forces herself to penetrate this inner sanctum, giving the impression of drifting or swimming towards him. As for Thomas, her presence not only bores but fatigues him. He refuses to give her or anyone else an accounting of his day. All he longs for is to remain alone. Their small talk, revolving around the weather and school, is brief; then he turns his head away from her "like an animal being offered something it does not like."

There is nothing decisive, authentic, or distinctive about Thomas. So much of him has remained unlived, secreted someplace in his unconscious, that it remains in its original unregenerate condition—like so much amorphous flabbiness. "His mouth and eyes expressed something, but not the whole of him; they seemed to be cut off from the central part of himself" (36). Like the house, he is a kind of echo, reverberating the ideas and thoughts of others, and never initiating any of his own. Yet he is sensitive at times, and when Portia, in all of her innocence, "looked through" him, he "felt the force of not being seen" (37).

The intuitive teenager with her "determined innocence" speaks through her "dark eyes," which keep observing and ferreting out key expressions, statements, and gestures that give her greater understanding of the psyches of those living at 2 Windsor Terrace. In time, she begins to accept the fact that there is "no point where feeling could thicken," where intimacy could be experienced, and love exchanged:

> Portia had learnt one dare never look for long. She had those eyes that seem to be welcome nowhere, that learn shyness from the alarm they precipitate. Such eyes are always turning away or being humbly lowered—they dare come to rest nowhere but on a point in space; their homeless intentness makes them appear fanatical. They may move, they may affront, but they cannot communicate. You most often meet or, rather, avoid meeting such eyes in a child's face—what becomes of the child later you do not know. (58)

Portia's shy and humble eye movements indeed mirror a deeply felt reticence and a sense of non-belonging, which may prevent her at this juncture from giving of herself.

Only with her friend Lilian, whom Anna does not approve of because she finds her overly developed for her age, does she feel comfortable enough to articulate her feelings. Matchett, too, the housekeeper, who, though she greeted Portia, when she first entered 2 Windsor Terrace, with "an austere, ironical straight face," is a caring person. Then, there is Eddie, Anna's "troubadour"—perhaps her lover (81).

From the start, Portia is smitten with Eddie, who is charming, handsome, warm, endearing, and a fine talker. As a *puer* type, he is uncommitted—a young man who goes from one job to another, and from escapade to escapade. Living a provisional life, never wanting to be pinned down, preferring to wander about in an undisciplined, indiscriminate way, Eddie needs to revolve around a strong woman like Anna, a mother figure of sorts. Solipsistic and immature in his attitudes, he is given to periods of depression, which elicit no end of pity from Portia. Eddie, therefore, answers a need in the teenager: an impulsion on her part to help others, and to expend warmth and love. An *arriviste* of sorts, he is an expert at selling himself, but no one really knew "how he *felt* about selling himself" (76).

Not long after Portia's arrival, Eddie is about to end a visit to the Quaynes; Portia runs to bring him his hat. So touched is he by her gesture that he writes her a thank-you letter in which he compliments her on her understanding of his moods, his unhappiness, and his sense of failure: "You wanted, you darling, to cheer me up." It means a lot to the *puer* to have someone fussing over him.

Eddie wants to be friends with Portia and relate to her, but only on his terms: that she makes no demands upon him. The inexperienced Portia does not understand the ways of this charming young man. What she seeks is "closeness" and "love," and she believes she experiences these feelings with him. How different he is, Portia thinks, from the "specious mystery" that is Anna. But the givingness of Eddie, whose smile is so open and whose ways are so gentle, is superficial, temporary, and virtually meaningless. Eddie does, however, enjoy chatting with Portia; never does he withdraw from her company, as does her foster mother, into "the shut-in room, the turned-in heart" (65). The fonder Portia grows of Eddie, the more she understands how useless it is to try to relate to the Quaynes: "Their privacy was surrounded by an electric fence" (109).

The adolescent runs true to form as she allows her mind to wander and to fantasize. "Sealed down under her eyelids," she visualizes a continent at sunset, rolling hills, shadows, luminosities penetrating the "dark hearts" of all those around her, and "like a struck glass, the continent rang with silence" (107). She sees herself seated with Eddie at the door of a hut: Light and darkness stream in on both of them as calmness and serenity take over—as if forever.

The reference to "dark hearts" suggests a poignant need to relate to the feeling world—to the heart, that central and vital organ in the human body. For Anna and Thomas, the mask, or cerebral cortex, is the focus of existence; for Portia, all revolves around the heart, the systole and diastole which see to the circulation of the blood and run parallel to a whole emotional complex. The heart, for Portia, is her very life principle; the continent she visualizes in her fantasy image is an inner land mass, a *topos*, where unity of purpose and harmony of spirit make sacred the world of passions and desires—her truth. The mention of glass in Portia's reverie—reminiscent of the opening ice image—suggests the interpolation of a brittle and cutting element to be encountered at the Quaynes'. It also may be construed as a premonitory or warning image: She, too, will have to be hard and aggressive if she is to strike out on her own. Only tough-minded action can lead to her own psychological and spiritual development. The darkness in the image refers to primordial darkness: gloom, primogenial chaos, nothingness, the path leading back to the profound mystery of each individual's origin, the gloom preceding the *fiat lux*—Portia's fall into the Quaynes' household. The light, the basic principle behind differentiation and hierarchical order, refers to Portia's desire to develop her potential and to illuminate those as yet unsublimated forces in the dark recesses of her unconscious.

Portia is flattered when Eddie invites her to tea; it is the first time a grown-up has made such overtures. He takes this opportunity to confide his problems to her: his poverty and debts, his loneliness, and the fact that no one really loves him. Once again he evokes torrents of pity from her, and, as to be expected, she reacts emotionally. Portia plays the role of a reassuring mother, but, as a teenager, she, too, needs to be reassured about Eddie's feelings for her. Since she considers each of his statements to be an eternal truth, she finds the reassurance she seeks. "You said I was beautiful," she reminds him much later, remembering how totally she believed him. Eddie does find her beautiful in a humorous and childlike way; she is utterly enjoyable, like a new toy. When he studies her face as she eats a crumpet, he cannot help but remark: "You've got a goofy but an inspired face" (125).

Eddie is also very entertaining. He is especially fond of impersonating Anna getting angry, but rather than finding this particular bit of mimicry amusing, Portia senses that he is smitten with Anna. Portia's inner disturbance and exhilaration at Eddie's antics are conveyed by Bowen semiotically: Portia feels "like a young tree tugged all ways in a vortex of wind" (132). Still unsure of herself, and far from being immovable and solidly implanted in the soil, since she has not yet developed a frame of reference, a center or focus to her world, Portia is pulled hither and yon, like the tree, in all directions. How should she react to Eddie, this rapturous being who has entered her life? Her emotions pull her one way; her thinking function, another. Her feelings give rise to hurricane power, after which may emerge a new creative breath—a new orientation to her life.

Portia is too young, too unsophisticated, to know how to handle Eddie, a consummate performer when it comes to playing on women's heart-strings. He also knows—when he so chooses—just how to imbue her with self-confidence:

> The force of Eddie's behaviour whirled her free of a hundred puzzling humiliations, of her hundred failures to take the ordinary cue. . . . The impetus under which he seemed to move made life fall, round him and her, into a new poetic order at once. (132)

Although different from one another, Portia and Eddie have, nevertheless, a good deal in common. Both are lonely; both are groping for someone or something to take them out of a world of conflict and distress and lead them into a domain where only happiness and serenity exist. They want to be able to leap over the fence enclosing them in their abysmal solitude, reminiscent of "two accomplices [who have] just discovered their common royal birth" (133).

The feelings of mutual *entente* and confidence Portia has for Eddie encourage her to let him read her diary, that work in which she has secreted her most precious thoughts and feelings. He alone will be able to understand, she thinks, statements such as the following: "I wish someone liked me so much that they would come to the door when I was out and leave surprises for me on the hall table, to find when I came in" (146). What she fails to discern, so wrapped up is she in her emotional reactions to him, is Eddie's complete lack of interest in her little book—and really in her. The focus of his world is himself. Self-indulgent, he is a taker, not a giver. As long as Portia can offer him comfort or entertainment of some sort, he will be friendly to her. The day she can no longer serve his needs, their relationship will terminate.

Polarities: "The Flesh"

The time is March, and the first yellow and purple crocuses set Regent Park ablaze with color. "No moment in human experiences approaches in its intensity this experience of the solitary earth's," Bowen writes (157). The sense of renewal in the above image is paralleled, on a feeling level, by Portia's burst of joy at the thought of her future happiness with Eddie as companion and lover. No conflict assails her fantasy world as she enjoys the full fruit of adolescent illusion—the dream that comes only once in a lifetime.

Like the Greek *Kore*, "the nameless one," who burst forth with such rapture each spring from her underground imprisonment, Portia looks upon the world as filled with infinitely pleasurable possibilities after the barren winter months spent at Windsor Terrace—an arid, empty space which provided her with neither a sense of wholeness nor intactness, but only animosity, hostility, and icy glare. For Portia, the onset of spring means the birth of new receptivity, and a fresh psychological experience.

"The Flesh," the title chosen by Bowen for Portia's second stage of development, is identified in the Christian West with evil. Unlike the Old Testament (in which it represents the fragile and transitory aspect of humankind), the New Testament considers the flesh sinful and the chief reason for humankind's downfall. St. Anthony believed the devil inhabited the body; St. Jerome tore his skin from his body with a stone; St. Bernard de Clairvaux stated that flesh inclines toward sin and prevents spiritual values from taking precedence. For Portia, however, the flesh opens her up to a new emotional foray, causing her pain and conflict, but increasing her ego-consciousness.

While Anna and Thomas vacation on Capri, Portia is sent to Mrs. Heccomb's home, Waikiki, at Seale-on-Sea, which contrasts sharply with 2 Windsor Terrace. Mrs. Heccomb's children, Dickie and Daphne, both in their early twenties, and their sophisticated friends flood the atmosphere with dynamism, spirit, and razzle-dazzle. Theirs is a high-voltage life, fast and fluid, but always lived within the framework of decency and decorum.

This new atmosphere allows Portia to experience a different matriarchal image: no longer cold and frigid, devoid of principles and feelings, but warm and understanding, compensating for her former deprivation. Yet, the dream Portia has when first arriving at Waikiki discloses a certain sense of trepidation—even terror:

> Portia dreamed she was sharing a book with a little girl. The tips of Anna's long fair hair brushed on the page: they sat up high in a window, waiting till something happened. The worst of all would be if the bell rang, and their best hope was to read to a certain point in the book. But Portia found she no longer knew how to read—she did not dare tell Anna, who kept turning pages over.

> She knew they must both read—so the fall of Anna's hair filled her with despair, pity, for what would have to come. The forest (there was a forest under the window) was being varnished all over: it left no way of escape. Then the terrible end, the rushing in, the roaring and gurgling started—Portia started up from where they were with a cry. (181)

The book in the dream symbolizes rational or mystical wisdom, science, and learning—not knowledge acquired directly from the life experience. Yet, important information can be gleaned in certain works, such as the Rosicrucians' *Liber Mundi*; the Sibylline books of the Romans, which see into the future; the sacred formulas revealed in the Egyptians' *Book of the Dead*. Such works speak to those who can *see*; they disclose certain correspondences existing between the visible and invisible worlds, between the spoken and the silent domains. For the psychologist, certain writings may divulge personality traits. To be able to look into people is to read them with ease—as an open book.

The dream frightens Portia because something is preventing her from pursuing her reading (her development, her understanding of her own inner world and that of others). Hair, which appears in the dream, is identified with the head and represents spiritual and rational factors, but also—and most particularly for poets such as Baudelaire—sensuality and instinctive life. In either case, hair represents the properties and values of a person: Samson, whose hair was shorn by Delilah, was divested of his strength. In Roman Catholicism, hair, venerated in saints' cults, takes on sacredness. For Portia, Anna's hair, which seems to be growing to such an extent that it covers the book she is reading, preventing her from seeing the print, is viewed as a threat. What Portia unconsciously fears is that she will be divested of her ego, that her conscious personality will be taken over by Anna, who will deaden her potential. Whatever identity Portia has developed thus far, and whatever relationships she has fostered, may be stifled—overwhelmed—by the long-haired Anna/Siren/Lorelei.

In real life, Anna has taken care of all of Portia's material needs—her clothes, schooling, and so forth—regulating her destiny as thoroughly as possible. Psychologically, she has dismantled her and denuded her of all that is her own. Such a divestiture, as attested to in the various images in her dream, unconsciously terrorizes Portia. She might even sense the fact that Anna has read her diary. Such an act may be looked upon, symbolically, as a kind of rape: the ravishing of what is most precious to a young girl—her own thoughts and feelings. In the dream, Portia has forgotten how to read, suggesting a complete neglect on her part of her intellect, but also, and more important, of her innermost self and her budding identity. The connection between hair and the forest image—Mother Nature in her undirected aspect—is linked by psychologists to subliminal spheres. Here, it emphasizes the chaos reigning in Portia's psyche. Feelings of loneliness and rejection parallel those of fear and despair; Portia feels constricted and imprisoned—with no mode of escape. The "gurgling" and the "roaring" of the water which nearly drowns Portia at the end of her dream may await her in her new environment. Water, associated with the collective unconscious—the deepest levels within the psyche—could, if she did not keep her head above this fluid element, drown her. Psychologically speaking, it could cause an eclipse of her ego, that is, of consciousness.

Water, the source of life, is now viewed as death-dealing and formless, as unknown patterns of behavior lying in the depths of Portia's unconscious. Her motivations, actions, and feelings are as yet untried and ambiguous. They will be tried now under a new set of circumstances. Water, the bearer and originator of life, as clearly stated in so many Creation myths, beginning with the Egyptian, the Japanese, and the Babylonian, and including the Judeo-Christian, is viewed as chaotic and dark and representative of a primal state, referred to in Chaldean mysteries as the Abyss or the Depths and in Genesis as the void.[7] Portia's dream suggests that, fearful, irresolute, nervous, and anxious, she is about to venture into new surroundings which could replicate the unsatisfactory conditions she already knows—or worse.

Portia is given a greater measure of freedom at Waikiki than she had in London. She finds herself adapting with relative ease to her new surroundings: a world ruled by youth rather than adults, a different social class, and working people rather than the Quaynes' upper bourgeoisie. More important, perhaps, is the fact that Dickie, Daphne, and their friends, although they work hard, are endowed with that marvelous capacity of being able to enjoy life.

The excitement and dynamism which reign at Waikiki are conveyed semiotically by waves of sunlight which flood the home, and a panoply of colors, including the cobalt blue and white of the breakfast dishes. Pain, however, is also present, in the shadows created by the harsh luminosities: the pain of growing up, the leap each adolescent must take as he or she passes from childhood to adulthood. Such distress is keenly felt by Portia in an example of active imagination. As she looks out upon the bay, her reverie encourages her thoughts to take on texture and form; they become visible signs of some new element about to enter her life. Portia views the steamers in the distance—and "the polished sea looked like steel: amazing to think that a propeller could cut it. The edge of foam on the beach was tremulous, lacy, but the horizon looked like a blade" (190).

The sea, considered as a dynamic, transformative, and eternally rich factor, may be the source of new riches in her life: beauty and love. Let us recall in this regard that Aphrodite was born from the sea; in Celtic lore, the sea brought divinities to Ireland—the Tuatha de Dannan, the tribe of the Danna Goddess—and it also gave access to the Other World. That Portia associates sharp, cutting, propeller-like instruments with the sea is significant. Such objects sever, and wreak havoc, death, and vengeance; they also serve in sacrificial and dismembering ceremonies, as attested to in *Bacchants*, *Prometheus Bound*, and Christ's crucifixion. Positive attributes may also be associated with cutting instruments: To sever what is whole, such as dividing a problem into its components, or analyzing a relationship by examining it from various angles, requires a cutting up of the whole image or emotional rapport. Portia's experience at Waikiki will be cutting and divisive; it will be positive in that she will gain new insights into her emotions and their involvement with others. The abrasions which will wound her, the feelings of betrayal she will suffer as a result, will sharpen her judging faculties, and will, by the same token, reveal the many levels in the structures that make up friendships. Her new understanding will give her greater independence; it will expand her consciousness. She will, so to speak, forget her mother. Not that she will block her out of her mind, but she will no longer need to look for her wherever she goes—she "no longer felt her mother's cheek on her own," Bowen writes (191). Psychologically, she will no longer yearn for a mother substitute—a figure she needed so desperately (and never found) when she first came to 2 Windsor Terrace.

At Waikiki, Portia enters another stage in her development: the patriarchal sphere. What her own father could not furnish, and what Thomas has failed to provide her with, she discovers in her special relationship with Eddie. Smiling, understanding, kind—or so she thinks—Eddie answers all her needs: "Portia saw Eddie in everything that could happen: she saw him in everything that she saw" (191). Eddie is her first crush, her first beau. His image permeates her world. Even when Dickie and Daphne give a party and Portia dances with some of their friends, she "saw her partners with no faces: whoever she danced with, it would always be Eddie" (209). When, however, Dickie's and Daphne's friends treat her like a "sweet little kid," she does take umbrage (218). How could she be just a kid now that she has a boyfriend? A thought, like a jagged blade, cuts into her at this moment: Does Eddie also look upon her this way? She begins to assess her situation, to cut it up and divide it, to view it from many angles and in terms of a variety of relationships. No longer as limited as it has been, her field of vision is expanding.

She asks Mrs. Heccomb if she can invite Eddie to visit her at Waikiki. He would enjoy the lavishness of their humor, their joy, and even the food they serve. Life at Waikiki is "unedited" and "frank." Doors bang shut; the plumbing makes all sorts of noises; the "upright rudeness of the primitive state," with its own rules and regulations, is "the fount of spontaneous living" (221).

When Eddie arrives, Daphne's friends look upon Portia with added respect: "The wish to lead out one's lover must be a tribal feeling; the wish to be seen as loved is part of one's self-respect" (231). Portia's sense of inferiority diminishes; she feels grown up, and her feelings of belonging to someone enhance her whole outlook on life. Portia, however, has not yet developed the discernment necessary to protect her from hurt. Still adolescent in her attitude toward Eddie, she is convinced that she is the only woman in his life, when, for him, she has ceased to exist. "The tender or bold play of half-love with grown-up people becomes very exacting: it tired Eddie" (245).

A particularly important image is delineated by Bowen in the empty house Eddie and Portia visit: "These rooms, many flights up, were a dead end: the emptiness, the feeling of dissolution came upstairs behind one, blocking the way down. Portia felt she had climbed to the very top of a tree pursued by something that could follow" (256). The visualization may be looked upon as a premonitory sign of Portia's inadequate understanding of Eddie. The upper stories of a house, frequently associated with the rational principle, suggest her inability to fathom what is going on, to discern, to evaluate, and to use her thinking function. Her emotions alone speak to her at this juncture—and all the more forcefully because she has been so deprived of love and affection since her parents' deaths. Only after witnessing Eddie's overt advances to one of Daphne's friends does she gain some clear insight into her situation. Later, when Eddie gets drunk and speaks freely, much to the annoyance of Dickie, Daphne, and their friends, "the autumnal moment, such as occurs in all seasons," takes place (248).

Portia demands an explanation. By cornering Eddie, however, she can only alienate him still further. When she reminds him that he has asked her to marry him, he retorts, "Only because you *were* such a little girl" (257). Since he knew it could never be, he was willing to commit himself. Portia feels the pain of a faltering relationship. Like the blade in the ship image, Eddie's rejection of her love is cutting it into pieces. And as she struggles to retain what little fondness for her remains on his part, he reacts sharply, unable to bear verbal, physical, or ocular constriction. He refuses to be judged, embraced, watched. Portia's "trying to piece" him together is anathema to him (258). Eddie, the *puer aeternus*, has to remain free. Never can he be leashed or taken seriously. His feelings, fluid as in the previous water images, forever alter and falter, depending upon times and circumstances. Eddie is that sharp vessel with cutting blades that

Portia saw in her reverie. At that time, she discerned only the mask—his charming, sweet facade—and not the shallow, solipsistic inner man.

Because rejection is too painful for Portia to handle, regression to a childlike state dominates at this point: "*Please* . . . You are my whole reason to be alive, I promise, please, I promise! I mean, I promise," she pleads, trying to mend what has been severed (261). She, who longs for commitment, cannot yet see beyond her needs and therefore cannot understand or accept Eddie's uncommitted nomadic nature. He is not one to be boxed in: "I cannot feel what you feel: I'm shut up in myself. All I know is, you've been so sweet. It's no use holding on to me, I shall only drown you" (279). The last image makes reference to Portia's premonitory dream at the outset of her stay at Waikiki. When Eddie warns her of his inadequacies, he speaks the truth: "What you want is the whole of me—isn't it, *isn't it?* and the whole of me isn't there for anybody" (280). How can Eddie give of himself when he himself has not evolved beyond the adolescent stage, and thus has no sense of his own identity? A typical *puer*, Eddie is an emotional cripple, a wanderer who can never settle down, nor probe his own psyche or soul, nor discover his own potential. Neither centered nor focused, he flees the very thought of being the prisoner of hearth/home. "*You must let go of me,*" he tells Portia (280). Her lancinating pain becomes an agony at the loss of yet another illusion. Accompanying him to the train station, Portia sobs outright as Eddie departs.

Portia needs time to assess and evaluate her experience with Eddie. That she does not cut herself off from her feelings, nor avoid suffering, is a positive step in her learning process. She is not morbid, and once the sharpness of her distress subsides, reason returns, and with it, reflection. Her strong instinct for self-preservation and her drive toward life are the basis for the illumination to come.

When a person is recovering from a physical wound, the formation of scar tissue indicates that healing is taking place. The coloration and texture of the scar tissue differ from the flesh surrounding the affected area. Highly sensitive, it reacts differently to light and touch. Analogously, Portia's psychic injury will help her develop a new understanding of her place in the world and in the family; accordingly, her ego-consciousness will be increased. When Portia returns to Windsor Terrace, readjustments, a new centering, and a fresh focus are in order. Now she has tasted of the flesh; and although it was raw and bloody, she has nevertheless been introduced to a feast for the gods.

Ego-Consciousness: "The Devil"

Symbolically, the Devil represents that factor in the human personality which struggles, doubts, and rejects, thus paving the way for growth and discernment. Lucifer (from the Latin *fiat-fer*) was a light-bringer. Thrust out of heaven into abysmal spheres for having disobeyed the ruling patriarchal power, his presence illuminated what had been dark, divided what had been whole, brought conflict where formerly there had been peace. Duality, though divisive, invites sapience. Only in a world of opposites can comparisons be made, evaluation occur, and increased ego-consciousness be gained.

Portia has suffered her first love tragedy. That she has not bottled up her pain, but has let it out, causes her a period of confusion and emotional turmoil. But, then, just as Aphrodite forced the despairing Psyche to sort out an enormous pile of seeds (corn, barley, millet, poppy, lentil, pea), Portia will have to learn to sift her emotions, to winnow, filter, and study each of her feelings, values, and motivations, so as to be able to understand them better and make them work on her behalf. Only by using her rational function—the book in the Waikiki dream which she no longer knows how to read—will she learn to defend herself and to carve out her destiny. Then she will no longer fear or be in danger of victimization by Anna's Circe-like personality. To gain consciousness and to develop identity by drawing on unknown factors in one's own subliminal world are no simple matter. The process entails the experiencing of what has been labeled the *horror vacui*: that emptiness which comes without knowing what will be; that leap into nothingness—the unprotected, detached, dark, and endless abyss. Portia's struggle with her undeveloped and unlived subliminal contents may lead to a higher stage of self-realization on her part.[8]

Portia returns to Windsor Terrace on a Friday afternoon in April. The house has undergone its yearly spring cleaning. Scrubbed from top to bottom, it shines and sparkles with mirrorlike reflections, "lanced through by dazzling spokes of sun, which moved unseen, hotly, over the waxed floors" (301). All appears fresh, new, and dazzling to the casual onlooker; the dust and grime associated with the negative archetypal parental image seem to have vanished. Yet a troubling image is interpolated: "The clocks, set and wound, ticked the hours away in immaculate emptiness," suggesting that the inhabitants of 2 Windsor Terrace have not changed; they still live according to their circular routine, their linear values (301). What has altered, however, is Portia's approach to these same conditions now that she sees into them with cleansed vision.

In the above image, Bowen's use of the phrase "lanced through by dazzling spokes of sun" recalls other jagged, cutting, and propelling sensations. A warring, contending Portia is now in evidence. No longer is she the awkward and obedient little girl that she was prior to her visit to Waikiki. An active and thinking person emerges, intent upon seeing to her own welfare. The lance and the "spokes of the sun" are associated not only with the wheel that carries one toward one's goal; they have a phallic meaning also. The end of Portia's love relationship with Eddie has aroused her fighting nature. An animus quality within her (that autonomous content in a woman's psyche which is alluded to as the inner man) has been catalyzed and so effects a change. In the Grail legend, let us recall that Christ's blood, after the centurion Longinus pierced his side, flowed into a golden chalice. Whoever came into contact with it was renewed. Blood, representing the life principle, is a catalyst. Psychologically speaking, Portia has been gravely wounded by her break with Eddie, but although this has caused her to bleed, it has also paved the way for a different attitude on her part—a new approach to people and the world about her.

Problems of adaptation emerging from newly acquired consciousness create different conflicts which must be assessed and dealt with as they arise. The Devil and his world of polarities, of doubts, of struggles, are now to be Portia's. How best to deal with the obstacles still besetting her is the focus of her next acts.

The spark that generates Portia's decisive move is struck by a conversation she overhears between Anna and Eddie at tea. She learns not only that Anna has read her diary, but that she and Eddie joke about its contents—about those things which she considers so personal and so painful. The tide turns. Aggressivity, and no longer reticence, is in order. Bowen writes:

> There is no doubt that sorrow brings one down in the world. . . . You may first learn you are doomed by seeing those vultures in the sky. Yet perhaps they are not vultures; they are Elijah's ravens. They bring with them the sense that the most individual sorrow has a stupefying universality. (355)

The Elijah of the Old Testament had a mission in life: to rid the world of Baal worship and to restore justice. To achieve his goal he had to experience the rigors of the desert. Alone, without food or water, he wandered about in the wilderness until he was about to die of starvation and dehydration. Suddenly ravens appeared and fed him (Kings 17:2–6). Psychologically, such manna from heaven may appear when an individual's ego is so depleted that, in order to survive, it draws on its most profound energies and resources. The transpersonal Self, identified with God in religious terms, comes to its aid.[9] So Portia, out of desperation, will draw upon the inner riches buried deep within her collective unconscious. Her psyche's ego/Self axis has learned from desert experience to communicate and to fluidify, thus providing her with greater insight into her difficulties.

Because life at 2 Windsor Terrace has become unacceptable to Portia, she decides to assert herself, to choose her way, and to claim her authority. With the emergence of *logos*, Portia sifts, selects, correlates, and evaluates the next steps she is to take. A sense of her own power and effectiveness—like Elijah's manna from heaven—helps her get through the dark and harrowing interludes awaiting her.

Portia first goes to Eddie's flat and demands to know if he is Anna's lover, what they talk about, and other details. Although he finds his position untenable, he again resorts to ruse and guile—or charm—as he attempts to explain his middle-of-the-course attitude to Portia, who still abides by her "lunatic values." For him, of course, she is nothing but an entertaining pastime. "I'd never dream of going to bed with you, the idea is absurd," he remarks, cutting her deeply (370).

After leaving Eddie, Portia decides not to return to the Quaynes' to live. She will visit Major Brutt, an older man who is one of Anna's votaries and also the butt of this modern Circe's ridicule. Arriving at his hotel, still psychologically bleeding from her latest encounter with Eddie, she "looked . . . like a wild creature, just old enough to know it must dread humans . . . she was like a bird astray in a room, a bird already stunned by dashing itself against mirrors and panes" (376). Although birds are representative of spiritual values and thoughtful factors, Portia's latest foray into the human sphere is flighty and impractical. Her offer to care for Major Brutt and even to marry him is not reasonable, and therefore is met with a refusal. She is, as the image describes, "dashing" herself against a brittle, transparent pane, still unable to accept some self-evident truths about the adult psyche. If she is to succeed in changing her course in life, she must resort to another route that will lead her out of the emotional maze which holds her captive.

Portia intends to fight back. Withdrawal into the courteous and civilized child's world is no longer effective. She must lash out and lacerate others verbally. Like Lucifer, Portia must play the role of light-bringer; like Satan (meaning in Hebrew "to persecute," "to be hostile"), she becomes Major Brutt's tormentor and his adversary, by revealing to him an excoriating truth.[10] She deflates Brutt's illusions concerning his adored Anna by telling him of the scorn and ridicule his Lorelei heaps upon the old man that he is. His hurt is deep; his color changes. No matter. In the long run, such knowledge will serve him in some way.

What should Portia do? Where should she go? An orphan, a refugee, she is most acutely isolated now. Her loneliness does not translate itself merely as an emotional condition, but is experienced realistically. The full meaning of the *horror vacui*—that archetypal void within which all exists as unformed mass and dark, undiscerned matter—takes hold of her when she finally understands that she "seemed to belong nowhere. . . . Stripped of that pleasant home that had seemed part of her figure . . . she looked at once harsh and beaten, a refugee—frightening, rebuffing all pity that has fear at the root" (385).

Portia must create her own world. One more step has to be taken: stand up to her persecutors, oppose and confront them. Only then will she acquire respect from others and independence for herself. Aggressivity, contention, and collision form the route she must take. If Anna's power play is not checked, if Portia cannot live with her on her terms, her growth will be stunted. To remain Anna's appendage, her shadow figure, would mean remaining, in essence, a little girl who has to follow a set path. Such comportment is now anathema to Portia.

Major Brutt tells her that he will call the Quaynes and ask someone to come and fetch her, since it is too late for her to be wandering around the London streets alone. He has decided never again to set foot in 2 Windsor Terrace: It is no longer "a clearing house for [his] dreams" (132). Moments later, he informs the Quaynes that Portia is with him. He intimates that she will return to their home only if they "do the right thing" (389).

The scene shifts to Windsor Terrace. St. Quentin, a novelist and one of Anna's admirers who is visiting the Quaynes, best sums up the meaning of Portia's demands, although they are still quite ambiguous: "If you are anxious to get her home—her 'right thing' is an absolute of some sort, and absolutes only exist in feeling" (404). What moves St. Quentin most deeply, perhaps because he is an artist and is sensitive to the workings of the human personality, is Portia's "extraordinary wish to love." The authenticity of such feelings, the purity of such a need, is not to be found among so-called civilized and sophisticated people such as the Quaynes. In a most telling move, which serves to underscore St. Quentin's remarks, Thomas draws the curtains and says, "People are looking in," as if still trying to cover up his failings and dissimulate the emptiness and hopelessness of his world and his marriage (404). Anna, however, reacts differently. She does not attempt to veil what she sees, and says in a semiconfessional tone:

> If I were Portia? Contempt for the pack of us, who muddled our own lives, then stopped me from living mine. Boredom, oh such boredom, with a sort of secret society about nothing, keeping on making little signs to each other. Utter lack of desire to know what it was about. Wish that someone outside would blow a whistle

> and make the whole thing stop. Wish to have my own innings. Contempt for married people, keeping on playing. Contempt for unmarried people, looking cautious and touchy. Frantic, frantic desire to be handled with feeling, and, at the same time, to be let alone. Wish to be asked how I felt, great wish to be taken for granted. (409)

Although Anna is far from knowing herself, she does for the first time reveal the turmoil corroding her being and the obstacles which prevent her from living and breathing the truth of her situation. Change, even for her, may be in the offing.

Matchett is sent to bring Portia back—on her terms.

Portia's ordeals and her drive for self-realization strengthened her ego to such an extent that she was able to stand up to the emptiness and pettiness of the vapid and self-indulgent personalities making up her world at 2 Windsor Terrace. No longer did she see herself victimized by the dull and solipsistic beings who prided themselves on the sophistication of their ways. The "Flesh" experience had created havoc in Portia; it had churned and catalyzed her emotions, resulting in extreme psychic distress. The "Devil" which emerged in her forced her to confront, to question, to act out her feelings. She stopped withdrawing into her own darkness and falling back into the womb, as do so many adolescents who yield thoughtlessly to the strictures of life at home. Portia followed the law of nature which decrees each person's right to realize his or her invincible inner power.

Reminiscent in so many respects of that marvelous adolescent created by Raymond Queneau in *The Complete Works of Sally Mara* (1947) and in *Zazi in the Métro* (1959), Portia outgrew her ineffective child's world with its illusions and fantasies. Her suffering, filled with cutting, jarring, and dismembering experiences, had to be taken seriously and acted upon if further change in her life were to be forthcoming. Because she followed the signs and signals her unconscious yielded to her in her dreams and reveries, she began the upward path of creating an identity for herself—of fulfilling her potential. As Shakespeare's Portia states in *The Merchant of Venice*:

> If to do were as easy as to know what were good to do, chapels had been churches, and poor men's cottages princes' palaces. It is a good divine that follows his own instructions: I can easier teach twenty what were good to be done, than be one of the twenty to

follow mine own teaching. The brain may devise laws for the blood, but a hot temper leaps o'er a cold decree: such a hare is madness the youth, to skip o'er the meshes of good counsel the cripple. (I, ii)

3 Isak Dinesen's "Peter and Rosa": An Alchemical Transfiguration from *Fixatio* to *Solutio*

Death, not life—spirit, not earth—is the focus of Isak Dinesen's tale "Peter and Rosa" (1942). The locus is northern Denmark, on the Sound, near Elsinore, a hundred years ago. A love experience between two fifteen-year-old children is narrated in a setting of a white, ice-covered landscape, with its seemingly endless mounds of glaciers and congealed mirrorlike surfaces. Dinesen's protagonists are not ordinary flesh-and-blood figures; rather, they are essences or collective beings who live in a space/time continuum.

Rosa is Peter's *anima* figure, an autonomous psychic content in his personality (his inner woman) who acts as his guide and inspiration. It is her image that he has carved as a figurehead on the mast of the model ship he has secreted in his room. Peter is Rosa's *animus*, the contrasexual element in her unconscious (her inner man). He will lead her outside of her world—into the unknown—to live out her destiny.

Viewed alchemically, Dinesen's tale enacts a transfiguration ritual: from a *fixatio* to a *solutio* condition. Alchemical theory is based on the notion of transmutation: Nothing disappears in the cosmos; everything merely alters in form and texture. Ancient and medieval alchemists, who were both scientists and metaphysicians, wanted not only to transform the imperfect into the perfect but also to raise human beings to the paradisiac state they had known prior to their earthly existence. Humanity longed to become reintegrated into the primordial unity (Eden), but in an altered and sublimed state. Since everything emerged from original oneness and became differentiated when entering the manifest world, returning to its undifferentiated state after death, it necessarily followed that everything that had been incarnated underwent the death/rebirth sequence.

The alchemical process reflects a parallel psychological condition: "the whole problem of the evolution of the personality . . . the so-called individuation process."[1] In "Peter and Rosa," then, events take us from a stultified, congealed, or, in alchemical language, *fixatio* life experience, to *solutio*, or the dissolution of psychological and spiritual problems through the water ritual. Such a transformative process may lead to expanded consciousness and rebirth, or to the eclipse of the ego and its annihilation.

At the outset of Dinesen's tale, Rosa's and Peter's empirical world represents a hard, ice-bound attitude toward life: "The earth and the air were equally without hope or mercy." Notions are congealed; attitudes toward spiritual and human matters are unbending and restrictive. No communication exists between unconscious and conscious contents, or between one individual and another. Each lives in his or her own silent and solitary sphere. Such an overly fixed condition may serve to anchor and steady individuals, thus affording them a certain sense of security. It may also immobilize them, force them to pursue unchanging and unwavering views, thereby preventing any kind of growth.

The patriarchal position prevailing in Dinesen's tale has virtually obliterated any possibility of psychological or spiritual evolution on the part of the older generation of protagonists. It has excised the aspects of the feminine principle, or a workable *eros* force—that is, the capacity to relate, to feel deeply for another human being. Woman exists only as a function, as a sublime, idealized, untouchable abstraction, or as a servant and procreating agent who sees to the survival of the brood and who services man when necessary. Rosa's father, a pastor, reigns supreme. Like the nineteenth-century Christian Pietists, he emphasizes earnest Bible study and places great worth on strict renunciation of earthly pleasures. Stress is placed on the next world and not on this one; spirit, not matter, is of import. A joyless domain prevails, which underlines humanity's sinful and guilt-ridden nature and its need for redemption. One can understand why such a stern and negative outlook, coupled with the long, dark winter nights and misty, cloud-filled days of northern Denmark, as well as the extreme poverty of the peasantry in this harsh and unyielding region, gives rise to Rosa's and Peter's lugubrious and tragic ideologies.[2]

Beneath this Pietist overlay, with its repressed spiritual and sexual views, exists the still active and powerful animist Norse religion, which prevailed prior to Christianity. Although the *Edda* (a collection of anonymous poems, some of which date to the ninth century A.D. or earlier) sing of the lives and loves of the Nordic gods, they also focus on the doom of both humanity and its creators. (Let us recall that the "Twilight of the Gods," with its final battle—Ragnarok, the tragic climax of the antagonism between the gods and giants which consumes the entire universe—dominates the environment.) Rosa and Peter, steeped in their nation's cultural and religious heritage, with the superimposition of a mournful Christianity, are filled with feelings of ominous foreboding.

Dinesen's narrative begins during the last days of March, when the frigidity of winter begins to give way to a warming atmosphere. We may suggest, psychologically, that the sun's fiery rays have started to melt brittle attitudes, paving the way for more moderate approaches to life and for relatedness, self-expression, and fulfillment. Dinesen writes:

> The hard, inexorable sky over the dead landscape broke, dissolved into streaming life and became one with the ground. On all sides the incessant whisper of falling water re-echoed; it increased and grew into song. The world stirred beneath it; things drew breath in the dark. Once more it was announced to the hills and valleys, to the woods and the chained brooks: "You are to live."[3]

The *solutio* process is liquefying what has been viewed as insurmountable glacial stumbling blocks. Like sugar or salt, whose individual crystals blend when placed in a bowl of water, rigid views become more malleable, appearing, at least on the surface, to be smoother and more comprehensive. Examined from a distance, Rosa's and Peter's problems are judged with greater perspective; the whole rather than the particular comes into consideration. *Solutio*, it must be emphasized, may also lead to drowning, regression, loss of identity, depression, or death.

Fixatio

Rosa, the parson's daughter, who wears faded and threadbare blue winter frocks, has a "classical and pathetic majesty" about her. When she wears her hair in an upsweep she is the picture of her mother, who died at her birth. The parson's feelings of loss after his wife's demise did not prevent him from taking his housekeeper, Eline, as his mistress, or from making her his wife when she gave him a son. Prolonged repentance for what he still considers his "infidelity" to his first wife has not only weighted his world, but it lies like a shroud over his family:

> In the house, overhung by the shadow of the grave, the other young people strove to keep alive; only the youngest inhabitant, the small, pretty child, seemed to fall in quietly with its doom, to withhold himself from life and to welcome extinction, as if he had only reluctantly consented to come into the world at all.

After the death of the parson's sister and brother-in-law, their son, Peter, comes to live in his uncle's home. Peter is to follow in the family tradition and become a parson. Daily, therefore, Peter sits by candlelight reading and studying *Fathers of the Church*. Book knowledge disenchants him, but God, about whom he feels most deeply, does not. Peter is not a thinking type. Intellectual and cerebral approaches neither answer his needs nor give him a sense of fulfillment. Only the natural world fascinates and nurtures him: winds, stars, glacial mounds, sun bursting through dense cloud cover. He spends long hours observing birds flying north or south, listening to their chatter and poignant songs. Their flight through infinite celestial expanses—the antithesis of the fixated ways at the parsonage—spells release and freedom for him.

For Peter, as for countless mystics, including the thirteenth-century Arab Ibn Arabi, the universe is an immense book which contains sacred formulas. Those who can decipher its arcana experience spiritual liberation, fluidity, and feeling, enabling them to interact with disparate and alien elements within the cosmos and psyche. When Peter is immersed in nature's flow, he no longer feels exiled or cut off from the ineffable—the *pleromatic* sphere—but at one with cosmic activity.

On one occasion, when Peter tires of reading *Fathers of the Church*, he gets up, walks toward the window (an image used throughout Dinesen's tale), and stares into the distant night. A paradoxical symbol, the window is both transparent and opaque; it enables the viewer's imaginative faculties to pass from within the closed, circumscribed house—an imprisoning, womblike inner space—to the free and far-off realms of the outer world. Psychologically, the window allows the ego (the center of consciousness) to leap out of the repressive, hermetically sealed conscious view and to exit into an abstract, atomized world where fantasy prevails.

Peter gazes through the window, listens to the gentle rhythms of the cleansing rain, and peers into the blackness beyond, a mirror image of the mysteries lying dormant in his own unconscious. Just as the process of germination taking place within black earth is invisible to the naked eye, so are Peter's dreams embedded in his unconscious. The warming weather encourages a breakthrough; emotions are energized, encouraging the burgeoning of unknown contents. Peter's brain seems to be able to tune into an outer dimension, to respond deeply to evanescent and mobile silences and sonorities. Tones, rhythms, and an entire musical score become audible, echoing from a hidden realm within.

The alchemists associated geese and other birds with *pneuma* (spirit and sublimated powers). Like angels for the deeply religious Peter, birds are soul images. They are unattached and uncommitted forces that have left their earthly climes to ascend to celestial heights; their wings are active instruments which transfigure them while also carrying them along. As Peter stares out of the window, his mind anticipates the warm August evening, and a sense of joy swells; time and space seem compressed: "All the pleasures of summer drew their course across the sky; a migration of hope and joy journeyed tonight, a mighty promise, set out to many voices." Like a "huntsman" searching for his prey, Peter is no longer satisfied with his passivity; he longs to wander off, in search of new horizons. Fulgurating forces take hold within his psyche and entice him to actively pursue a new course, putting an end to the cloistered environment within the parson's radius.

The epithet "huntsman" is particularly applicable to Peter's new approach to life. The Norse god Odin, whose quest for knowledge was insatiable, frequently assumed the guise of huntsman and traveler. Thirsting for the untried, he sought to drink from the well of wisdom. Mimir, its guardian, however, demanded the surrender of Odin's eye as a pledge of good faith. Odin was also the god of poetry and magic, of love, and of water, which he could rouse and calm; but he was primarily the god of the dead and ruler of the underworld, which enabled him to pass with relative ease from life to death and back again. It was on Odin's command that dead warriors were burned on funeral pyres and that they went to Valhalla, an area described in Snorri's *Prose Edda* as a giant hall with many doors, symbolizing the grave. Here the dead rested and were received by their ancestors.[4]

Like Odin, Peter longs for knowledge—not the arid information gleaned from books, but those infinite riches that lie beneath the waves or exist in supernal spheres. Peter may also be alluded to as "the fisher of men," seeking what is invisible to the naked eye, what is buried deep within the blackness of those endless seas that are identified, psychologically, as the collective unconscious. Meister Eckhart, the fourteenth-century German mystic, analogized his ardent inner struggle as a hunt, and Christ as the prey he was seeking. Like Odin as well, Peter is a poet, not of written verse, but of the creative factor in life; his sensitive inner eye is forever transfiguring reality.

Rosa, too, has reached an impasse in her world. We see her in a parallel image, stepping away from her loom and walking toward the window, gazing out and enraptured by the sight:

> Her mind was balancing upon a thin ridge, from which at any moment it might tumble either into ecstasy at the new feeling of spring in the air, and at her own fresh beauty—or, on the other side, into bitter wrath against all the world.

That Rosa is tired of weaving indicates an unconscious need to stop accumulating and multiplying her fantasies, to cease accepting her patterned existence, to step out of the enclosure associated with the square loom and the window frame. The move away from her loom is a sign of her need to carve out her own destiny and to restructure her compartmentalized and segmented personality.

A medium figure, responding always to the needs of others in her entourage, Rosa reflects the lugubrious atmosphere that permeates the parsonage—a world where only the hereafter is important. Because a negative view of life prevails, she is convinced that "something horrible would happen to her." Like the rest of her family, she is drawn away from the "vain and dangerous task of living."

Unlike Peter, who seeks to escape and live out his fantasy as a navigator sailing the high seas, Rosa breaks away from the untenable atmosphere by withdrawing into her fantasy world—"out of reach" and "inaccessible to the others." Only the secluded and protected domain of her own manufacture brings her some semblance of comfort and happiness. Increasingly her subliminal meanderings invite her to dwell in an inner space, where she seems to be able to understand and speak an unknown language and feel a part of nature's multiple dimensionality. In fact, Rosa is proud that no one can penetrate within the magic circle she has created for herself—except for Peter. When speaking of the universe—its moon, stars, and sun—he alone possesses the power to enthrall her. What he says "rang strangely in Rosa's mind, like echoes of hers." Is he duplicating her very feelings and thoughts? Is he invading her private realm? She is both attracted to and fearful of such a possibility. For then he might succeed in dominating her thoughts and feelings, thereby substituting a different condition for the claustrophobic one enclosing her.

The month of March, with its harsh rains but warming winds, also affects Rosa's psyche. Less frigid, she warms to the thought of questioning her feeling world. She also worries at the thought that her dream world—within which she has felt such a sense of well-being—might be in jeopardy. Who is this symbolic huntsman? this ravisher? this "unknown seducer" who penetrates her inner sanctum, her secret world of fantasy?

An animus figure, Peter is a projection of her own unconscious masculine nature. He is an autonomous figure—a heavenly spouse or guide—who could become the source of her renewal or death. Since she is Peter's anima—the collective image of woman that he carries in his psyche—their relationship is fated to grow closer. They will be drawn to each other as Tristan was to Isolde; as Channon was to Leah in *Dybbuk*; as the young boy was to the girl to whom the Chinese goddess Kuan Yin tied him with an invisible cord prior to their births.[5]

Neither animus (Peter for Rosa) nor anima (Rosa for Peter) is to be looked upon as an abstraction or concept. Rather, they are active, independent powers and potent forces pulsating in the unconscious, demanding the ego's obedience and allegiance. Because Rosa and Peter have done little to realize themselves (she withdrawing deep into her unconscious and he leaping into external spheres), they have projected onto each other, both creating their ideal images, compensating in this manner for the sorrow in their lives. The excitement and novelty engendered by Rosa's animus and Peter's anima send out flames from their subliminal realms, driving them to seek fulfillment.

The most powerful urge dominating the lives of Peter and Rosa is *eros*—the primordial personification of creative union in love. Since Rosa and Peter have been cut off from their *feeling* world because of the reigning Pietist consciousness, the mother as a warm, nurturing, and comforting force is virtually nonexistent. Even Peter's and Rosa's relationship is impersonal and indistinct, existing in the realm of universals. Their feelings toward each other are never acted upon, but are sublimated. As C. G. Jung wrote, "The more concrete the feeling, the more subjective and personal the value it confers; but the more abstract it is, the more general and objective is the value it bestows."[6] Never have Rosa and Peter touched each other; they keep their distance in their rarefied worlds.

When Rosa first feels her dream world invaded by some exterior force (her animus), she is both fascinated by this living power within her and angered by the intrusion. This "huntsman," "adventurer," and "betrayer" has made inroads into her hidden world—that cloudy, bleak sphere lying beyond consciousness and serving as her refuge. She blames Peter for spoiling her reverie and the joy such introversion brings her, and for forcing her to transcend the womblike atmosphere which comforts—but also stifles—her. A world of tension and conflict, of painful and lugubrious moods that must be dealt with on an empirical level, has been born to her because of Peter. The disturbance of Rosa's hitherto uninterrupted enjoyment of her pacifier—her fantasy world—so troubles her that there are moments when she wishes Peter would go to sea and die.

There are other times when Rosa penetrates Peter's inner sanctum and knows his turmoil and dissatisfactions. Then a "tremendous stream of longing" absorbs them both. Peter allows his books to collect dust while he looks out of the window toward new horizons, which rise "afresh with each morning's sun." He sees himself thrillingly sailing across the seas on the *Esperance*, a ship similar to the small barque he has carved and rigged with such precision and which he has named *Rosa*. Picturing himself lying at the bottom of the sea, deep currents of water passing through his eyes, small and large fish rushing along his body in an endless underwater pursuit, he accepts such a fate.

Water is Peter's element: It represents both freedom and death. Analogously, the liquefying process of *solutio*, which is included in the alchemist's transformative operation, takes a solid and concretized chemical, metal, or element and renders it virtual, informal, and fluid, allowing for fertilization and, thereby, development. During the *solutio* process, the alchemist triturates and burns the compounds with which he is working. Rid of unclean deposits, sediments, and sludge, matter is re-formed; or, expressed psychologically, outdated conscious orientations are dissolved and cleansed. The Egyptians referred to such transmutations in religious terms, as a kind of "Night-Sea Journey"—a perilous and painful period when the dead (symbolized by Osiris) left the world of the sun to enter lower abysses, thus exposing themselves to the perils of the deep, after which they were resurrected and their reentry into the world was assured. Similar trajectories were experienced by the biblical Jonah, who was swallowed by a whale and spent three nights in its belly before returning to land; by Joseph, when cast in the pit by his brothers; and by Virgil and Dante during their voyage in hell. Norsemen similarly placed their dead heroes in ships, sending them out to sea to be burned. These ship-graves, or funeral ships, symbolized the journey the spirit had to take to reach other shores. There is evidence from archaeological remains dating back to the seventh century A.D. that women and girls were also cremated in ships—some consenting to be sacrificed alive. The harsher the fire, the swifter the bodies burned, and the sooner they reached Valhalla. A link between fire and water—between the cult of springs, natural wells, and pools and burning passage to an afterlife—was prevalent throughout the Viking world.[7]

Travels in subterranean watery depths symbolize the ego's penetration into the fluid realm of the collective unconscious, where it must be purified while also cohabiting with unknown and perhaps fearsome forces. Such periods of regression may be looked upon as fulfilling a need on the part of an individual or group to return to that infinite yawning abyss that existed prior to creation: Niffleheim, a domain made up of clouds, shadows, and mists for the Norsemen, where the fountain Hvergelmir spouted her glacial waters. In these aqueous spheres, emotions are reshuffled and obstacles liquefied, bringing about alterations of outlooks, emphases, and attitudes.

In keeping with Peter's cultural heritage and his own psychological conditioning, he fantasizes about sailing forth on the *Esperance*. Unlike the vessels of Odysseus and other great navigators of past centuries, Peter's must be looked upon as a ship of death or a ship of transcendence. Like Plato and Plotinus, among other mystics who believed in the mystery revolving around the cyclical reorganization of matter, Peter considers sailing as a means for taking an individual into deeper planes of existence.

More and more drawn into abstract worlds, Peter believes Rosa to have taken on the countenance of a Sibyl. Reminded of the time he saw her gazing out of the window onto the garden outside, with its bare-branched trees etched starkly under the light of a night sky, he remembers her as spanning linear time and having the prophetess's ability to peer into mythological or cyclical dimensions. Let us mention that the Norse goddess of love, Freyja, one of Odin's wives, had started the practice of *seidr*, the divination ceremony. It was usually presided over by a *volva*, or seeress, who sat on a special scaffold or high platform as she entered a trance state brought on by the incantations sung by the participants, whereupon she invoked spirits, whose languages she understood and translated once she awakened.[8]

Rosa is such a figure for Peter. She can penetrate and understand higher truths and spiritual messages from transpersonal spheres, drawing out and absorbing secret thoughts and feelings. There are times, nevertheless, when Rosa is earth-drawn and involved in rectifying problematic situations. For example, her stepmother wants to buy a cow whose milk can feed the family; the parson vetoes her proposal because Christ is due to appear at any moment and one should not "hoard up treasures in this world."

The cow, a feminine force associated with the moon, represented for the Norse people the primogenial goddess Adhumla. Born of interacting cold and heat in primeval abysses, she became the wet nurse to the original frost giant, Ymir. From her udders flowed four streams of milk.[9] Such a fecundating force would represent a threat to the parson's harsh, cold, and fixated surroundings and is, therefore, inadmissible.

Still, there are moments of release in this frigid and stultifying household, when, for example, to the delight of the parson's little son, a butterfly that had remained alive throughout the winter months has "awakened with the first rays of spring." Ephemeral and inconstant, attracted toward and purified by light, the butterfly is frequently identified with metamorphic spirit, the chrysalis being the container of the potentiality of being.

Rosa tries to catch the butterfly for the little boy, but as it keeps eluding her grasp, she realizes that it, too, seeks freedom. In a gesture of supreme kindness, she climbs onto the sill, opens the window, and lets it out. Peter, who is walking toward the house, sees her framed in the window space and is transfixed by the vision. She "was so like the figurehead of a big, fine ship," he thought, "that for an instant, he did, so to say, see his own soul face to face."

By liberating the butterfly, Rosa has in essence freed her own soul, and, by extension, Peter's. Having taken the first step toward escaping her inner condition, and unconsciously attempting to choose her essence, Rosa, the catalyst, sets the pace for the alchemical change which is to occur: a departure from a patriarchally bound home divested of the cow and the world of abundance with which it is identified.

Solutio

After the butterfly's release, Rosa feels like a "benefactress"—a mother figure able to bring happiness to the little boy. For Peter, she is the sea, the barque, and the figurehead he has carved. She spells freedom and happiness. Her presence as an anima figure has taken on magnitude in Peter's world. Guide and totem, she is that feminine power able to help him navigate through troubled waters to safety—that other side where freedom and beatitude exist—or to death.

As the figurehead on Peter's ship, Rosa stands above the earth—the ideal blond and beautiful maiden in Peter's mind's eye. Reminiscent of the Sirens Odysseus encountered during his travels, and the Loreleis or undines, those water maidens who enchanted everyone who came within their reach, Rosa is the focus of Peter's dream—which is her dream as well. Lost in each other's subjective world, they both build up their own elaborate imaginings, compensating for the dreariness and lugubriousness in which they are entrapped.

The Siren, the undine, the Lorelei, and water maidens in general, representing inferior woman, have been considered throughout the ages—be it in the works of Aristotle, Pliny, or Ovid or in the medieval bestiaries—as fascinating but corruptive forces. It is they who lure man toward a primitive stratum of life, thus encouraging him in his bent for self-destruction. Although their hypnotic songs and ever-alluring breasts arouse passion, they are essentially negative beings. Temptresses only, they can neither satisfy man nor be satisfied by him, since the lower part of their torso is a fish tail instead of legs. The many men who have been captivated by these elemental, half-human powers are beguiled and bewitched into a deathlike condition—a dormant or quiescent state. To be dominated in this way by an anima figure is to miss one's destiny, to disavow any sense of commitment to the real world, and to regress into a state of continuous reverie and oblivion. Such a feminine power has been looked upon in patriarchal societies as a devouring vampire, an infernal deity, a seductive force which arouses obscure pulsions but never fulfills them. Unlike Odysseus, Peter does not tie himself to the mast of his ship (psychologically, to hard reality—the vessel's center and his own), and thus he lets himself be carried into an illusory world.

Rosa, the Sibyl, the Siren, the figurehead, captivates Peter. Her image and wistful nature blind him to earthly ties, destroy his rational thought, and entice him into an inner ocean where his nascent ego may be fated to annihilation. Mesmerized as he is by her image, be it at the helm of a ship or against a window frame, he is no longer in command of his fluidifying emotions. Energies triggered by his anima propel him ever deeper into his mirage. He trusts Rosa and wants to confide in her; he asks to come to her room at night. She need not fear discovery; no one will hear him climb the ladder outside of her window.

Peter chooses March 21, the night after the vernal equinox, when daylight hours begin to lengthen, to *ascend* to her room. He tells her that he has not honored God; rather, he has injured him by not making something of himself: "If I am no good, God is no good." Peter wants to give living proof of God's magnificence and grace, by realizing his lifelong dream of running away to sea. "God made those great seas, and the storms in them, the moon on them" as an expression of the mysterious relationship between the infinite and the finite. As Peter talks of the affinity between the animate and inanimate world, between water and land, and air and fire, new feelings constellate within him—and, by association, within Rosa as well. Energy passing from one to the other arouses fiery charges and pulsations, triggering in each a sense of excitement. How can she help him? By telling her father that she wants to go to Elsinore to visit her godmother and that Peter must accompany her. Once at Elsinore, Peter will be able to board the *Esperance*, which is anchored there, and travel to the North Sea; Dover, England; and round the Horn. What if he should drown? "But all people are to die some time, you know," he answers, "And I think that to be drowned will be the grandest death of all."

Reality vanishes momentarily; linear time vanishes; the past flows forward, and Peter sees Rosa once again framed in the window space. So moved is he by this archetypal image that he can barely speak. Rosa, the totem, the figurehead, has obliterated the empirical domain. Now that he is in the clutches of his anima, little separation exists between reality and illusion. No mast is left to grasp. His center of gravity founders as his ego sinks beneath the churning waters of the collective unconscious.

As Peter lies on Rosa's bed and talks on, never do their bodies touch. Only for a moment does he touch and finger her hair; afterward, he leaves, swept up in a state of unsurpassed bliss. To touch Rosa's hair indicates a need to feel, to palpate some living being and to prolong the livingness of those qualities the person in question represents. Cults of saints' relics, which include the preservation of their hair, indicate not only a veneration for these beings, but a desire to participate in their virtues and to eternalize their values in love and intimacy, through objects belonging to or related to them.

Ascension and descent are symbolized by the ladder Peter climbs to enter Rosa's room, that sacred space where rituals are performed. That Rosa's quarters are located at the top of the house suggests that spiritual spheres are being sounded out. Communication is taking place between two different verticalities or levels of existence: terrestrial and spiritual. Step symbolism, alluded to when referring to the rungs of the ladder Peter climbs, dates back to distant times—to Egyptian pyramids, Mesopotamian ziggurats, and the teocallis of South and Central America. Let us recall that the seventy-two rungs of Jacob's ladder, of which the top ones disappeared into the clouds, permitted angels to ascend and descend, their movement symbolizing a fluid relationship between formerly irreconcilable terrestrial and celestial differences. That Peter sought to "beatify" Rosa, to render her "unapproachable," is in keeping with the reference to Jacob's ladder in Dinesen's narrative. Rosa is not a living entity for Peter any more than he is for her.

Peter sees Rosa as an object of veneration—a hierophany (manifestation of the sacred) of sorts—which he can worship from a distance. For Rosa, Peter is the messenger, guardian, conductor, and annunciator of the sacred journey ahead. Both are signs of unknown and silent worlds.

As the butterfly image indicates a breaking through for Rosa from one level of existence to another (the chrysalis in the process of evolving from an undeveloped to a developed state), so the ladder implies a similar transformation in Peter's outlook. He has ascended to higher spheres and has drunk, so to speak, from the oxygenless atmosphere. As a result, he feels a "wild, overwhelming longing to beatify" Rosa. So disoriented and dizzied does he feel by the influx of new and powerful sensations that he sits down on the lowest rung of the ladder to assess the meaning of the strange sense of peace and beauty which has come over him—this "mystic accord with all the world"—and to steady himself in the process.

After Peter's visit to Rosa, he sees himself as a "challenger" and a "conqueror," while Rosa has a nightmare from which she awakes crying. Although she is unable to remember the details of her dream, it has left her with feelings of emptiness, as if she has been "let down and deserted by someone." Peter's need to run away to sea is interpreted by her as an abandonment and an unwillingness to interest himself in her plight. Forlorn and lonely, she envisages herself as rejected and forever enslaved in the glacial *fixatio* of her home environment. When, however, she soon realizes that she, too, is a power with whom Peter must reckon, her sense of bereavement at the thought of separation vanishes. No longer will she allow him to consider her a passive and yielding force and a mere object. How to show her strength? Through deception. She will speak to her father about the Elsinore project, but she will also (though the reader does not find this out until later) tell him of Peter's plans.

To elicit her father's sympathy, Rosa purposely wears her hair swept up, as her mother had. No sooner does the pastor cast his eyes upon her than tears well up in his eyes, fluidifying his formerly fixated stand. Under the spell of his inferior function—feeling—he grants his daughter anything and everything she seeks, unaware of the consequences.

"The ice is breaking up. . . . The Sound is free," Peter tells Rosa, who is stunned by his strangely radiant facial expression. Emotionally traumatized, as her father was in her presence, he suddenly becomes metamorphosed and takes on the stature of a hero, in whose presence she feels powerless. Like the ancient Norsewomen, she, too, will follow her huntsman, her Odin-like wanderer. Henceforth, Rosa and Peter are to live out their imaginary visions as a transference and countertransference in a world of fantasy.

Now that Rosa and Peter have drunk of the brew of feeling, *eros* has taken over; each becomes the talisman for the other. Unaccustomed to the sharp, rhythmic pulsions ejaculating from their feeling world, they are thrown off-balance and run the risk of capsizing in the process: "Peter had walked on in a state of blissful intoxication, with the sea before him and dragging him like a magnet."

As Rosa and Peter start to walk out on the chunks of breaking ice, the world seems to grow ever lighter and increasingly radiant, blinding them by its resplendence. The sun's fiery charges strike the congealed whiteness of the frozen masses in the water. Water blazes; it gleams in refracted prismatic hues. This kaleidoscopic visual symphony is so intense that any remaining evolutive principle in either Peter or Rosa has been obliterated. Like Odin, who lost sight out of one eye, Peter can no longer see into the world of reality. As for Rosa, her hero/animus has taken over, transforming her into a passive follower. The once-rigid ice condition has now been transformed into *solutio*.

Peter has thoughts and eyes only for the water element, since it is the only vehicle capable of taking him to far-off places. As the two walk far out on the ice crags, he tells the story of a skipper's wife who is jealous of her husband's ship and of its figurehead—a duplicate of her—which he had carved: "Is she not gallant, full-bosomed; does she not dance in the waves, like you at our wedding?" When, after helping save the life of a native king, the skipper is given two precious blue stones as a reward, rather than give them to his wife for earrings, as she has demanded, he has them set into his figurehead's eyes. One day when the skipper has to absent himself from his ship, his wife orders a glazier to remove the precious stones and insert blue glass instead. Unaware of the substitution, the skipper sails to Portugal, confident that his talisman will *see* to his safety. Soon thereafter, his wife's sight begins to diminish. When doctors tell her she is going blind, she vows to return the stones, but it is too late:

She learns that the skipper's ship has crashed, in broad daylight, into a rock which rose out of the sea, and all have been drowned.

The blue stones (perhaps sapphires) are to be looked upon as sacred objects endowed with magic powers. As such, they must not be used for personal reasons but for the good of the collective. Because the skipper's materialistic wife did not understand the powers vested in the stones, she did not treat them with sufficient reverence, and punishment was meted out to her. Interestingly, in medieval times blue sapphires were believed to have ophthalmic value: If placed on the eyelids, they effected a cure. That alchemists identified blue sapphires with the element of air—*sublimatio*—indicated their ability to see, in a space/time continuum, something which the naked eye could not discern. Divested of the sapphires (transpersonal entities and organs of perception and *voyance*), the skipper was incapable of directing his vessel through life's course and unable to deal with his wife in both the domain of reality and the domain of his own psyche (his anima). Unlike Senta, in the *Flying Dutchman*, who sacrificed her life to save a soul, the skipper's wife was more interested in fulfilling her own desires than in thinking of anyone else. Her physical blindness was a manifestation of her spiritual blindness. The skipper's inability to see the rock jutting out of the sea in broad daylight suggests an abdication of his earthly responsibilities—that is, his responsibilities to his wife and crew. Dominated by his anima, he was unable to *see* the danger confronting him. He became psychologically blind, lulled into a state of laxity as the sailors of Odysseus would have been had their ears not been filled with wax, which prevented them from listening to the songs of the Sirens. Odysseus dealt with the anima problem realistically and constructively, unlike the characters in Peter's tale.

The Vikings considered the figureheads they carved on the helm or wooden posts of their ships as protective powers and guides which worked in harmony with nature. To pay allegiance to these totem figures or titulary guardians or deities, as the skipper had done, is to identify with them, to become possessed by them and their nonhuman side. Only danger, then, is in store.

The skipper's ship—and by analogy, Peter's, for he, too, has carved his Rosa on its helm—may be looked upon as the vehicle used to accomplish a rite of passage, from life to death. Let us recall that the Egyptians, Babylonians, Celts, and Vikings considered the ship sacred. It assured protection from the many perils of the deep. From the Bronze Age onward, corpses were placed inside funeral ships, which were fitted with brilliantly colored sails, mastheads, and pennants or vanes incised with figureheads of various types and dimensions. A source of pride as well as fear, for the rite of passage had to be accomplished with technical perfection, the ship then sailed out into the unknown.[10]

We may suggest that, from a psychological point of view, the ship, like the cradle, womb, and tomb, may lull and anesthetize its passengers into a state of oblivion. Under such conditions, the voyager returns to an *illo tempore*, rediscovering and basking in a soothing and comforting beginning or infancy. Like Noah's ark, the ship may also be viewed as a prefiguration of God's covenant with mortals: a saving and binding force which protects from danger and heals what has been severed.

Peter's story is a warning to both himself and Rosa to see out into the world ahead and to face their acts, past and present, so that the rite of passage may be accomplished successfully. To allow the abdication of the ego is to encourage the unconscious to dominate. In Rosa's case, feelings of guilt take on dimension—a positive sign, to a certain extent, since it indicates her awareness of her betrayal and her self-centeredness, paralleling in this instance the skipper's wife's solipsism. Significant also is her identification with Judas Iscariot: Rosa has betrayed Peter to her father and has also kept the silver coins he gave her to buy the cow.

Why does Rosa believe she is living out Judas's fate? In Matthew we read: "And as they were eating, Jesus said, Verily I say unto you, that one of you shall betray me" (26:21). For many, Judas is not considered a traitor, but rather a sacrificial agent who, because he was the most beloved of the disciples, had been *chosen* to accomplish the most excoriating task of kissing Christ, thereby pointing him out to the Romans and thus fulfilling the prophecy of the crucifixion. Although Rosa betrays Peter, however, her father, unlike God, does not sacrifice him; rather, the pastor allows him to live out his destiny. Other parallels are in order also. In the Syrian *Acts of Thomas*, Judas is considered Christ's twin brother. Accordingly, Rosa may be viewed as Peter's sister. Their fates are inextricably sealed, one to the other. Viewed in this manner, Rosa becomes a redeeming power enabling a destiny to be fulfilled; Peter, the instrument that has awakened her to consciousness.

As Rosa and Peter walk joyfully—yet solemnly—on the vast expanses of brilliantly white ice, blues and grays shimmering as far as the eye can see, pastel hues are juxtaposed with harsh, fiery reds and golds, falling like sheets onto seemingly endless congealed water crystals. Soon, their footing grows uncertain; they begin to sway amid the breaking and melting blocks of ice. The water ritual that follows is of rare beauty.

As Peter takes Rosa's hand, she feels a sudden "stream of energy and joy" invade her being; a "sense of *universal moisture intoxicated her*," seeping into her very bones and arteries, as it does into Peter's, immersing them both in the alchemist's whiteness, or *albedo* condition.

For the medieval scientist and metaphysician, *albedo* indicated a whitening stage in the process of creating the philosophers' stone and a washing of the elements or metals through ablution or baptism. In the process of *solutio* or *dissolutio*, that which is imperfect within the object (or individual) is washed away in the holy water, bringing about a state of sinlessness. The incorruptible glorified body thereby created is the philosophers' stone for some, and for others it is a sign of Christ or the Self.

White, symbolizing an absence of, as well as unlimited, color, represents a world *in potentia*. Like dawn, it connotes futurity: a new beginning, paving the way for gestation and the development of heretofore dormant aptitudes. *Albedo* in Dinesen's tale suggests a vaporous condition in which body is made spiritual, consciousness yields to the unconscious, and the created to the uncreated.

As Rosa and Peter walk into infinite whiteness, faith in the *livingness* of their imagination increases powerfully. Some of the blocks of ice they see before them they identify with Elsinore; others, with Rosa's godmother's house near the harbor where the *Esperance* is docked. From there, Peter will board to sail northward to England and then on to the South Pole. The incandescent hues which dazzle and blind also excite and energize the archetypal images which leap forth in rapid sequences. Reality intrudes, but only momentarily, when Rosa notices water-filled crevices in the floe: The ice is starting to break up, but there is no use screaming for help, since no one on land would hear them. When she and Peter hold hands, tension vanishes; calmness, instilled by feelings of relatedness, envelops her: "That fate, which all her life she had dreaded and from which today there was no escape—that, she saw now, was death. It was nothing but death."

Peter holds the mystical keys leading to the land of the dead, but like Peter of the Bible, he fears to leave the world he knows. Only Jesus can dispel Peter's fear of walking on water:

> And when the disciples saw him [Jesus] walking on the sea they were troubled, saying, It is a spirit; and they cried out for fear.
>
> But straightway Jesus spake unto them, saying, be of good cheer; it is I; be not afraid.
>
> And Peter answered him and said, Lord, if it be thou, bid me come unto thee on the water.
>
> And he said, Come. And when Peter was come down out of the ship, he walked on the water, to go to Jesus.
>
> But when he saw the wind boisterous, he was afraid; and beginning to sink, he cried, saying, Lord, save me.
>
> And immediately Jesus stretched forth his hand, and caught him, and said unto him, O thou of little faith, wherefore didst thou doubt? (Matthew 14:26–31)

Faith, no matter what the religion, is the source of miracles.

Rosa, as her name indicates, is associated with the Holy Rose: the symbolic flower Christians identify with the Virgin Mary, and the feminine principle that fuses with the male cross. The departure of Rosa as the sacred flower—as anima—will be mourned by the patriarchal sphere which her father represents. His world cannot tolerate the loss of such gentility, beauty, and love: "So much loveliness, so much inspiration, so many sweet benefactions were to go from it now." The mysteries of the Rose, a universal symbol, are also identified with the Greek Aphrodite and the sexual mysteries connected to her worship, and with the cosmic Triparasundari, the Divine Mother of the Hindus, who is associated with perfection. Sufi writers such as the thirteenth-century Attar, author of *Conference of the Birds*, associated the rose with spiritual love: "I know the secrets of love. Throughout the night I give my love call. . . . It is I who set the Rose in motion, and move the hearts of lovers. Continuously I teach *new mysteries*."

Because Rosa (redness) is also identified with blood (holy communion), she may be considered the most important element in the death/resurrection ritual, which plays out the demise of the spiritual and sexual mortal (individual) and the birth of the immortal (universal) being—through *solutio*.

Clear water flows on all sides of Rosa and Peter as they walk on, their hearts "aflame" at the thought of meeting the captain of the *Esperance* and of flowing out into eternity. Seemingly guided by some unknown power, Peter bores a hole in the slowly receding ice chunk upon which they are standing, and into the ice he sticks the tree branch which he has been carrying, and onto which he has tied a large red handkerchief. The impression from a distance is that he is sailing on his ship—clear ahead. Now that the separation is at hand, Peter and Rosa will experience the sacred moment of holy sacrament. He takes out a flask of gin he carries in his pocket, gives Rosa a few drops, and then takes some for himself. Horizons expand; feelings dilate; and Peter, for the first time, has the courage to ask Rosa to untie her hair, to let it flow freely in the wind like strands of gold.

Associations between Rosa and the Virgin Mary are now fused with those of Lorelei: spirit with unfulfilled sexuality. "The soft, glossy mass of hair loosened and tumbled down, covering her cheeks, neck, and bosom, and, just as he had foretold, the wind lifted the tresses, and gently swept them against his face." A transfiguration has taken place; she is the living incarnation of the figurehead Peter had carved onto his barque. As Rhine maiden, water Siren, river goddess, Aphrodite, and Virgin Mary, all in one, she has become that superior force capable of healing man from the pain of living through death. Rosa now exists beyond the world of human vicissitudes. As an archetypal figure, she is the echo of Divinity's voice, an instrument of his will, and a repository for his most primitive revelations. (Let us recall that the Germanic peoples considered women to be endowed with the gift of prophecy. They were, it was believed, more open to the unconscious than men, more receptive to the collective sphere, and therefore more in tune with the transpersonal realm—the space/time continuum. Odin himself went to see Vala to learn his fate.)[11]

Rosa follows her animus as she stands unafraid upon the breaking ice under her feet. He, under the spell of his anima, is equally calm as his feet slowly sink beneath the waters in an eternal baptismal ritual. "In one great movement [Peter] clasped his arms round Rosa and held her to him," and Rosa, groundless, her being submerging in the fluid mass, "squeezed her face into his collarbone, and shut her eyes. The current was strong; they were swept down, in each other's arms, in a few seconds."

For the alchemist, water is both the source and end of life: the *fons et origo* that purifies and regenerates. Because of its fluidity it may be looked upon psychologically as a compensatory image for an overly static or fixated life condition. Because Peter and Rosa came from a rigid, unbending patriarchal environment, each desperately sought a fresh way of relating to the world and a means of adapting to the feeling function that had been shorn from them virtually at birth.

The death of Rosa and Peter in the icy northern waters of the Sound may be viewed as the first step in unbinding, fluidifying, and dislodging an overly burdensome terrestrial worldview. It can also be understood as an aspect of the creative process—of Dinesen's in particular. Rosa's allusions to Peter as "seducer" and "huntsman," and his characterizations of her as seductress and transpersonal force, are appellations which belong to Dinesen's artistic credo:

> You call an artist a seducer and are not aware that you are paying him the highest of compliments. The whole attitude of the artist towards the Universe is that of a seducer. For what does seduction mean but the ability to make, with infinite trouble, patience and perseverance, the object upon which you concentrate your mind give forth, voluntarily and enraptured, its very core and essence? Aye, and to reach, in the process, a higher beauty than it could ever, under any other circumstances, have attained? I have seduced an old earthenware pot and two lemons into yielding their inmost being to me, to become mine and, at the same moment, to become phenomena of overwhelming loveliness and delight.[12]

Peter's and Rosa's initiation into infinite waters—numinous spheres—is beneficial to the artist, who withdraws during the creative process into a world *in potentia*, drawing from this fluid realm the riches within reach, and concretizing these in the written work.

Once "Peter and Rosa" emerged from the alchemist's *aqua permanens* and reentered the finite domain in the word, *fixatio* again took precedence, to be followed by *solutio* and another death and resurrection in Dinesen's following work. We may suggest that, in "Peter and Rosa," she took seriously the alchemist's maxim: "Until all be made of water, perform no operation."

4 Natalia Ginzburg's *All Our Yesterdays:* The Introverted Cocotte and the Insect

Natalia Ginzburg's novel *All Our Yesterdays* (1952)[1] focuses on the drama of children growing up in Mussolini's Italy. The narrative movement of her novel, with its cumulative energy and suspense, fleshes out not grandiose deeds or spiritual intents, but rather the minute feelings and thoughts of young people trying to understand the meaning of lives bereft of security, continuity, and love—and the absurdity of it all. Ginzburg's episodic sequential style is garnished not only with captivating tongue-in-cheek humor, relieving the pathos of virtually hopeless existences; it has also an unusual visual aspect, which adds to its dynamism. She frames events and feelings in cinematographic arrangements, prompting readers to follow the day-by-day happenings as though they saw them unwinding on a reel. Images, people, streets, and mountain villages seem to flow by intermittently, discursively, and dramatically, each segment linked or cut off from the other, depending upon the psychological and emotive situation of the moment.

The two young girls to be focused upon in our analysis are Concettina, the introverted cocotte, and Anna, alluded to as the "insect." They are idiosyncratic because of their seemingly robot-like natures, due not expressly to a depressed condition familiar to so many readers, but rather to a kind of fundamental inertia, as if their egos had been detached from the Self and as if two separate parts of the personality were acting independently. Concettina and Anna, unable to communicate with family or friends, seemingly uncaring and uninterested in their own welfare, live isolated existences, dissociated from the rest of the world as they are from themselves. Strangers in their own home, unrelated beings, they rarely, if ever, experience empathetic relationships.

Neither esoteric nor mystical, Natalia Levi Ginzburg deals with the world of reality in *All Our Yesterdays*—the world she had to face during the difficult war years of World War II. Born in Palermo (1916) into a bourgeois family of Jewish intellectuals, she moved to Turin when her father became a professor of anatomy at the university in that city. During Mussolini's dictatorship, Levi's home was a meeting place for well-known anti-Fascist thinkers. In 1938 Natalia married Leone Ginzburg, a Slavicist; they had three children. Tortured for his anti-Fascist activities, Leone died as a result of his imprisonment. In 1950 Natalia married Gabriele Baldini, a professor of English and American literature in Rome.

All Our Yesterdays begins prior to World War II, in a small northern Italian town. Signora Maria keeps house for an anti-Fascist widower and his children: Ippolito, Concettina, Giustino, and Anna. Directly across the street live the owner of the local soap factory and his children: Emanuele, Amalia, and Guima.

Concettina: The Introverted Cocotte

Concettina's father, more interested in his anti-monarchist and anti-Fascist activities than in rearing his children, has been unaware of the importance of love during a child's early years. Concettina's world has been divested of tenderness; she lives in a void. Nor has the father understood the significance of integrating an ordered masculine principle into the home. He is an idealist as well as a recluse. His home is divided: the father on one side, and the children, forever catering to the irascible patriarch, on the other. After Mussolini's rise to power, the father suddenly—and for no explicable reason—loses faith in socialism and in life. As for his religious inclinations, God simply does not exist, and if he does, he is certainly on Mussolini's side, Concettina's father has told his children.

Concettina resembles her father in certain ways; she is introverted and spends most of her time in her room. Unlike him, however, she is not an intellectual. Rather than reading and thinking, she spends her time brushing her hair and deciding what dress to wear. If she can't find just what she wants among her things, she begins to cry, annoyed by the family's lack of money, which obliges her to wear the clothes Signora Maria makes for her out of old curtains or spreads. It is Signora Maria who tells Concettina that she looks like a cocotte.

The absence of the mother figure in Concettina's life, and the presence of a remote and dictatorial father principle, create a disturbance in the primal relationship between child and parent. The result: There is virtually no sign of any nascent conscience developing in Concettina's psyche, no ethical sense, no concern or caring for others—factors that help in the maturation process. The developing of awareness exists *in potentia* in the human psyche; it must be cultivated and nurtured in order to flower. Such was not Concettina's case.[2] She focuses exclusively on herself. She has no concern for others, no compassion, but she is not cruel or hurtful to family or friends. She is simply indecisive, uncommunicative, and detached. There is no foundation in her for moral development or emotional germination, no code of ethics, no building of a personality or strengthening of an ego. Although Concettina lives unconnected with and alienated from the rest of her family, she adjusts emotionally to their world by creating one of her own manufacture.

Since Concettina's father allows no visitors in his home, either male or female, Signora Maria is the only mother image she knows. Active and competent, Signora Maria does her best to keep the household together. Nevertheless, she lacks the qualities necessary to nurture warmth and tenderness. Forever critical of Concettina—her hips are too broad, her chest too flat, her clothes unbecoming—it is Signora Maria who tells her she looks like a cocotte. Strangely enough, Concettina seems to be covered by a hard carapace and impervious to Signora Maria's criticisms.

Preoccupied with clothes and weight, Concettina's focus is strictly physical. Her ability to attract young men to her orbit fills her with joy. She wants to be sought after and longs to be the hard-to-obtain treasure. Concettina has many boyfriends, alluded to by everyone in half-mocking tones as her fiances. One, in particular, Danilo, waits for her outside of her home, though he knows he will never be invited inside. Despite her need to attract young men, Concettina is not a hetaera type—the courtesan companion to man, who may also play the role of *femme inspiratrice*. Like the hetaera, however, Concettina forms few if any relationships; in fact, she does not know how to relate to people at all.

That Concettina weeps when something goes wrong—if she should lose one of her fiances to another girl, or if she should be unable to find the right dress to wear—is her way of expressing distress. An almost mechanical reaction to disappointment, tears, and not words, help her release what has been constricted within her undeveloped psyche; they aid her to ward off pain. Tears, however, can have negative results: They may draw a curtain in front of a person's eyes, dulling their vision, preventing them from seeing the world and coping directly and overtly with real problems. Such is Concettina's condition: Incapable of facing herself, her situation, and her destiny, she feels little or no conflict on the conscious level and cannot, therefore, evolve emotionally.

Nor does Concettina develop a sense of responsibility. She never thinks about the past or the future, living merely from day to day in her own solipsistic world. She is sad when her desires are not fulfilled, happy when they are. Psychologically, she exists in a paradisiac realm—in the *uroboric* state of original totality and self-containment prior to the birth of consciousness—as had Adam and Eve before the Fall. Her ego has not been born out of the collective unconscious; it "exists only as a latent potentiality, of *primary identity* with the Self or objective psyche."[3] Concettina lives in a state of undifferentiated wholeness. Although she sees light and darkness and knows what she likes and does not respond to, there is no understanding of the notions or concepts involved, and no capacity to discriminate between opposites. Never, for example, does she question or sound out situations; instead she reacts only with smiles or with tears.

For example, Concettina hates to go to the family's country home, Le Visciole, during the summer months. There is nothing for her to do there but to sunbathe and grow fat. She has no feeling for nature, or for the garden which "stretched down to the high road, a big, uncultivated garden full of trees," or for the surrounding fields of corn and maize, or even for the vineyards (15). She expels her rage at her own weakness by weeping profusely prior to her yearly departure, unconsciously revealing her inability to counter her father's orders. Ruled by his iron hand, she can do nothing but obey. The manner in which Le Visciole is furnished adds to her dissatisfaction: The guns and horns hanging on the walls take away whatever charm and warmth the home may have. A patriarchal atmosphere reigns, whereas she longs for a matriarchate.

After her father's death, Concettina seemingly feels a twinge of real pain. There is nobody now to give orders and direct the children's activities. A vacuum has been created, in which fear and distress reign. Who is to be the family's guiding light? Since the father's interdiction of visitors no longer prevails, one of Concettina's brothers invites Danilo into the home. Concettina turns bright red; she makes believe she does not even see him. Why? When she and Danilo had gone for a walk together some time ago, he had made a vulgar remark to her, and she told him outright that she did not want to see him again. He refuses to obey her wishes, however, and each time she leaves her house, he is there, wearing "a threatening look on his face" (33). Concettina's so-called fiances are fleeting encounters. Not with one of them has she formed a real, vital, or profound relationship.

Alienated as she is, Concettina has never known what it means to be accepted or valued for herself. Nor does she have any capacity for enjoyment and happiness. Moods of depression plague her and increase her sense of deprivation. Unconsciously, she views her mother's death—which she had been unable to understand as a child—as an abandonment and a rejection, disfiguring her very notion of the maternal image.

The life urge is deficient in Concettina. Stunted emotionally, she is attracted to persons of the opposite sex. The physical urge based on the instinct of sexuality exists, but nothing else. There is little in her psyche which leads to mutual understanding. Nor can she think logically or perceive connections between others and herself. Her feeling world functions, but on the most primitive level: Existence is determined according to whether something is perceived as pleasant or unpleasant, acceptable or to be rejected—as if she were immersed in a stream of events, unable to distinguish outer from inner worlds.

Concettina lacks self-awareness; she has no real identity. Nor does she feel rebellious or guilt-ridden, as does an adolescent when expelled from the paradisiac childhood state. She has experienced her separation from her primal beginnings passively, as though she were the recipient of events. Her suffering is pathological.[4] That she was cast into a wilderness, not by her own doing, but due to a "flaw" in her early environment, is at the root of her unhappiness, neuroses, and inherent despair.

Concettina performs as a fundamentally alienated and lethargic personality. When she does not have to go to school, she sleeps late, selects her wardrobe as she does her fiances, and prepares her thesis (on Racine)—a requirement for graduation—in the same desultory fashion that she does everything else. Only one event occurs to excite her enthusiasm: Danilo's imprisonment for political reasons. Suddenly, as if from nowhere, a hero figure is born. She, who had rejected him, now dreams about this strong, powerful being who exists in a realm beyond hurt, interested only in making revolutions. No sooner does she learn of his release and of his marriage than her ideals are dashed. As she was bereft of a mother figure, so she now finds herself divested of a dream—a deity.

Feelings of rejection set in. Days pass. Concettina decides it is time for her to prepare her trousseau. When her brother suggests that a suitable husband first be decided upon, she informs him that such a one has been found.

Although Concettina's family does not like the man of her choice, Emilio Sbrancagna, because he is a Fascist who takes part in Mussolini's parades, she marries him anyway, leaves her home, and goes to live with her husband's family. She becomes pregnant on her honeymoon and, after her return, is coddled and petted by her in-laws. Grandmother, mother, aunts, and maids surround her in order to help her during her period of morning sickness and, later on, after the baby's birth. Concettina has opted for a matriarchate over the patriarchate she had known. But will she fare any better?

In her new environment, as in her old way of life, everything is taken out of her hands. No responsibilities are imposed upon her: no thinking, no feeling, no apprehension—nothing. Concettina has become a vessel, a procreating force. Nor does her situation alter once she becomes a mother, or when her husband is called to war. She has nothing really to do with the infant except to nurse it; all else is carried out as in tribal custom, by the women of the household. She remains a *puella*, retreating, as does a child, to the domain of tears when sadness overcomes her. A period of growth could be in the offing now that she has become a mother. For such a situation to occur, however, she would have to become involved in events, situations, and the feeling world. Her detachment— even toward her own child—is startling: She pursues her life as if floating on water, pushed along by the ebb and flow of the wishes and desires of her adoptive family.

Tears, to which Concettina always has recourse in times of distress, are, for the psychologist, a solvent, a momentary *solutio*, allowing problems to stream out of an individual. A spiritual and physical panacea, in that tears dissolve and wash away obstacles, they may be said to be double-edged. Though a remedy of sorts, their fluidity prevents Concettina from facing concrete reality. Problems vanish, trickle down the drain, never compelling her to face those factors which make for her distress. *Solve et coagula*, stated the ancient alchemists: Concettina could conform to the first part of the saying, liquefying her problems; but not to the second, which demands that coagulation take place, that hard fact come into being. Only then can one confront and wrestle with one's inadequacies—in Concettina's case, her childlike views, her infantile reactions, and her unevolved ego. What bothers or hurts her, however, is excreted, along with her tears, making her incapable of assessing or understanding her situation and of developing any kind of identity. Because she cannot act overtly, she allows herself to be acted upon as a passive recipient.

Only through ego development and an awareness of her own free will—the notion of duality and the ability to act on her own—would she be able to deviate from the automatic instinct which determines her life. Only through "deviation" or separation between consciousness and unconsciousness can inner growth occur, and the individual be born—an individual responsible for her life as a person and that of her family as a whole. Concettina's marriage does not alter her situation; at the mercy of the matriarchal sphere rather than of the patriarchal domain, she has merely exchanged one mode of life for another.

For consciousness to come into being and for an adult to function, choices have to be made. An individual has to learn to give up the desire to be cared for and loved exclusively, and must, in turn, care for and feel deeply about others. Even after the birth of her baby, Concettina continues to abdicate her right to be a real mother, preferring to remain the child herself and to function as a birth passage, a vessel, a funnel—never an entity in her own right.[5] Distortion, mutilation, and a pathological injury to the archetypal image of parenthood account in part for her antisocial behavior and her inability to grow into adulthood.

Anna: The Insect

Anna, Concettina's younger sister, suffers even more desperately from the distortions of an unintegrated ego. Her mother's death, shortly after her birth, had divested her also of a primal relationship: the archetypal mother image. For Anna, however, there had been no paradise and no fall, nor any intense and instinctive relationship between mother and child. She just existed, as in a vacuum, never lamenting former joys, nor anticipating future ones, not knowing the meaning of anxiety, nor suffering guilt, nor even terrors of the night. Anna has a negativized ego, which, egoistic and egocentric, reaches pathological proportions at times. Uncorrected, it serves to increase her already powerful sense of forsakenness and insecurity.[6]

Signora Maria is also Anna's compensatory mother image, albeit a highly inadequate substitute. In a normal primal relationship, a mother's love brings the security and confidence necessary to a child's ego development, and the stability and integration upon which a personality can be built and individuality take root. At this early period, when a child considers itself the center of the mother's world, such anthropocentricity is not only considered normal, but it acts as the foundation for further development.

Anna, even more than her sister, lives a lonely life. Her only source of contact with the outside world is one friend at school and the music teacher who comes to the house to give her and Concettina piano lessons. After their father's death she is invited, along with her brothers, to visit the family across the street—the wealthy owners of a soap factory. That one of the sons, Guima, takes a fancy to her surprises Anna. Her father had always said, "Make yourself useful, seeing that you're not ornamental" (22).

The above remark sums up not only her father's opinion of her, but her own: She feels inferior to others, physically as well as mentally. Unlike the child who has known paradise and who is ejected from this idyllic state or rebels against it, Anna has no basis for distinctions or comparisons. Good and evil, right and wrong, are abstract concepts without meaning for her. Because she has no real sense of danger, she might not always know how to take the necessary steps to avoid it. Anna accepts her father's denigration of her as something completely natural; he is realistic, she thinks. Since she is not beautiful, she must be told so. Nor do her feelings of inferiority overly oppress her, since she has never thought of herself as an individual, but rather as a composite of what others—mostly her father—think of her. She is a mirror image, a reflection, and a projection—not a flesh-and-blood being.

Like her sister Concettina, but even more pronouncedly, Anna has no ego or self-awareness. Life flits past her, leaving little or no trace upon her consciousness. Like a reel of film, her existence is a composite of fleeting images which just roll on and on, always following the same patterns, encrusted in the same black and white spatial background. There is no center of consciousness, no shading, no tension, no memory or mind, and few somatic responses.

Anna suffers from what could be called non-experience. How can she know about life when she lives in such cloistered quarters? Guima is the first person who pays any attention to Anna. Her sense of her own worth has been so damaged that she is convinced from the outset that she and Guima will never be friends, and therefore it makes no difference to her what he thinks of her.

For some strange reason that Anna cannot as yet understand, Guima invites her to his home on a daily basis. Although Anna prefers to spend time with her schoolmates, she does not have the courage to refuse him. Besides, she is proud to be invited by such a high-class person.

Anna is always either passive, indecisive, or lethargic with people in general, and with Guima in particular. She feels cut off from everyone—and from her own inner being. But inertia does have a positive side. It allows an individual to come into contact with the vegetative process upon which all life depends and which modern people have a tendency to dismiss, identifying instead with the ego and its conscious goals. In Anna's case, no such identification exists. She neither nourishes her body's energies nor emancipates herself through a wild effort of consciousness. Lassitude takes possession of her in her schoolwork, curbing her activities, her responses, and the demands she might make upon her intellect. Anna may be said to be suffering from an illness described as a depletion of reserves of vital energy. Libido (psychic energy) has been withdrawn from the outside world and shunted inward, but for no creative purposes. Anna neither grows nor deteriorates.

In time, Anna's relationship with Guima takes a turn for the bizarre—perhaps for the perverse. The first few times they meet, they play Ping-Pong. Guima's needs change, however, and he becomes distinctly sadistic: He likes to reenact certain violent scenes from old films he has seen. Almost daily, he ties Anna to a tree, then holds a flaming piece of paper in front of her as he dances round and round. She remains mute, tolerating these antics and the soreness in her wrists from the tightly tied ropes. Guima also enjoys telling her of his heroic deeds: of the rugby prizes he has won and the boat races in which he has participated. He sees himself as invincible—a macho figure. In contrast, his brothers and sister label him the "buffoon."

What does Guima's obsession with such games symbolize? Games in general represent struggle as well as a need to dominate the elements and oneself. They also demonstrate a certain hostility to the outside world. Even though sports are supposed to be enjoyed, a spirit of contest is the catalyst. When, therefore, Guima tells his rugby stories to Anna, the very act of relating them arouses and excites him. He identifies with the players, their heroic adventures, and their physical prowess. He becomes these people. As for the sadistic rituals implicit in the games he concocts, he sees himself unconsciously as a master of ceremonies or a grand marshal, who can substitute established order for anarchy, spontaneity and fantasy for constraint.

In ancient times, Greek and Roman games had a sacred function: They were ceremonies accompanying religious feasts. Trained athletes and acrobats, musicians, and poets gave of their best. Guima's games, however, although smacking of ritual and fantasy, have a sadistic side to them. That he binds Anna to a tree indicates a certain lust for power on his part, as well as a need to dominate, master, and control his woman victim by tyrannical means. Its sexual overtones are obvious.[7]

The tree is a cult object for Hebrews (the Tree of Life and of Wisdom), for Christians (as represented in the wooden cross), for Buddhists (the bodhi tree under which Buddha attained enlightenment), for the Chinese (the Kien-Mou stands at the center of the world), and for others. The tree also signifies the phallus (fertility). In certain Iranian and Hindu tribes, young women adorn their bodies with tatoos of trees, the roots starting from their vaginas. Let us recall that Attis castrated himself on a tree at the height of his paroxysmal delirium brought on by his mother's passion for him.

Why does Guima need such spiritual and sexual play? This is a complex question and one which we could only begin to answer by suggesting that sadism may in part be a means of compensating for a sense of inferiority. Sadists seek to maim that part of "another" that they unconsciously consider inadequate, ugly, deformed, and misguided in themselves. It is, then, in psychological terms, a denial of one's *shadow*—that aspect of the unconscious which the ego considers unacceptable and, accordingly, rejects.[8]

The shadow may become destructive if split off from consciousness: "Everyone carries a shadow, and the less it is embodied in the individual's conscious life, the blacker and denser it is."[9] In Guima's case, it is repressed and split-off. Were he to acknowledge its existence and assimilate the tendencies which give rise to it, he would be able to bring these archaic contents to consciousness. Once the ego's control is extended over the unregenerate darkened sphere of the psyche, the hazards involved diminish. By ignoring and rejecting his shadow, Guima does not develop sentience; he is oblivious to what lies behind his drives, his pain, his hostility, and his impulsive acts. He is instinct-bound and not free to decide upon his future.

As Anna's ego is negativized, so is Guima's. Each in his own way is cut off from the outside world. Ego-rigidity, alternating with profound feelings of inferiority, lead to anger and sadism on his part, and lethargy, inertia, and masochism on hers. Both reactions are pathological.[10]

That Guima dances around Anna, who is tied to a tree, is also significant. Dance, an expression of an inborn mechanism (instinct) which has been organized into form and shape, reveals the needs of both the personal and collective unconscious. Reminiscent of psychodrama, pulsions and feelings are lived out through gesture—an inner necessity which cannot be conveyed through language but only through the body.

For sadism to exist, masochism must also. Although Guima never lacerates Anna's arms and feet, he does hurt her, thereby expressing the inner rage he feels toward both the feminine principle in general and his own deficiencies in particular. "Anna sat on the grass and her neck ached from so much nodding and her lips ached too, from pretending to smile" (28). Although bound and fettered both physically and psychologically, Anna does not complain; nor does she feel free to converse with Guima. On one occasion, he ties her to a tree at nightfall:

> . . . he told her he was going to the kitchen to fetch a knife so that he could cut her throat and eat her. So she was left alone in the almost dark garden, and tied up too, and suddenly she was frightened and started shouting, "Guima, Guima!"—and it was getting darker and darker and her arms were hurting her. Then Emanuele came out and cut the knot with his penknife, and took her into the bathroom and put vaseline on her arms where the skin was grazed and purple. "That brute of a brother of mine," he said. (28)

Anna's continued passivity is, indeed, masochistic and not incommensurate with the notion of the sacrament and the activities of the Christian Penitentials in the medieval Catholic church.[11] Penance means punishment—a penalty for sins or for other infractions—and the hope of salvation. Anna perhaps feels unconsciously guilty for her mother's death, since it occurred following Anna's birth. Her need for redemption, sacrifice, and atonement may be one of the factors involved in her dispassionate—and pathological—reactions to Guima's games. We may even suggest that Anna's impassivity, identified with death rather than with life, verges on the perverse. Indeed, she seems to enjoy the mortification and pain she experiences at Guima's hands to such an extent that after he leaves for the French Riviera, where he is to spend the winter, she is bored in the company of her school friends. Their games have no appeal for her anymore. Penance and self-blame disculpate Anna from all other concerns and may even help her, unconsciously, to reshape or remold her outlook on life. As Franz Kafka wrote: "One learns when one has to; one learns when one needs a way out; one learns at all costs. One stands over oneself with a whip; one flays oneself at the slightest opposition."[12] For Anna, Guima's game ritual may be looked upon as a cultivation of *mortificatio*: a salting of wounds.

Anna's masochistic bent may also be associated with the *eros* factor: the sense of isolation and alienation from which she suffers. Let us recall that the ancient divinity Eros was both cruel and compassionate. His wounding arrows tore into his victims' flesh, compelling them to love and hate more and more deeply. To torture others may be the only way *eros* can be heard and the sole manner in which one part of the psyche can break through to another, thereby paving the way for psychic change.[13]

Anna, like Guima, is fascinated by struggle and contest. She loves to talk about revolution, though her understanding of it is, at best, rudimentary. When she hears her brothers and the youngsters across the street discuss Mussolini's Fascism, the Maginot and Siegfried lines, the concentration camps, and the Red Army, she is fascinated. She likes the excitement these subjects arouse within her. Never for a moment does she begin to fathom the complexities of the political, economic, and philosophical maneuverings involved in these power struggles. Intellectual questions are virtually of no importance to her.

When Guima sees Anna at a get-together after spending a summer on the French Riviera and a winter in a Swiss school, "his lips curved into a contemptuous smile" (85). He invites Anna to the movies the following day. Anna agrees, passively as usual; and although "fatigued and frightened" in his presence, she admits to being proud of his invitation (86). They see *The Mark of Zorro*. Guima is scornful about everything in this film except the duel. He is attracted by this energetic contest as he had been by other manifestations of power, violence, and brutality. When he launches into a complicated story concerning dueling, rather than display her ignorance, a silent Anna maintains her customary nonverbal attitude and remains silent.

Guima has turned into an intellectual who flaunts his knowledge of modern art by showing Anna reproductions of pictures on which triangles and circles have been painted, and of literature by quoting the poems of the anti-Fascist Eugenio Montale. As Guima explains Montale's sober, intense, and melodious themes, dealing with the grimness of the human condition, Anna looks on in silent ignorance. Nevertheless, in the days to come, as she listens to Guima recite more and more of Montale's lines, their rhythms and images begin to dance in her head. Although she does not dare question Guima about the meaning of such mysterious words as *bomba ballerina*, nor ask him to elaborate upon the identity of the people alluded to by Montale, she enjoys this newly discovered side of Guima.

As for Guima, he tells Anna he is happy only in her company and then kisses her. Such a declaration is understandable, since she is the only one who is kind to him. His family and acquaintances have only scorn for him, considering him an arrogant, overly cerebral, and pedantic show-off.

As the days go by, Anna notices that each time she kisses Guima his face becomes "gentle, tender, brotherly . . . " (92). Despite this seeming transformation of personality, there is something frightening that she sees emerge in him: his "wolf-like teeth." By identifying Guima with a wolf, Anna lends an archetypal flavor to the relationship. She experiences something extrahuman about him: He exists on a plane which goes beyond human consciousness and therefore is connected with the "daemonically superhuman" or "bestially subhuman." Devaluation of human attributes is not always the case when probing the wolf image. As with other animals, the wolf has attributes that humans do not have. In fairy tales, for example, thanks to their knowledge of magic, helpful wolves lead lost children and adults to safety. There are others, of course, like the Big Bad Wolf, who devour the young and old as well.[14]

In Anna's case, the wolf is not identified with the mother figure as a nourishing force (cf. the paradigmatic wolf who fed Romulus and Remus, the founders of Rome). It is identified instead with a person given to wild, unsociable, combative, and sometimes brutal behavior. The psychological characteristics inherent in Anna's wolf are associated with a paternal chthonian force—her own father, who, like the big bad wolf in *Little Red Riding Hood*, terrifies children, or like an evil sorcerer dressed in a wolf-skin cape, his head hidden under the animal's gaping jaw, as he practices lascivious rituals high on a mountaintop.

The concept of lycanthropy—a person's willing or unwilling change into a wolf or vampire which chews up its prey—symbolizes, in psychological terms, the fears of childhood. For Anna, Guima represents a negative father image. Destructive, monstrous, and fearsome, his "wolf-like teeth" are ready to cut, crush, and dismember everything within their reach.

Teeth, representing aggressive forces, take from the outside to nourish the physical being. By dismembering the prey, they also divest it of its identity and strength.

That Anna identifies Guima with the wolf indicates a primitive identity with this theriomorphic force in her unconscious. It is a dark, destructive, and threatening shadow factor, which exists inchoate in her subliminal sphere. There is, on the other hand, another aspect to the wolf. In Greek mythology this animal belonged to Apollo, the sun god, and represented the principle of consciousness. Since the wolf is a nocturnal animal, it sees at night. The Greek word for wolf is *lykos*, associated with the Latin word *lux*, meaning light, perhaps because the wolf's eyes shine in the dark. The wolf may be looked upon both as a destructive inner power and a well-developed intelligence. One must, therefore, treat it with care and approach it from a distance, so as not to be engulfed in its gaping maw, from which there is no return. One must also learn to perceive the secrets of the wolf in the darkness of the night.

Guima as wolf may be identified, psychologically, with Anna's internal animal, forever hungry for freedom, trying desperately to wrench herself free from her repressive state and from the constant punishment her masochistic bent metes out. How long will she endure the penance inflicted upon her world of instinct? When will she stop enjoying such a relationship?[15]

As a projection of Anna's unsatisfied instinctual world, the wolf symbolizes the unfed, unloved, and rejected part of herself. Guima's wolf-like teeth are a constant reminder of her own ferocity—an aspect of that nonpersonal power buried deep within her being. It, too, is ready to devour the child's weakly structured and undernourished nascent ego. The beast of prey who sees deep into darkness is in search of food. Until now it has been kept at bay, locked in and repressed, as has Anna's shadow. To keep the wolf outside and to restrain its appetite require rituals powerful enough to contain its power. Until now Anna has remained silent and passive, yielding to the wolf-Guima's every demand. As long as she can maintain this exterior stance, she is relatively safe. Within, however, Anna, further dehumanized and alienated, is being consumed by the wolf and is unable to make human contact with others.

Anna does have moments of respite from her anxious thoughts. When alone in her room, she allows her fantasies to roam: Revolutions rage and volleys of shots are fired, as she sings out the battle anthem and Guima mounts the barricades:

> These were thoughts that she allowed to grow in secret within her, every day she added a new adventure, the flight of herself and

> Guima with guns over the roofs, Fascists . . . whom she and Guima led in chains in front of the people's tribunal. And she and Guima, after the barricades, would get married, and they would give the soap factory to the poor. (101)

When reality intrudes, however, she is ashamed that she has allowed her reveries to take over. Although she pushes them aside, they quickly blossom forth again, provoking moods of rapture—and jealousy. Anna knows that Guima goes skiing on Sundays and that his partner is the beautiful Fiametta. The images of the two together that emerge in Anna's reverie terrify her. She fears losing Guima. When she broaches the subject, he assures her that he is not in love with Fiametta, that she is only his skiing partner. As for Anna, she is for kissing. When she cries bitter tears, they make love for the first time, behind some bushes in the park, in silence, without tenderness, divested of feeling.

On her way home after the experience, Anna realizes she should not have yielded to Guima and longs to find some member of her household who might tell her not to see Guima anymore:

> But no one came to say anything to her, no one even came to see if she had come home. . . . She was alone, she was alone and no one said anything to her, she was alone in her room with her grass-stained, crumpled dress, and her violently trembling hands. She was alone with Guima's face that gave her a stab of pain at her heart, and every day she would be going back with Guima amongst the bushes on the river bank, every day she would see again that face with the rumpled forelock and the tightly closed eyelids, that face that had lost all trace both of words and of thoughts for her. (110)

No one seems to care what she does or where she goes. Her sense of isolation is crushing. Despair, melancholy, and inertia corrode her being. Nothing arouses her enthusiasm. She feels useless and unwanted—*de trop*—in a sordid and cold world. That Guima does not love her, but only makes love to her, increases her sense of worthlessness, adding to it feelings of humiliation.

Apathy, despair, and the listlessness which follows cripple any initiative and also serve to shatter her already feeble ego. Like Persephone, Anna seems to be descending into the dark and gaping mouth of Tartarus. Unlike the Greek goddess, she does not find her Pluto—her riches. Anna's psyche just penetrates the endless waters of her subliminal spheres, unaware of the dangers to which she is opening herself.

Immersion in the collective unconscious may lead to an eclipse of the ego. A depletion of libido from the outer world into subliminal domains, drawn there by heavily charged complexes, means that psychic energy is no longer at the disposal of the ego. As a result, Anna's already weakly structured adaptation to reality falters increasingly. Her inability to create a life and personality of her own, or to mobilize new forces to alter her situation, has led to depression and sloth. Anna cannot see beyond her immediate problem. Only an understanding of the magical side of the psyche could open her up to new situations and a fuller life experience. Anna feels only a sense of injury, without understanding.

Realizing she is pregnant, she longs for bombs to rip the world—and her—apart. Then she fantasizes. Perhaps Guima would marry her? No, the idea is impossible, she reasons. At first, Anna keeps her pregnancy a secret from Guima. She tries every—naive—way possible to get rid of the fetus: rapid walking, swimming in the lake, and so forth. Finally, the words escape her. Guima is outraged. When Anna suggests they marry, he immediately counters the suggestion: They are too young, the war is on, they are not in love. Guima gives her quinine pills to get rid of the fetus, and money for a midwife to perform an abortion, should all else fail, and then leaves on his summer vacation. Anna is desperate. The quinine has not worked, and she has not gone to the midwife.

Ginzburg offers the reader a *deus ex machina*. One rainy afternoon, as Anna walks alone in the street, she runs into an old friend of her father's, Cenzo Rena. She remembers him and his kindnesses from childhood: the wonderful postal cards he used to send from distant lands, and the chocolates he brought the family when he visited. Though her father had quarreled with him and he had not visited since, Anna runs to him now in her moment of need. She hugs him and weeps profusely at the same time. He comforts her as a father would a child. Later, she confides her problem to him. Although a confirmed bachelor, he agrees to marry Anna. His unusually perceptive statement to her sums up Anna's personality: "He told her that up till that day she had lived like an insect. An insect that knows nothing beyond the leaf upon which it hangs" (149).

Why the appellation of *insect*? Usually identified with a trivial person, the insect behaves according to inherited modes of functioning: It flies about, alights here and there, seeking nourishment for short periods of time—never on a permanent basis. It may be suggested that Anna, like the insect, has no cerebrospinal nervous system—only a double chain of ganglia, which function as reflex automata.[16] As such, she has an insect-like personality; she lacks the ability to function consciously and thus yields perpetually to an unconscious and instinctive pattern of behavior. Her actions, impulses, and relationships are always predictable: She flits here and there, playing with an idea, such as revolution, without ever *thinking* about the complexities involved. Nor does she ever try actively to construct a life of her own, face the workaday world, and deepen her relationships. Like the insect, she lacks the powers of concentration and attention, never engaging in life's multiple struggles.[17]

When Cenzo Rena compares Anna to an insect, he is suggesting that she lives mechanically, on a very primitive level. Unable to integrate outer and inner worlds, her psychic energy, activated in subliminal spheres, expresses itself in archaic terms, fragmentarily.[18]

Cenzo Rena marries Anna and takes her to live in his village, Borgo San Constanzo, in the southern part of Italy, where life is lived as it had been centuries before—primitively. He hopes that Anna, as future wife and mother, will no longer run in different directions, appearing and disappearing at a moment's notice, but will learn to run a household and act consciously. She does, to the best of her abilities, developing a relationship with her husband which grows deeper as the years go by. After Cenzo's death, Anna returns to her hometown. Guima, now married to Fiametta, seeing Anna's little girl, turns red: His daughter and he "looked at each other with intensity and distrust, and they laughed with their wolf-like teeth" (298).

Inertia and alienation plague both Concettina and Anna. Because the energy that usually emerges from subliminal spheres has either never issued forth or has fallen back into its depths, the psyche as a whole has been deprived of this catalytic power. The condition of sloth that reigns perpetuates unawareness and psychological stasis. Neither Concettina nor Anna is open to life's possibilities; neither is fully awake. They simply flow along with the tide, devoid of the initiative necessary to take their lives in hand. Unfulfilled, their infantile personalities and the painful turn of events their lives have taken do nothing to alter their dismal and portentous destinies.

In today's world, inertia, as lived out by Concettina and Anna, is antithetical to the cultural values of many nations. It is looked upon as regressive—a pulling back or return to a more primitive psychological condition. For Judeo-Christians, sloth is a negative quality; for the Chinese, it spells the dark and heavy earth spirit that clings to certain beings when asleep; for the Buddhist, it indicates *avidya* or unknowing, a state of bondage to the world of instincts, preventing perception of the higher consciousness of *atman*.[19]

A plethora of Concettinas and Annas—sufferers of sloth—exists in the universe today. Because their inertia is unconscious, it is dangerous, leading in many cases to a paralysis of soul and psyche. As expressed in *The*

Secret of the Golden Flower: "Laziness of which a man is conscious and laziness of which he is unconscious, are a thousand miles apart. Unconscious laziness is real laziness; conscious laziness is not complete laziness, because there is still some clarity in it."[20]

5 Flannery O'Connor's "Everything That Rises Must Converge": Sacrifice, a Castration

Flannery O'Connor's short story "Everything That Rises Must Converge" (1956) may be looked upon as a religious ritual which discloses the dark side of the human experience. Sacrifice is its core; the parasitic/castrating relationship between a mother and son, its essence. O'Connor conveys the decadent, ugly, worn, and destructive visible atmosphere and the equally fungal invisible order by means of her sharply etched descriptions, her dramatic use of objects, and her restrained and incisive dialogue.

Although the title of "Everything That Rises Must Converge" is taken from Teilhard de Chardin's *Phenomenon of Man*, O'Connor's story does not posit his progressive view. While Teilhard believed in an evolutionary progression from diversity toward an ultimate unity or Omega point, incarnated in Christ, O'Connor's characters do not broaden their views, nor do they grow psychologically or spiritually, until, perhaps, the end of her story. The question remains moot as to whether the protagonist, after knowing true agony, opens himself up to a deeper life experience. What is certain is that, like the Greek Erinyes, personifications of conscience and remorse who pursued and punished wrongdoers, so guilt and sorrow will plague O'Connor's nonhero for the rest of his days.

Autobiographical elements are present in "Everything That Rises Must Converge," such as the locale of the tale, Milledgeville, Georgia, where the O'Connor family moved after Flannery's father came down with the lupus that killed him in 1941. Her mother worked hard managing the farm she had inherited from her brother. As for Flannery, she attended parochial schools and then Georgia Women's College in Milledgeville, after which she won a fellowship to the Writer's Workshop at the University of Iowa, where she earned an M.A.[1]

Having moved to New York in 1949, then to Connecticut, O'Connor spent her time writing. Not until 1951, when she was diagnosed as having "disseminated lupus," did she think of returning to Georgia. The years remaining to her were spent in and out of hospitals, where, from 1952 to 1964, she underwent radical treatment for her disease. Due to the lupus, or the drugs used to arrest its destructive course, O'Connor suffered from a softening of her bones, which forced her to use crutches, further restricting her movements. Although her suffering, both physical and psychological, was acute, she never stopped writing. Outside of a trip to Lourdes and the giving of some lectures, O'Connor's movements were limited to her mother's home at Milledgeville.

Although she and her mother did get along well, O'Connor's physical dependence upon the older woman made terrible inroads on her emotional life, fostering, certainly, the growth of insalubrious emotions in both women. Whereas other young people live away from home, strengthening themselves in order to gather reserves to lead independent lives, O'Connor's physical condition forced her back to her childhood home, to live in close—perhaps stifling—rapport with her mother. There was no escape for her. She endured the vise. Rather than allow her spirit and psyche to be destroyed, she transfigured what festered within her into the work of art which is "Everything That Rises Must Converge."

Fiction, for the deeply religious Roman Catholic that O'Connor was, may be looked upon as a kind of confession, a purification, and a progressive shearing off of facades. O'Connor's expert use of objects, metaphors, anagoges, sardonic humor, and increasingly concentrated action and dialogue reveals the protagonists' souls. Shock is the technique used to elicit the moment of truth: a violent confrontation endowing the victim with a sense of his (or her) own fallibility, blindness, and mortality.

"Everything That Rises Must Converge" deals with a mother/son relationship. Each feels he (or she) has sacrificed for the other: The mother has worked hard to pay for her son's college education: the son, Julian, yields to his mother's demands, believing he is making life pleasanter for her. The tale begins on a Wednesday night. Julian is about to take his mother by bus to her reducing class at the Y. Because of her high blood pressure, the doctor had told her to lose twenty pounds. Heretofore, she had always taken the bus alone. Since integration, however, she insists that her son accompany her. Julian, therefore, must shoulder the task. Because "the reducing class was one of her few pleasures, necessary for her health, and *free*, she said Julian could at least put himself out to take her, considering all she did for him. Julian did not like to consider all she did for him, but every Wednesday night he braced himself and took her."[2]

Sacrifice

Sacrifice (from *sacrificare*, to make holy) is "an act whereby an offering is made to a god or divine being, and thus the object offered is made holy."[3] The goal of such an act is to establish or maintain a relationship with deity, be it for the purposes of love or appeasement. Cases in point are numerous and include Abraham's sacrifice of Isaac (Genesis 22) and Christ's crucifixion (Hebrews 8–10). According to some scholars, the Eucharist in ancient liturgies was considered a prolongation of the sacrifice of Calvary, and for this reason Roman Catholics call the Mass "the holy sacrifice."

Psychologically, sacrifice implies a divestiture of one's individuality in favor of another person, as well as a renunciation of one's personal claim over another individual. Sacrifice is a wholly altruistic act which does away with egoistic desires. Once a child has grown into adolescence, a mother's sacrifice entails an annihilation of the maternal instinct within herself, i.e., her compulsion as mother always to be the giver. Her goal, to a certain extent, is to allow her offspring to function on their own and to work toward detachment.

The opposite is true in O'Connor's tale. Instead of freeing mother from son and son from mother, psychic energy (*libido*) is caught up in each of them, binding them together still further in a blinding, viselike union. Rather than lessening the demands they make upon each other, each is determined to have his or her own way, covertly or overtly. The parasitic relationship between them invites mother to feed on son and vice versa: Each is living on the other's organism, deriving sustenance and/or protection without making compensation. Such a relationship can only be destructive.

The mother in O'Connor's tale is never given a personal name. She is a collective figure. Archetypal, she is a woman who has existed from time immemorial. She indulges her desire to mother her son; her destiny and his are indissolubly linked. She is proud that she has sacrificed her own comforts to send her son to college. Since she became a widow, she "struggled fiercely to feed and clothe and put him through school," and is still supporting him "until he got on his feet." True sacrifice exists only when a mother is able to release her grasp (conscious or unconscious) over those she loves best. Only then can she begin to understand the *Eros* principle at work. As Meister Eckhart, the fourteenth-century German mystic, wrote, God is "born anew within the soul," because *Eros* transcends personal desires. Until the mother and the son can experience real love, which comes with the renunciation of desirousness and possessiveness, neither spiritual nor psychological fulfillment can be experienced.[4]

The notion of sacrifice is presented from the very outset of O'Connor's tale. As Julian waits for his mother at the door, with "his hands behind him," he "appeared pinned to the door frame, waiting like Saint Sebastian for the arrows to begin piercing him." Such a metaphor concretizes Julian's need to identify with the notion of sacrifice and martyrdom. To consider himself a Saint Sebastian justifies his weakness; it serves as an excuse for not carving out his future.

Saint Sebastian, a third-century Christian martyr and the subject of paintings by Titian, Perugino, Memling, Mantegna, and others, was an officer of the Praetorian guards and was favored by the Roman emperor Diocletian until he discovered Sebastian was a Christian. He then ordered his archers to shoot arrows into Sebastian's body, but warned them not to kill him. Left for dead, with many arrows piercing his flesh, Sebastian recovered only to be beaten to death on the order of Diocletian.

That Julian identifies with Saint Sebastian takes him out of the human and individual sphere and plunges him into the divine and collective domain. *He* sees himself as truly heroic, unusual, and worthy of admiration. Not so for O'Connor, who satirizes such hubris. The image of Julian "pinned to the frame" replicates Saint Sebastian's ordeal (pinned down by arrows) and Christ's (by nails). It also suggests that pain and suffering, as well as immortality, will be part of his destiny. Objects such as nails, pins, and arrows are penetrating and lacerating forces which pave the way for both dismemberment and death and, symbolically, for illumination and fortitude. As stigmata, they are attributes of divine power in the form of punitive forces or manifestations of love. Transcendence of physical pain, motivated by passion for deity, indicates a sanctification or an anticipation of conquest beyond terrestrial spheres. It symbolizes unification and synthesis on both the human and divine plane. Let us mention the fact that arrows, nails, and other sharp and cutting instruments are also phallic symbols signifying man's search for the feminine element—the center, or the heart.

Why the comparison between Julian and Saint Sebastian? For a partial answer, let us turn to the world of objects as used by O'Connor in her narrative scheme. Objects, for her, play a crucial role. They serve to concretize an emotion, feeling, thought, or act. Objects in "Everything That Rises Must Converge" speak; they are real and must be dealt with. At times they participate in the protagonist's (or antagonist's) unfolding drama; in other instances, they add to the story's unity and singleness of effect.

The object which is the tale's pivotal force is a hat, a *deus ex machina* of sorts. Julian's mother has just spent $7.50 on a purple and green velvet hat. Although she takes joy in the fact that she won't "meet herself coming and going" in it, she regrets having spent the money to gratify a desire: "I'm going back to the house and take this thing off and tomorrow I'm going to return it. I was out of my head. I can pay the gas bill with that seven-fifty." The mother feels comfortable in the role of sacrificial agent which she plays out. Julian is adamant: He wants her to keep the hat. He catches her arm "in a vicious grip" and says, "You are not going to take it back. . . . I like it," underscoring, at least outwardly, his altruistic attitude toward his mother—his wish to see her happy.

The hat as object is a *sign*. Worn on the head, it represents the thinking function and the spiritual domain. It corresponds, symbolically, to the crown, which stands for authority and sovereignty. That the mother hesitates about keeping the hat indicates her irresolution. The colors of the hat are equally significant: Purple, for the Roman Catholic, signifies power, but also sorrow and penitence. It is the liturgical color for Advent and Lent, the seasons of preparation and penitence.[5] Green is a reassuring and happy color: It spells spring and renewal, growth and fertility, and, above all, hope. The hat itself, then, represents duality: sorrow and resurrection.

Landscapes are also signs of an invisible and unlived dimension. As Heraclitus wrote, "The Lord whose oracle is at Delphi neither speaks nor conceals, but gives signs."[6] When, for example, mother and son step out of their home to take the bus, O'Connor depicts a mournful and lugubrious landscape: "The sky was a dying violet and the houses stood out darkly against it, bulbous liver-colored monstrosities of a uniform ugliness though no two were alike." The panoramic image of the protagonists' neighborhood gives the impression of a dark, ugly, grotesque, and uniform environment. O'Connor's depiction of an insalubrious and miasmic locale is in keeping with her vision of reality, which is based on the notion that spirit is incarnated in matter.[7]

The epithet "dying violet" is a premonitory image. The color worn frequently by the Virgin Mary after the Crucifixion, and by such penitents as Mary Magdalene, violet indicates deep sorrow. Painters in the Middle Ages featured Jesus wearing a violet robe during the Passion. For this reason, the *choeur* of churches is draped in violet on Good Friday. That O'Connor describes the heavenly sphere as "dying violet" not only suggests the agony of death, but also a sacramental view of happenings.

The "bulbous" houses in O'Connor's panoramic depiction are paradigms for enlarged tissues and organs in both the body and psyche. Something, then, is out of proportion and deformed in the relationship of the protagonists. As for the liver (in the "liver-colored monstrosities"), the organ from which bile is secreted, it has always been linked with the emotions of anger, animosity, and bitterness. Saint John of the Cross, interpreting Jeremiah's Lamentations, identifies bile with the death of the soul when deprived of the Godhead. Everything alluded to in O'Connor's panoramic vision is prosaic, conventional, freakish, malformed, and in a state of decay. Such a climate fosters a condition of alienation, of self-hatred, and of antagonism between mother and son. Julian, unconscious of his dependency upon his mother, seems to limp along, as he lives out his psychologically incestuous relationship, like the "swollen footed" Oedipus.

A love/hate connection is evident in O'Connor's metaphors and interior monologues. Whenever Julian's mother enjoys herself, for example, he is determined "to make himself completely numb during the time he would be sacrificed to her pleasure." Looking at the "dumpy figure" of his mother "surmounted by the atrocious hat," he is caught up in a panoply of tangled emotions: "saturated in depression, as if in the midst of his martyrdom he had lost his faith." When the mother notices his "hopeless, irritated face," she feels "grief-stricken" for the wrong reasons, and she tells her son she is going to return the hat. Anger follows Julian's depressed state; he grips her arms "viciously," then tells her to shut up and enjoy her hat. Nor can he accept the fact that his mother, in some instances, may be right. He loses patience with her when she congratulates herself upon having moved into a neighborhood that had been fashionable forty years before and would eventually return to being so.

Verbal interludes between mother and son indicate the misplaced values. Instead of sacrificing for each other as they believe they are doing, each adheres to rituals without ever understanding deeper meanings. Both indulge in spiritual and psychological mortification, not because they are doing away with their ego-driven natures, but because they are nailed to an unconscious condition from which they are unable to break away. Each fastens onto something which neither understands. The stasis or deathlike situation they suffer brings no inner development for the mother. Rather, it invites a kind of disguised suicide. For the son, it remains ambiguous.

The ego (center of consciousness) in the mother and son's understanding of martyrdom is unable to give up its hold—that is, its vision of what is right and wrong. Had their sacrifice been authentic, it might have paved the way for growth and healing, but it turned against them instead. Rather than allow something greater (Divinity or the Self) to take over, they allow the ego to maintain its vigilance and authority. Stasis is invited to dominate; blindness, to lead. The surrender of a self-conscious personality in mother and son to a higher authority—to a transpersonal principle—does not take place.[8]

Stasis is felt most acutely when the mother looks back upon her past with longing and indulgence. Her upbringing has been of the finest; she thinks she knows how to act and how to be gracious to everyone. She feels secure in the knowledge that she is rooted. The fact that she takes comfort in knowing "who she is" is double-edged; it invites her to consider those around her as inferiors, socially as well as racially. Unlike the others, she comes from good stock. Her grandfather had been governor of Georgia; her father had owned a prosperous plantation with two hundred slaves; and her family had lived in a beautiful home, with antiques and a double stairway, in an atmosphere of luxury. Her heredity and class endow her with a sense of belonging to a paradisiac state, preventing her from seeing out into the present world, from relating to others, and from keeping up with the times.

The more the mother dreams of a past that is no longer, the greater is Julian's "irritability." The feeble and psychologically impotent surreptitiously revile those forces and people which they are unable to openly contest. Rather than move out of his mother's house to live an independent existence, Julian remains, preferring to speak with "contempt" of the rundown home which had spelled happiness to his mother, and still does. Because he identifies himself with her and her past—the luxurious childhood and adolescence of which he was deprived—he fails to take the difficult steps necessary to carve out his own existence. In fact, he dreams of the old mansion regularly. The symbiotic relationship he lives out with his mother deprives him of the possibility of creating any kind of independent identity.

Acrimony, anger, distortion, and ugliness find their place in O'Connor's narrative, heightening the moral sense of her tale and forcing readers to understand the *livingness* of the sacred drama taking place—that of the impersonal mother and her son. Perhaps O'Connor chose to call the son Julian after the apostate Roman emperor (A.D. 361–63) who tried unsuccessfully to restore paganism. In so doing, he encouraged momentary confusion and chaos. So, too, does Julian, in O'Connor's tale, constantly attempt to reverse the mother's values, convinced of his own maturity and detachment. His efforts are, in fact, indications of his extreme dependence and involvement with the mother principle.

The son in O'Connor's tale is not a hero. Like Oedipus, he longs for the mother's protection and love, as is evident in the house image about which he dreams. Identified by psychologists with the womb and the tomb, the house is a protective refuge to which Julian unconsciously longs to return, in what could be called "an incestuous backturning of the libido."[9] O'Connor's house may be considered as a sanctuary, an enclosed and secure space which harbors both the living and the dead, the profane and the sacred. At crucial moments, mother (consciously) and son (unconsciously, in his dreams) return to the serene atmosphere of the house image. A pacifier, it allows them to regress to those infantile stages when a child is cared for, loved, and made the focus of attention.

When a son reaches manhood and still remains under the protective care of his mother, he virtually sacrifices himself in allowing her love to dominate his every move. Such a condition has been depicted symbolically in many ancient myths with which O'Connor was conversant, having read Erich Neumann's works on the subject. That Aphrodite's beloved Adonis was killed by a wild boar, and Cybele's Attis was struck mad by a stag, resulting in his castration and suicide, are paradigms of the destructive and vengeful nature of the Great Mother's primitive side. When Julian's mother is unconsciously faced with her son's childish dependency upon her, she feels weakened by his softness. She fights such a psychologically undermining situation by being oversolicitous—destroying him in the process. Unwittingly, she castrates him as in the ancient myth. Julian, in turn, submits to his mother's advances and becomes so subjected to her so-called kindnesses and indulgences that he becomes powerless to resist this force of nature.[10]

That Julian's mother has sacrificed her comfort to give her son an education seems to be a grand and marvelous gesture to the outside world. Nevertheless, she extracts her pound of flesh. Rather than renounce her personal claim to her son, as a truly sacrificial act warrants, she dominates and indulges him to such a point that he becomes incapable of any objectivity. He has not given up the demands he makes upon her, as manifested in his bouts of anger and deprecation. As for his self-analysis, it is rudimentary and childish. Only once does he see authentically into himself: Telling his mother that someday he will make money, "he knew he never would." Neither has been weaned from the other.

To sacrifice requires a killing of what is most precious to an individual—a conscious annihilation of the ego so that it may be allowed to experience the transpersonal:

> It [sacrifice] reenacts on the conscious human level what is prefigured on the divine, archetypal level in the sacrifice of Christ by himself. According to Chrysostom, Christ was the first to eat his own flesh and drink his own blood. This action then becomes a model for the ego which has reached a sufficient level of consciousness to understand its meaning.[11]

Because Julian's mother has never divested herself of her personal claim upon her son, she is determined to have her own way, to make demands of one sort or another upon him. Nor has she ever recognized his individuality. By bringing up the subject of the sacrifices she has endured on his behalf, she not only emasculates him still further, but she also cultivates his weaknesses, encouraging him in his childlike and self-pitying conduct.

Because of her inability to deal harshly with him, she undermines his manhood and drains him of his virility—*castrates* him—thus encouraging him to withdraw from the contest which is life. This mother, walled up in her own past and her own set of values, has imprisoned her son in her coffinlike existence. Julian is her votary, as Adonis and Attis had been worshippers of their divine paramours.

Had the son really sacrificed for his mother, as he claims to have done, he would be able to give up the demands he makes upon her, including the providing of a comfortable home. Nor would he denigrate her ways—an easy escape mechanism which serves only to involve him still further in a state of parasitic dependency. To detach himself from her orbit, to leave and carve out an exogamous relationship of his own, would prevent him from unconsciously clinging to her. To accomplish such a task, however, requires immense courage. He would have to forgo the luxury of being his mother's "little lamb," renounce her protection and shelter, withstand her tears and sorrow, and remain unafraid in the face of her emotional turmoil. Of crucial importance would be to withdraw from her need to be a giver, compelling her to relinquish her psychologically dominant position over Julian, which also serves to prolong her sense of superiority over others.[12] Julian, then, would also have to summon up sufficient energy to battle the pain and suffering that must be encountered in the outer world. Only then could he fulfill the requirements needed to complete successfully the rite of passage taking him from adolescence to manhood. The child in him would have to be sacrificed so that the man might be born. The waning of the moon in ancient myths indicated the death of the Son of the Mother; during the following period of darkness, the Son was reborn, able to live out his independent existence.

The Giver

As mother and son wait at the bus stop, Julian looks at his mother's "preposterous hat, [worn] like a banner of her imaginary dignity." He has "an evil urge to break her spirit," attempting in this way to destroy what she represents rather than setting out on his own and sacrificing his state of dependency. His weakly structured ego encourages him to do whatever goes counter to her ideas on decorum. He pulls off his tie. Her reaction is predictable: She is embarrassed and tells him he looks like a "thug." When she threatens to go home, he puts his tie back on, thus restoring his class. "True culture is in the mind, the *mind*," he says to her. She retorts, "It's in the heart and in how you do things and how you do things is because of who you *are*." Although there is validity in his mother's notion, her heart is so cramped with bitterness and domination that little feeling remains for love. She devours the object of her affections. At times she resorts to threats: "I'll just go home . . . . I will not bother you. If you can't do a little thing like that for me . . . "

By the same token, the son feels superior to his mother and above "the general idiocy of his fellows." He has a college degree; his mind, therefore, is well developed, he believes, whereas hers is primitive. He prides himself on his use of the advanced thinking principle to battle his mother. Whenever faced with a crisis he cannot handle confrontationally, he withdraws into his own territory, where he feels comfortable, as his mother withdraws into her past.

The bus arrives. The mother enters the public conveyance "as if she were going into a drawing room where everyone had been waiting for her." As the hat in the first episode was a metaphor for a way of life, so the bus is to be looked upon as a microcosm. As opposed to the house, in which egocentrism reigns, this mobile enclosure, which takes mother and son on a predetermined journey through time and space, contains the collective's rules, codes, and conventions. Mother and son are required to deal extrovertedly with the people on the bus.

No sooner does the mother sit down than she engages two other ladies in conversation. She takes great pride in informing her listeners that her son has graduated from college and that he wants to write; he is selling typewriters only temporarily. After looking around to make certain there are no blacks on the bus, she comments, "I see we have the bus to ourselves." Julian "cringes," gets up, sits across the aisle, and opens the newspaper which had been left, "withdrawing into the inner compartment of his mind where he spent most of his time."

Sequences of indirect interior monologue follow as Julian assesses the "idiocy" of his fellow beings, while also probing "with absolute clarity" his mother's world and his own by extension. His superior thinking function, as suggested before, allows him to look condescendingly upon others, as does his mother because of her aristocratic heritage. Like his mother, he, too, withdraws into his fantasy world for solace, where he will also find justification for his acts and thoughts.

Julian's thinking principle is so limited in its range, so warped in its outlook, so lacking in objectivity, that his reasoning processes are distorted. He marvels, for example, at the fact that he has "turned out so well" despite the poor college he had attended; regardless of his mother's small mind, he "had ended up with a large one." Furthermore, he considers himself free of prejudice. As for his insight into himself, he feels it to be virtually infallible. He has neither been warped nor "blinded by love for her as she was for him," because he has "cut himself emotionally free of her and could see her with complete objectivity. He was not dominated by his mother."

Julian, possessed by a mother figure, is unable to see clearly into his own psyche. Walled up in regressivity, he fantasizes and sees himself as a kind of hero, having "miraculously" escaped his mother's dominion and feeling free of guilt and sin. He views the hatred that he harbors for his mother as a rejection of everything she stands for, when actually it represents his resentment of her autocracy over his infantile ego. Unable to see into his paradoxical situation, he hides behind the mask he has crafted for himself, living out a kind of cramped existence where he rages against his mother's behavior, never delving into the reality of his own.

The bus stops to pick up a well-dressed black man carrying a briefcase; he sits down, unfolds a newspaper, and "obscure[s] himself behind it." When Julian's mother casts an "approving look" as the woman seated next to the black man rises to take another seat, Julian gets up and sits down next to the black man, observing his mother's face as it "turned an angry red." Julian wants to further anger his mother by trying to talk to his neighbor, who pays absolutely no attention to him.

War between mother and son has been declared. He will teach her a lesson, he reasons. He will do so, but only in his fantasy world—not overtly. He muses: Perhaps he won't call for her at the Y at ten o'clock, after her lesson. Then she would have to return alone, thereby proving her independence. At one point he feels like slapping her as one does "a particularly obnoxious child." He tries to imagine other ways to humiliate her: by bringing a black professor or lawyer, or a "beautiful suspiciously Negroid woman," home with him. To persecute her is his intent, and such is the unconscious goal of many an adolescent who has achieved neither independence nor fulfillment.

The bus stops with a jerk, wrenching him out of his reverie. A "giant" black woman enters:

> The downward tilt of her large lower lip was like a warning sign: DON'T TAMPER WITH ME. Her bulging figure was encased in a green crepe dress and her feet overflowed in red shoes. She had on a hideous hat. A purple velvet flap came down on one side of it and stood up on the other; the rest of it was green and looked like a cushion with the stuffing out. She carried a mammoth red pocketbook that bulged throughout as if it were stuffed with rocks.

She sits down next to Julian, while her four-year-old child takes a seat next to Julian's mother. The white mother smiles at the little boy: He is so "cute," she tells her neighbor. Seconds later, however, her face turns "almost gray," as if she had become "sickened at some awful confrontation." The black woman is wearing the same hat she is!

At this moment, the hat is much more than a personal possession. It takes on the power of a hierophany; it has become a sacred object. That such different people should be wearing the same hat not only indicates a mysterious affinity and a bond between the two mothers, but it is also the manifestation of a synchronistic event—a meaningful coincidence. A heightening of tension is thus obtained, from a narrative point of view, and it also demonstrates a point of convergence, as the title of O'Connor's tale suggests.

Julian sees the hat incident as the ultimate punishment to be meted out to his mother. As such, it makes his joy virtually complete:

> The vision of the two hats, identical, broke upon him with the radiance of a brilliant sunrise. His face was suddenly lit with joy. He could not believe that Fate had thrust upon his mother such a lesson. He gave a loud chuckle so that she would look at him and see that he saw. She turned her eyes on him slowly. The blue in them seemed to have turned a bruised purple . . . . Justice entitled him to laugh. His grin hardened until it said to her as plainly as if he were saying aloud: Your punishment exactly fits your pettiness. This should teach you a permanent lesson.

His joy at his mother's embarrassment indicates the degree of his involvement in her world, but even more important is the fact that his rage, projected outward onto her, is unconsciously focused on himself. He is ashamed of his own feebleness, his impotence, his failure, and his inability to stand up to his mother.

The two parallel images drawn by O'Connor reveal another dimension of the mother/son relationship. The black child seated on one side of the aisle with the white mother may be looked upon as her shadow or her unconscious, infantile ways, which her ego cannot accept and constantly attempts to repress, limit, punish, and ignore. The "giant" black mother sitting next to Julian is a paradigm of his shadow, Mother Earth, which spells the unredeemed feminine principle existing within him. Never has he allowed this autonomous earth force to come into its own, to nurture his wan ego. Like his mother, he has repressed his dark and unlived side, which O'Connor has incarnated in black and white.

The more the white mother smiles at the little black boy, the more the "bristling presence" next to Julian angers, "rumbling like a volcano about to become active." The black woman resents the white mother's use of "cute," considering it condescending when directed to her giggling black child.

The four get out at the next stop. Julian has a "terrible intuition": He knows his mother wants to give the child some money and warns her to refrain. She disregards his advice. No sooner does she hand the child a bright new shining penny than the child's mother reacts in kind: "The huge woman turned and for a moment stood, her shoulders lifted and her face frozen with frustrated rage, and stared at Julian's mother. Then all at once she seemed to explode like a piece of machinery that had been given one ounce of pressure too much." As she swings her red pocketbook toward his mother, shouting, "He don't take nobody's pennies!" Julian closes his eyes, opening them to see his mother seated on the sidewalk, dazed by the blow. The woman and child have already made their way down the street.

Why did the black woman react so powerfully to the gift? Charity is as complex a notion as sacrifice. It, too, may be misunderstood and misinterpreted by both the recipient and the giver. Such an act, particularly when offered to someone who is not in need, may be unconsciously motivated by feelings of superiority as well as of condescension. When Julian's mother offered the black child a bright new penny, it masked her true feelings. Her unconscious intent was to humiliate the blacks, whom she dislikes. Such a cover-up is evident to the black woman, the Earth Mother, who is not only accustomed to such overt acts of charity bestowed by whites, but who also *feels into* situations and into people. She knows only one way to fight degradation, humiliation, and hurt: by brute force.

Julian's mother, even while giving charity, is in fact working for destruction and not for construction; for death, not for life. She is an evil force—a demon—hiding behind a mask of sanctimony. No higher consciousness can possibly emerge from her penny-giving act, which was intended to downgrade the other. This was her pathetic way of prolonging an existing state of subservience of blacks to whites; it is the same tactic used to continue her son's dependence upon her. Giving, when combined with discernment, understanding, wisdom, and true self-abnegation, is an act of love, as the Latin origin of the word, *caritas*, implies.[13]

The Kratophany

The explosion, which we call a kratophany, will bring about a partial resolution of O'Connor's tale. Kratophanies are manifestations of power: thunder, lightning, volcanoes, tidal waves, and earthquakes. These have been "feared" and "venerated" since time immemorial.[14] Because such concentrations of energy, when projected onto human beings, objects, or natural occurrences, lend sacred value to what some may consider only an ordinary entity, kratophanies, as any magico-religious rite, must be approached with great precaution.

From a psychological point of view, kratophanies may bring about emotional upheavals of the most violent types, sending shock waves reverberating throughout the psyche of an individual or of a community. The terrifying conditions brought into existence can alienate or drive to madness and death. Some mystics, such as Jacob Boehme, Meister Eckhart, and Saint John of the Cross, believed that kratophanies, viewed as chaotic events or situations, may pave the way for revelation.

The experience of turmoil and shock—which Julian and his mother undergo when the black woman swings her bag at her—serves to confuse, to dazzle, and to shock her. That Julian closes his eyes indicates his need to block out the workaday world in which he cannot function. In so doing, he is oblivious to the real meaning of the explosive event and interprets the drama as another lesson for his mother. His warped thinking faculties, rather than opening his mind and his heart, have blinded him to the reality of his mother's condition. He even tells her that he hopes the incident will teach her a lesson:

> "That was the whole colored race which will no longer take your condescending pennies. That was your black double. She can wear the same hat as you, and to be sure," he added gratuitously (because he thought it was funny), "it looked better on her than it did on you. What all this means," he said, "is that the old world is gone. The old manners are obsolete and your graciousness is not worth a damn."

Julian's mother gets up and walks ahead, oblivious to the fact that her son wants to take her home by bus. So deeply crushed is she that she has become incoherent, losing all contact with the real world. The past, comforting and warm as always, comes to her aid again. She asks that Grandpa or Caroline come and call for her, after which she slumps forward and falls on the pavement. "Mother! . . . Darling, sweetheart, wait! . . . Mama, Mama!" he cries out in vain. It is too late. She is dead: "Her face was fiercely distorted. One eye, large and staring, moved slightly to the left as if it had become unmoored. The other remained fixed on him, raked his face again, found nothing and closed."

Julian runs here and there, crying for help. The world, secure until now, has been transformed into a gaping maw ready to devour him. Only now does he begin to understand the closeness of his bond with his mother: "The tide of darkness seemed to sweep him back to her, postponing from moment to moment his entry into the world of guilt and sorrow."

That primitive shadow factor within Julian's mother—and lived out in the black woman, with tidal wave force—had drowned her ego, bringing death in its wake. The Black Mother, the source of the kratophany, the paradigm of the unredeemed power that lives in the depths of individuals, societies, and nations, had taken it upon herself to destroy the contrived self-image which both mother and son had so carefully nurtured. She was that transpersonal force that explodes and dismembers unnatural patterns of behavior.

Now that Julian is bereft of his mother/enemy, his life, spent battling that domineering force, has become meaningless. Alienation, nihilism, and absurdity arise in one whose heart has been laid bare, leaving him—unlike Saint Sebastian, who experienced God's radiance—emotionally lacerated, bloodied, and eviscerated. Yet, perhaps open to experience? Like Julian the Apostate, who said when dying, "Thou hast conquered, Oh Galilean."

Although Julian understands the power of his love for his mother, the trauma which brought on the revelation fosters nothing but feelings of "guilt" and "sorrow," all the more powerful in that the patina of memory wipes out the image of a castrating mother. What remains in his loneliness and pain is the image of a beatific, loving, and gentle presence. Her demise, rather than decreasing Julian's psychologically incestuous relationship with his mother, increases it. Feelings of guilt and remorse will provide him with the emotional sustenance needed to prolong the regressive pattern of behavior set forth by his sacrificing/castrating mother.

6 Jean Rhys's *Wide Sargasso Sea*: Mother/Daughter Identification and Alienation

Jean Rhys's *Wide Sargasso Sea* (1967), a deeply troubling novel, fleshes out the problems confronting two embryonic psyches in a mother/daughter identification and alienation situation. The action for the most part takes place on two islands (Jamaica and Dominica) in the West Indies in the 1830s. Communication with the outer world is possible only by ship, and this accentuates the isolation and helplessness of the feminine figures involved. The imposition of the white man's patriarchal law, depriving women of most of their rights, adds to their distress, as does the hatred of the newly emancipated Negroes, who take revenge for their former condition by burning, pillaging, and raping.

The manner in which Rhys's remarkable narrative unfolds—in elliptical sentences, brief dialogic sequences, well-chosen epithets, and fleeting sensual images of tropical landscapes—is all the more dramatic and mysterious because of her fragmentary style. So much remains unsaid; so much is silent and invisible. Her symbology is also arresting: Words such as "marooned," "looking glass," or "empty," repeated in key spots in the novel, create rhythmic effects which lull readers even while shocking them, and also create a climate of desolation and mounting emotional paralysis.

Jean Rhys (1894–1979), born in Roseau, Dominica, one of the Windward Islands in the West Indies, was the daughter of a Welsh doctor and a Creole mother, whose white family had settled on the British island many years earlier. After having attended convent school, Jean left for London in 1910, with an aunt, to study acting at the Royal Academy of Dramatic Arts. After her father's death the following year, the family's income declined and Jean's school years ended. She took a job as a chorus girl and toured the English provinces, discovering in the process the meaning of being set adrift, or "marooned," in a cold and alien culture. After her marriage to a Dutch poet and journalist in 1919, she led a rootless existence on the Continent, which she depicted in *The Left Bank* (1927). A daughter, Maryvonne, was born in 1922; five years later, Jean and her husband were divorced. Married twice more and widowed both times, Rhys continued to write novels, though her works neither sold nor were appreciated. She published *Quartet* (1928), *After Leaving Mr. Mackenzie* (1930), *Voyage in the Dark* (1934), *Good Morning, Midnight* (1958), and short stories. Only with the publication of *Wide Sargasso Sea*, which took ten years to write, did critics finally recognize her great talent.

For many years Rhys had been drawn to the mysterious figure of Edward Rochester's mad West Indian wife, Antoinette, as depicted in Charlotte Brontë's *Jane Eyre* (1847). Who was this strange woman? How had she managed to attract the handsome and wealthy Rochester? What had her life been like as a young girl? These were the haunting questions Rhys broached and answered in highly stylized form in *Wide Sargasso Sea*. "The Creole in Charlotte Bronte's novel is a lay figure—repulsive which does not matter, and not once alive which does," writes Rhys. "She's necessary to the plot, but always she shrieks, howls, laughs horribly, attacks all and sundry—*off stage*. For me . . . she must be right *on stage*. She must be at least plausible with a past, the *reason* why Mr. Rochester treats her so abominably and feels justified, the reason why he thinks she is mad and why of course she goes mad, even the *reason* why she tries to set everything on fire, and eventually succeeds. (Personally, I think *that* one is simple. She is cold—and fire is the only warmth she knows in England.)"[1]

Wide Sargasso Sea is divided into three parts. The first, narrated by Antoinette, takes place in Jamaica, on the isolated estate called Coulibri. The second, situated on Dominica, is recounted for the most part by Rochester. The last, placed in Rochester's manor house in England, is told by Rochester's housekeeper, Grace Poole, as well as by Antoinette during her moments of lucidity.

Mother/Daughter Identification

The locus of Rhys's tale is an island—a word which comes from the Latin *insula*. As an island surrounded by water is cut off from a large body of land, so the mother, Annette, and her daughter, Antoinette, in *Wide Sargasso Sea* feel an extreme sense of isolation and loneliness. In psychological terms, we may say that the island of our story, representing an autonomous complex with a life of its own, remains unrelated to the conscious personality. A split-off area within the psyche, it floats adrift in the fluid expanse of the unconscious. Under such conditions, the conscious personality knows little or nothing of what is going on within the subliminal domain.

This subliminal domain is analogous to the mysterious and dangerous Sargasso Sea in the novel's title. The Sargasso, which lies between the West Indies and the Azores, is characterized by a great swirl of ocean currents and by the incredible abundance of surface seaweed that obscures the visibility of its depths. So, too, are mother and daughter incapable of perceiving a clear image of themselves; their motivations and needs are caught up in an opaque web of subsurface growth, entangling them in a murky and mephitic psychological condition.

Neither mother nor daughter experiences a sense of belonging to others or to herself. When Annette first married and moved to Jamaica, she was rejected by the English community because she came from French Martinique. After the death of her first husband and her ensuing poverty, the wealthy plantation owners looked down upon her economic inferiority. Following the emancipation of the blacks, when the "white people . . . close[d] ranks," they cut her and her daughter off from their group. For the blacks, both Annette and Antoinette were "white cockroaches." Alienated from the islanders, they lived like pariahs.

The imposition of a puritanical and patriarchal European Christian culture on Annette and Antoinette, the latter born and bred in Jamaica, where the indigenous way of life was matriarchal and animistic, added to their emotional deprivation. The so-called "civilized" ways of the English were always at odds with the "primitive" indigenous culture. What increased the psychological conflict in the feminine protagonists was the incongruity between the ideal behavior pattern of so many Christian men and their secret sexual debauchery. Comportment and ethics were antithetical. The blacks, on the other hand, lived in harmony with their instinctive natures. Jung wrote in this regard:

> The world of instinct, simple as it seems to the rationalist, reveals itself on the primitive level as a complicated interplay of physiological facts, taboos, rites, class-systems and tribal lore, which [and now we come to another factor] impose a restrictive form on the instinct from the beginning, preconsciously, and make it serve a higher purpose.[2]

Many men in the English community were so victimized by the repressiveness of their religion that they tried to escape from a corrosive sense of guilt by going to the other extreme. They allowed themselves to be swept up by the world of instinct, or what they looked upon as darker powers hidden deep in the personality. When reason returned, they could not help but look upon themselves with revulsion.[3] To escape the repugnant image, they looked outside of themselves and found a scapegoat upon whom they could heap the blame for their "insidious" conduct. This was not a difficult task, since Western patriarchal cultures label woman either as saint or sinner, equating her either with the sublime Virgin or Mater Dolorosa, or with the Terrible Mother, Dragon, or Witch, capable of dismembering or depotentiating the male.

As the tale begins, hatred abounds on the island that the widowed Annette and her daughter, Antoinette, call their home: Whites are pitted against whites, blacks against whites, half-castes against whites and blacks, bastards against legitimate children, men and women against each other and themselves. The two hapless women live imprisoned in poverty on the estate called Coulibri, which grows more run-down each day. Tension permeates the world of these psychological refugees, whose nutrients consist of exile, emptiness, and solitude. It is a world where "nothing [is] safe" (17).

Annette's sole source of pleasure is horseback riding. It alone permits her to leave Coulibri and to relate in the most minimal way to the world outside. One morning, she finds her horse dead, poisoned by angry Negroes. Henceforth she is unable to venture out of her estate, out of her house, out of herself. "Now we are marooned," she says. "What will become of us?" (19).

The psychological introversion that sets in forces libido (psychic energy) inward. Annette's attention is focused almost exclusively upon herself and her retarded son, Pierre. Virtually no time is left for Antoinette. Unable to clarify the reasons for her inner chaos now that energy is pouring into her, Annette feels a mounting sense of isolation and hopelessness.

Two key images reveal Annette's psychological condition: the looking glass and the horse. Each time she passes in front of a mirror, she cannot help but admire her own beauty. Unlike Narcissus, who was captivated by his exterior image, Annette is not obsessed with her physical form to the exclusion of other elements of her makeup. She is aware that her body is an object of attraction for men and an object of hatred and contempt for the ultra-proper British ladies. What she sees in the mirror enhances her sense of personal worth. The same youthful image of herself seen in the looking glass repeats itself throughout the book. Like Narcissus, she has no urge for self-development; rather, she seeks to remain the beautiful young girl—the *puella*—uncommitted and never achieving any independence or freedom. Since the mirror is the vehicle through which her soul passes and her instincts free themselves, the looking glass becomes the paradigm of both the real and the ideal, the spirit and the body. As such, it takes on almost mythical proportions for Annette.

The horse image likewise becomes archetypal in stature. Associated since ancient times with both life and death, with destruction and triumph, and with energy, passion, sexuality, and youth, the horse is also identified with the feminine, as in *mare*. Unlike most other animals, the horse is ridden; it carries a person as does a ship or a vehicle, thereby linking the individual's and the animal's destinies. The poisoning of Annette's horse is an analogical indication of a sudden withdrawal or deadening of her "instinctive" and "primitive" life forces. As a result, Annette's behavioral patterns alter: She lets herself exist rather than actively participate in events; she feels "marooned," unable to function or move. Psychological paralysis sets in. As Rhys wrote, "The extreme poverty and isolation of the family at Coulibri in 1834 cannot be sufficiently stressed."[4] Divested of outside influences and of men in particular, Annette's life impulse diminishes, and the artificial state of introversion in which she now lives causes her to grow increasingly wan, "thin and silent."

Antoinette, who narrates this section of *Wide Sargasso Sea*, is the one through whose eyes we experience the dramatic and psychological vicissitudes. She feels increasingly neglected now that her mother, who is virtually incarcerated in her house, focuses all her attention and emotions on Pierre. Because of this consistent rejection, Antoinette craves any show of feeling that might be cast her way. Never, however, is there discussion or understanding of any kind between mother and daughter. Annette exists as a fleeting image for Antoinette: a remote figure, present but unresponsive, beautiful but distant; a stranger. Although the daughter is alienated from her mother in the true sense of the word, parallels do exist between them. Neither experiences her ground-bed; neither has any sense of identity; both are disconnected and fragmented beings.

Antoinette suffers from a negative mother complex: Her mother's personal behavior simply does not correspond to the inborn image of a nutritive force.[5] She is not warm; she is not kind; she is not caring. As a result, Antoinette longs desperately for a helpful, comforting, and understanding mother figure. Her psychological divestiture is reflected in the descriptions of gardens, forests, mountains, and seascapes at crucial times in the novel. Antoinette maintains that the "tree of life"—referring to the one in the biblical Garden of Eden—is growing in her garden, near her house. Whereas that Garden of Eden was ordered and cultivated, Antoinette's is overgrown and wild, with "the smell of dead flowers mixed with the fresh living smell" (19). No pattern or direction exists in her garden/world; only fear and loneliness reign. Beauty is present, however, in the form of fecundating forces and delicious aromas—but these always seem to be out of reach or intermixed with dangerous and even lethal elements.

The tree, then, has special significance for Antoinette, who was born and bred in the West Indies. For practitioners of Voodoo, referred to as *Obeah* by the natives, the tree is a cult object within which exist the spirits of ancestors—powerful mana forces which, if approached with respect and according to appropriate rituals, can bring about positive results. In that the tree rises from the depths of Hell to the far reaches of Heaven, it is also used as a means of communication between the dead and the living, or between good and evil, depending upon the invocation used. For Antoinette, so immersed in the religious beliefs of the native culture, trees are living forces with personalities of their own, as are other fetishes, such as amulets, certain stones, chicken feathers, or parts of the body. That tree, in touch with Mother Earth, is for Antoinette a positive, stable, and nutritive force, as well as a restorative and healing power, able to put her in touch with herself and root her.[6]

Antoinette describes her garden as follows:

> Orchids flourished out of reach or for some reason not to be touched. One was snaky looking, another like an octopus with long thin brown tentacles bare of leaves hanging from a twisted root. Twice a year the octopus orchid flowered—then not an inch of tentacle showed. It was a bell-shaped mass of white, mauve, deep purples, wonderful to see. The scent was very sweet and strong. I never went near it. (19)

Orchids, symbols of fertility, beauty, and spiritual perfection (certain varieties live solely on air), also remind Antoinette of octopi (because of their twisted roots). Resembling dangerous entities that grab unsuspecting people with their tentacles, clutching and strangling their victims, the twisted roots suggest an abnormality, a deviation from the norm, a coiling, spiraling, and encircling authority. One orchid is described as "snaky," implying a cold, gluey, secretive, and sexual influence. Reminiscent also of the Gnostic symbol of the *uroboric* snake (the snake eating its own tail), which stands for "the original psychic state prior to the birth of ego consciousness," the image reveals Antoinette's inner world.[7] Its trees and flowers are overgrown and in disarray—a paradigm of the daughter's (and, by extension, the mother's) undetermined and identityless personality. A *puella*, a child of nature, she will have to be cared for and nurtured by others, or she will run wild—as do the plants, trees, and shrubbery in her garden.

As for Annette, the only time she emerges from within her house is when she walks up and down the *glacis* (a paved, roofed-in terrace which runs the length of the house). From this vantage point, she can view the sea; but people passing by can and do stare at her. When they begin to snicker and mock her, Annette closes her eyes as a means of self-defense, shutting them all out from her world; then she clenches her fists and frowns so deeply that the furrows could "have been cut with a knife." So sensitive is Antoinette to her mother's moods at times that she touches her brow, attempting to smooth it out and wipe these deep lines away. Rather than respond to her daughter's concern with a show of warmth, however, the mother pushes her away, "not roughly but calmly, coldly, without a word, as if she had decided once and for all that I was useless to her" (20). Antoinette realizes instinctively that her mother wants only her son to be near her, or to be left alone in peace and quiet. On other occasions, in a desperate attempt to attract her mother's attention, Antoinette fans her during her afternoon nap; or, when she just wants to be near her, she watches her brush her hair, which she looks upon as "a soft black cloak to cover me, hide me, keep me safe" (22). Always, Annette waves her daughter away.

The rejected and neglected Antoinette seeks solace in a former slave, Christophine, her surrogate mother. Given to Annette by her husband as a wedding present, Christophine came from Martinique. She is described as being different from the other Negro women on the island: "She was much blacker—blue-black with a thin face and straight features. She wore a black dress, heavy gold earrings and a yellow handkerchief—carefully tied with the two high points in front" (21). Christophine's blackness makes her more potent and more magical in the eyes of both blacks and whites. Her name is paradigmatic of her function: Like Saint Christopher, who was weighted down by the Christ child, whom he carried on his shoulders across a river, she will support the personalities of two *puellae*, Annette and Antoinette.

A Great Earth Mother archetype, Christophine is a timeless, solid, and nutritive force, capable of bearing the pain and heartache of mother and daughter, even though they are unaware of the powerful role she plays in their lives. She represents the connecting force between the rootless *puellae* and the original source of power. Psychologically, she may be looked upon as a positive shadow figure, "a composite of personal characteristics and potentialities concerning which the individual is unaware."[8] Unlike Annette and Antoinette, who are not three-dimensional but are silhouettes or cardboard replicas of women, neither belonging to herself or others, Christophine is tied to the earth. She is body and matter. Stable and steady, understanding the problems of others as well as her own, Christophine is life, activity, and vitality, in contrast to mother and daughter, whose melancholia and morbidity may overwhelm them. A maternal, protective, and generative force, Christophine stands for continuity.

Important, too, is the fact that she is a practitioner of Obeah. A black ethos that includes ancestor cults, Obeah keeps worshippers close to their community, and allies them not only with the living but with the great African families of the past. Two worlds exist in Obeah: the physical, inhabited by visible beings and objects; and the abstract and invisible, a spiritual homologue of one's ancestors. An animistic religion, it includes the belief that the unrevealed powers existing throughout the universe also inhabit a variety of objects—hair, dolls, materials, fruits, herbs, blood, fowl, goats, songs, words—which, through transmission of thought or feeling, may be used for positive or evil purposes.

Christophine, different from other black women, has the power to attract covert energies to her being. She is a *Mamaloi*, or high priestess, an ancestral mother, a medium, and the receiver of offerings. It is she who determines the potions or libations necessary to carve out the destinies of friends and enemies.[9] The women in the community, both young and old, fear her, bring her gifts of all sorts, and labor for her free of charge. She is the wielder of energy and the figure of authority on the island. For Antoinette and her mother, she is the only secure, warm, and loving person they know.

To be safe is Antoinette's prime concern. Instinctively, therefore, she spends long hours with Christophine. Like her mother, Antoinette rarely leaves home, preferring to imprison herself in her garden, with its soft moss, or in the kitchen, with Christophine, her friend Maillotte, and Maillotte's daughter, Tia. Such withdrawal arrests the outward flow of her libido; she becomes stuck in her inner world of the house and garden. By ignoring the laws of life, her personality atrophies and stagnation follows. This *puella* creature is helpless in all ways, and her needs are never served. In keeping with Western tradition and the rational Victorian order, Antoinette represses her instinctual world, and hence remains disconnected from the deeper levels of her feminine nature. Those so-called darker aspects of the psyche, which were damaged at an early age and so never really took root, cause Antoinette's world to remain static and, psychologically, putrescent.

Under such psychological conditions, it is not surprising to discover that Tia, the daughter of Christophine's friend, becomes her only real companion. Antoinette admires this strong young girl who runs barefoot over sharp stones and never hurts her feet. Tia lives in harmony with herself and her people, physically and emotionally. She represents the antithesis of the vulnerable, sensitive, fearful, tense Antoinette, who is not in tune with herself and is forever looking for safety zones. Loyal always to those forces that sustain her, Antoinette never thinks of evaluating the role she plays in Tia's life. Because she believes so strongly in Tia's friendship—complete and reciprocal—her naive faith dooms her from the start. One day, when the two go swimming, Tia gets out of the water first, puts on Antoinette's clean, starched, and ironed frock, and departs, leaving her old and soiled dress on the riverbank for her friend. Antoinette's shock and dismay at what she considers to be Tia's treachery are interpreted as a sign of her friend's hatred for her. When Antoinette arrives home and bears the brunt of her mother's anger ("Throw away that thing. Burn it"), shame descends upon her; a sense of hurt and betrayal floods her psyche. Antoinette has no other dress except for an old, torn one, which she puts on. Her habitual way of dealing with her problems—and this incident is no exception—is to hide and withdraw still further from the real world.

Clothes frequently represent the persona—the "public face," mask, or disguise that individuals put on to conceal the inner person. When Tia stole Antoinette's dress, Antoinette felt divested of whatever personality she had—of herself. After donning what was not hers, she felt unclean and hateful. Thick-skinned Tia, familiar with the ways of her world, knew how to protect herself in any situation; she could wear anyone's dress and be herself. The undiscerning *puella*, on the other hand, a mirror image of her mother, was always on the outside of things, drifting, and led on by powerful forces which took hold of her, guiding her blindly onward.

The word "marooned," used at crucial times in the novel, is particularly apt in depicting the inner topography of both mother and daughter. From the American Spanish *cimarron*, meaning wild and savage, as used in the West Indies it meant a fugitive or a descendant of a Negro slave; or a person who, as a punishment, was put ashore in some desolate place and left there—isolated and helpless. Annette and her daughter are both refugees, set adrift on an island amid lonely seas.

The theft of Antoinette's dress has yet another meaning. In Obeah, as already mentioned, objects such as clothes, or hair, or any part of a person take on a dynamic power of their own. If stolen or acquired by another person, the energy inherent in the object or body part can be used for possession purposes, such as casting a hex on an enemy. A dress, therefore—and Antoinette's dress in particular—might be used as a fetish, or a hostile charm to persecute or dominate her and, through her, perhaps her family.

So important an incident is the theft of Antoinette's dress that it triggers the following dream:

> I dreamed that I was walking in the forest. Not alone. Someone who hated me was with me, out of sight. I could hear heavy footsteps coming closer and though I struggled and screamed I

> could not move. I woke crying. The covering sheet was on the floor and my mother was looking down at me. (27)

The dream clearly spells terror and a state of anxiety on the part of one suffering from a negative mother complex. In the forest in the dream, nature grows thickly and uncontrollably, hiding the sun and bathing the area in darkness. Identified with the unconscious, this darkened realm conceals monstrous forces which may creep up on the unsuspecting individual, as did Tia. Danger stalks the dreamer everywhere. Invisible and unexpected, the unknown becomes a constant threat to her well-being. The "heavy footsteps" coming closer to her indicate the dread that prevents her from connecting with the earth. So frenzied is she by her auto-inspired fear that she finds herself unable to move to extricate herself from the forest. Unconscious forces, riddled with menace and death, paralyze her.

The forest in Antoinette's dream symbolizes Mother Nature in her devouring, perilous, hateful, and destructive aspects. That Antoinette awakes to see her mother standing over her and scolding her ("You were making such a noise. I must go to Pierre, you've frightened him"), rather than comforting her, plunges her deeper into a life-threatening emotional situation. As compensation for her mother's rebukes and the fear the dream itself has inspired, she has recourse to an inanimate world: the steadiness of the "friendly furniture" in her room, the garden outside, and the cliffs and sea in the distance. "I am safe. I am safe from strangers," she thinks.

Antoinette's dream, archetypal in dimension, reaches back into her remotest memories, "to the one who was always there for the child": the eternal, unborn, primal cause.[10] So powerful is this dream that its images (forest, tree, footsteps, etc.) contain enormous energy charges which serve to drain the ego of its vitality, accounting in part for Antoinette's increasing withdrawal. Hence it is not surprising to find her walking alone the following day to parts of Coulibri she has never ventured into before. Although the high grasses cut her legs, white and black ants bite her, the rain wets her, and the threat of snakes is always present, she goes on, like a zombie. She is cognizant of nature's painful side, but nature is "all better than people," and so she is prepared to deal with its eventualities.

As Antoinette walks on, she comes to a clearing. Looking toward the open spaces before her, she feels entranced by their vastness and their prismatic colorations and multivalent reflections. A kind of self-hypnotic state is engendered in which her ego (center of consciousness) diminishes concomitantly in importance as it becomes increasingly filled and paralyzed by the immensity and beauty of the world outside. The more the unconscious impulses contaminate her consciousness, the greater is the dissociation between reality and fantasy. A kind of schizophrenia takes hold, and while the luxurious tropical vegetation connecting her to the deeper layers of her subliminal sphere holds sway, she is in a dangerous—but fortunately temporary—condition.

In time, Antoinette is informed of her mother's impending marriage to a certain Mr. Mason. While, heretofore, Antoinette has told her story in strongly visual images, she now becomes *listener*. She hears bundles of hateful remarks leveled at her mother and at Mr. Mason by both whites and blacks. She also learns new things about her own father: He had been a drunkard and libertine; he had fathered bastards; he had let Coulibri go to ruin.

No sooner does her mother marry Mr. Mason (we are never told his first name) than Coulibri is repaired and made to look new. Despite this fresh, living force in the person of Mr. Mason, something seems awry: Coulibri "didn't feel the same" (30). Annette senses danger, intuits a silent rage on the part of the natives. She begs her husband to leave Jamaica with the family and to go to Grandbois, her estate on Dominica. He refuses. A true Westerner, he insists upon a logical approach to life and needs to know her "reasons" for wanting to leave. He even accuses her of imagining an "enmity which does not exist," of being illogical and unreasonable. What he fails to recognize is that knowledge gleaned from instinct does make sense. She sees both sides of human nature; he, only its positive side. He can, therefore, be caught off guard.

Antoinette's dream was premonitory. It revealed her own anxieties and mirrored those of her mother, with whom she is unconsciously identified. The fearsome footsteps in the dream conveyed the pulse of the natives—unsuspected instinctual powers which might erupt at any moment.

Antoinette sleeps fitfully one night soon after, and awakens to hear her mother tell her to get dressed and come downstairs. "Drunken Negroes" are pelting stones at the house; "a horrible noise swelled up, like animals howling" (38). Mr. Mason tries to calm everyone down. All will be well, he declares; everything will be forgotten at dawn. His wife thinks differently, and as she wrings her hands, "her wedding ring fell off and rolled into a corner near the steps" (39). The mood outside grows fierce. Flames envelop the house. Annette rushes up the stairs to get Pierre. The girl in charge of watching over him had run away at the first sign of trouble. Pierre dies. Hysterical, Annette heaps abuse on her husband. His innocence, his misplaced trust, and his blindness have all turned into evil. Reviled by the natives, who scream out at him, ironically, "But look the black Englishman! Look the white niggers," he begins to pray, "May Almighty God defend us," and drags his struggling wife out. Antoinette remarks, in one of Rhys's most extraordinary ironies: "And God who is indeed mysterious, who had made no sign when they burned Pierre as he slept—not a clap of thunder, not a flash of lightning—mysterious God heard Mr. Mason at once and answered him. The yells stopped" (42). As the family hurries to their carriage and escapes the frenzied mob, Antoinette looks back: "The house was burning, the yellow-red sky was like sunset and I knew that I would never see Coulibri again. Nothing would be left, the golden ferns and the silver ferns, the orchids, the ginger lilies and the roses . . . ." (44).

Before leaving the island, Antoinette sees Tia ("she was all that was left of my life as it had been") and runs toward her to embrace her, blocking out all sense of danger. Unnoticed is the jagged stone the black girl is holding in her hand and which she throws at her. "We stared at each other, blood on my face, tears on hers. It was as if I saw myself. Like in a looking-glass" (45).

Tia, Antoinette's shadow figure, is a complex of opposites and a bundle of hate and of love. The emotional pain she caused Antoinette when she took her dress has now been translated into physical hurt. As for the drawing of blood, caused by the abrasive stone, it symbolizes a diminishing of the precious life force and a deleting or diluting of the remaining energetic factor. (A similar situation occurred for Annette when her horse was poisoned.) Tia's show of wild hate (the stone) and immense love (tears) reveals both forces existing in Antoinette's unconscious: a longing to relate to people; and an undifferentiated sense of humiliation and loss, which is conveyed in aggressive acts.

After the burning of Coulibri, Antoinette lies ill—virtually unconscious—for the next six weeks. All she can recall about the night of the fire are her mother's wild screams directed toward Mr. Mason: "Don't touch me or I'll kill you if you touch me. Coward. Hypocrite. I'll kill you" (45). Once recovered, Antoinette is taken by carriage to see her mother. The experience is traumatic. She opens the door to the little cottage where her mother is living and sees "a coloured man, a coloured woman, and a white woman sitting with her head bent so low that I couldn't see her face" (48). Everything about her mother has changed; her hair alone is recognizable. She clasps her mother tightly and wants to say, "He [Pierre] is dead. But I am here, I am here." She is incapable of saying the first sentence, however, and merely shakes her head and mutters the second. Her mother quietly answers "No," then adds "no, no no" very loudly, and forcefully pushes her daughter away from her (48). Antoinette falls against a partition and hurts herself; the man and woman in charge hold Annette by the arms. Sorrow has driven Annette insane. Later, Antoinette learns another horrible truth: Her mother has been sexually abused by these black attendants, who were hired to care for her.

Antoinette is sent to a convent school, where she remains until the age of seventeen. Looked upon as a refuge at first, the convent in time becomes a place of "sunshine and of death." It is a complex of opposites: a place of sin and the terrors accompanying it; and a world endowed with serenity, an oasis for new understanding and in-dwelling. "That was how it was, light and dark, sun and shadow, Heaven and Hell, . . . " *from the inside* (57).

Mr. Mason visits Antoinette during her convent years. Now that she is a young lady, she can no longer be "hidden away," he tells her. "Why not?" she questions, content to live out her uneventful life in this protected, though imprisoning, place. Mr. Mason's decision prevails, and as Antoinette leaves the convent, she is overwhelmed with feelings of "dismay, sadness, loss." She knows that an unmarried girl, a virgin, "belongs to *herself*"; that when she marries, this will no longer be true. Furthermore, to live outside the cloister is to live in a dangerous world divested of a safety zone. Antoinette's second dream takes place at this juncture:

> Again I have left Coulibri. It is still night and I am walking towards the forest. I am wearing a long dress and thin slippers, so I walk with difficulty, following the man who is with me and holding up the skirt of my dress. It is white and beautiful and I don't wish to get it soiled. I follow him, sick with fear but I make no effort to save myself; if anyone were to try to save me, I would refuse. This must happen. Now we have reached the forest. We are under the tall dark trees and there is no wind. "Here?" He turns and looks at me, his face black with hatred, and when I see this I begin to cry. He smiles slyly. "Not here, not yet," he says, and I follow him, weeping. Now I do not try to hold up my dress, it trails in the dirt, my beautiful dress. We are no longer in the forest but in an enclosed garden surrounded by a stone wall and the trees are different trees. I do not know them. There are steps leading upwards. It is too dark to see the wall or the steps, but I know they are there and I think, "It will be when I go up these steps. At the top." I stumble over my dress and cannot get up. I touch a tree and my arms hold on to it. "Here, here." But I think I will not go any further. The tree sways and jerks as if it is trying to throw me off. Still I cling and the seconds pass and each one is a thousand years. "Here, in here," a strange voice said, and the tree stopped swaying and jerking. (60)

Antoinette's dream is premonitory. Just as, after the fire, she was forced to leave the "sanctuary" of Coulibri, so now she must leave the convent.

Back in the forest, her unconscious archetypal images of wild, untamed, unchanneled powers are rampant, adhering to no rules, regulations, or traditions. Chaos floods her world. Although trees frequently signify an inner process, a symbolical development of human life both on the physical and spiritual level, here Antoinette sees them as specters, and their ghostly appearances terrify her. They are harbingers of destruction. Identifying with her mother, she sees herself as wearing a long dress and thin slippers. Unlike the thick-skinned Tia, who is wise to the ways of the world, the immaculate virgin Antoinette wears thin-soled shoes and feels hurt whenever she steps out of her intimate, imprisoning, and fixed world. As for the man, who at first seems solicitous of her well-being, he shows his real nature (his hate-filled face) once he penetrates the forest.

Antoinette's negative vision of men is not surprising. Her father, a debauched drunkard, allowed Coulibri to go to ruin; Mr. Mason's naivete has been the cause of the destruction of her home, her brother's death, and her mother's insanity. As for the purity and beauty associated with the "sacred" concept of virginity taught in the convent school, Antoinette knows that it is in reality a farce. The notion encourages its opposite: lewdness, lasciviousness, and uncontrollable sexuality, with their religious and psychological concomitants of sin, guilt, contrition, and punishment.

A mirror image of her mother, Antoinette must go through life as an unrooted, identityless being set adrift in the universe—the plaything of others. Unlike her mother, however, she has not yet discovered her sexuality, nor does she know how to entice men. Passivity rules her, and she makes little or no effort to extricate herself from an arranged marriage to a man whom she has never met. In the dream, the dirt on her dress and the tears she sheds during a symbolic rape convey her ingrained sense of pain—her fear of the male's autonomy over the female in marriage. That she finds herself "enclosed" in an unfamiliar garden surrounded by a stone wall sets the stage for a new orientation in life—a different kind of incarceration. As she ascends to her new station in life, that of bride, she stumbles in her dream: darkness and imbalance prevail. The tree to which she clings to steady herself jerks and sways as it does during a tempest. Although the man points the way, Antoinette can go no further. The tree steadies itself for a while, as does her marital relationship at the outset: another precarious safety zone. Soon afterward, however, another danger presents itself: Antoinette's ego risks drowning amid the stagnant waters of the collective unconscious. Unable to maintain its official position as the center of consciousness, indicating to her the right way to proceed, her ego becomes contaminated by unconscious impulses, and feelings of dissociation intrude. Danger lies ahead.

Imprisonment

Narrated by Antoinette's husband, Edward Fairfax Rochester, the happenings in Part 2 of *Wide Sargasso Sea* are seen from a patriarchal point of view. Like Antoinette, Rochester has been rejected by a parent: His father, according to the laws of primogeniture, has willed his estate to an older son. Rochester comes to Jamaica to seek his fortune and to prove his worth to his father. Since Mr. Mason has left a large sum of money to Antoinette, she becomes a most desirable heiress. According to British law, once a dowry is given over to a husband, the wife is divested of all power over her money. Mr. Mason is as blind to the economic dangers awaiting Antoinette as he was to the physical dangers when he refused to leave Coulibri. Antoinette, as stated earlier, is basically indifferent, and so the marriage takes place.

For three weeks after the wedding, Rochester is bedridden with a bad fever. After he recuperates, the couple moves to Grandbois (High Woods), Annette's estate in Dominica. Rain greets the couple's entry onto the island—as if the "sea crept stealthily forwards and backwards"—and this is symptomatic of the ebb and flow of their relationship-to-be; it is also an indication of the struggle between consciousness and subliminal impulses. Antoinette thinks that her tendencies toward introspection and self-enclosure may diminish now that she is married. Rochester has no illusions as to his feelings about his wife. From the very outset he looks at her critically: Her eyes "are too large and can be disconcerting. She never blinks at all it seems to me. Long, sad, dark alien eyes. Creole of pure English descent she may be, but they are not English or European either" (67).

That Rochester should have focused on Antoinette's eyes is significant. As sources of light, intelligence, and spirit, eyes reveal an inner climate; they mirror a soul. Within Antoinette's eyes dwell feelings of melancholia, alienation, and distress. Solitude shows in the dimness of their silence. Solipsistic, dwelling on his own problems, Rochester never bothers to ponder his wife's needs. Nor are his demands—those of a nineteenth-century husband—surprising. A woman's place is in the home; she has a role to fill. Her reactions are unimportant; the man's well-being alone counts. Since woman is not represented in the Holy Trinity, she does not warrant admiration. She may, of course, be venerated as a Mater Gloriosa or Dolorosa, or reviled and feared as seductress or whore. There is no relational image that connects Antoinette to her husband.

Dominica is a "very wild place," Rochester is told shortly after his arrival; it is "not civilized" (68). Why has he come to the island? asks a "Young Bull," all body and brawn, a paradigm of the island's physical and visceral orientation. An archetypal inseminator, a phallic force, this vigorous youth could also be compared to a cock strutting about hens. Indeed, Rochester mentions the crowing of a cock, remembering the one that had awakened him the previous night. Symbolizing the rising sun, solar energy, and consciousness, the cock sheds light on situations, be they happy or sorrowful. A sacrificial animal for the Greeks (cocks were killed in honor of Aesculapius, Apollo's son and the god of medicine) and for the practitioners of Obeah, who consider it a cult object, this fowl will be instrumental in opening up the sexual dimension in the lives of husband and wife.

The wildness of the topography on the road leading to Grandbois is symptomatic of the couple's new proclivities: "on one side the wall of green, on the other a steep drop to the ravine below," then hills, mountains, and the blue-green sea. The countryside is "menacing," Rochester notes. The hills seem to close in on people, and the green is "extreme" (69). Like Antoinette in Part 1, he now experiences a sense of imprisonment and a closing in on him, in a threatening atmosphere. Rochester is, indeed, a prisoner of tradition, of society, and of his own inner desires. He needs a love he has never known. The "extreme green" he notes in the landscape may be interpreted as an awakening of primordial emotions and "irrational" powers, which are anathema to him. His Victorian upbringing causes him to fear their "sinful" dominion over him, but they promise a kind of madness he longs for.

The color green, to which he refers, although associated with the pope's emerald, was also worn by Lucifer when he was cast out of paradise. So we may look at Rochester's move to Dominica as a fall from grace: from a state of not knowing, or unconsciousness, into its opposite, or "extreme" pleasure, with its concomitant moral conflicts.

> Everything is too much, I felt as I rode wearily after her. Too much blue, too much purple, too much green. The flowers too red, the mountains too high, the hills too near. And the woman is a stranger. Her pleading expression annoys me. I have not bought her, she has bought me, or so she thinks. (70)

Rochester notes that despite the colorful natural surroundings and the brilliant sun, the natives look sad: "sombre people in a sombre place" (68).

Each time Rochester seeks to steady himself, to justify his acts, and to balance things out, he writes to his father, a paragon of strength, authority, law, willpower. His father embodies the rational approach, and Rochester seeks to emulate him:

> I will never be a disgrace to you or to my dear brother the son you love. No begging letters, no mean requests. None of the furtive shabby manoeuvres of a younger son. I have sold my soul or you have sold it, and after all is it such a bad bargain? The girl is thought to be beautiful, she is beautiful. And yet . . . (70)

Rum punches await the couple, and they drink "to happiness." More and more will Rochester and Antoinette have recourse to intoxicating brews. Associated with Dionysus for the Westerner, drink, or spirits, encourages individuals to divest themselves of all conscious responsibilities, hence releasing the pleasure principle.They enjoy sensations of lust without fear of retribution. Once initiated into the world of the senses, Rochester writes: "I breathed the sweetness of the air. Cloves I could smell and cinnamon, roses and orange blossom. And an intoxicating freshness as if all this had never been breathed before" (73).

The word "intoxicating," from the Latin *intoxicare*, means to inebriate or excite beyond the point of self-control, or to drive one to a state of frenzy or rapture; the word is also connected with *toxin*, a poison or drug. Let us recall Agave's ecstasy and the dismemberment of her son in Euripides' play *Bacchants*. The stage is set for Rochester's and Antoinette's Dionysian experience. Dionysian blood (liquor) is imbibed, with all its resulting wonders and horrors. The rational sphere yields to all that titillates and excites, all that goes counter to the puritanical subjugation of passions.

To prolong the state of wonderment and of trepidation the couple knows in Dominica, Rhys has recourse to an interplay of luminous effects: candlelight, brilliantly shining stars, fireflies, groups of flickering and fearsome shadows peopling the forest and the outside of the house. The inclusion of such effects is not merely for artistic purposes. Candle cults and juxtaposition of various colors are important in Obeah, the density of hues depending upon the age and sex of the person sought to be brought under control. Are Antoinette and Rochester being dominated by outside forces?

Antoinette tells Rochester of a frightening incident experienced at Grandbois when she was a little girl. One night she awakened to see "two enormous rats as big as cats" on her windowsill. Although they stared at her, she was not frightened. In fact, she saw herself staring back at them in the looking glass on the other side of the room. Only after falling back to sleep did she awaken again, frightened; she left her bed and went to sleep in the hammock on the veranda in the light of the full moon. When Christophine heard the story, she was aghast: To allow lunar rays to cover one's inert body is an ill omen.

Christophine feared the power of rats: They were a scourge that propagated so rapidly they could denude entire areas and render them unsafe. As for the moon, a celestial body deprived of its own light and dependent upon the sun's rays for its visibility and its transformative powers, it has been compared to subliminal spheres, which can be understood only in the light of consciousness. For Antoinette to expose herself to this dangerous lunar force was to encourage the dominion of her unconscious, thereby diminishing the ego's control. Passivity—allowing external forces to determine her future as her unconscious held sway—coupled with her inability to develop a personality and life of her own, would bring disaster.

The morning after the newlyweds' arrival at Grandbois, as Rochester is about to put his arms around his wife, Christophine interrupts, with breakfast, what was to be an interlude of lovemaking. Antoinette, having enjoyed the previous night's pleasures, leans "back against the pillows with her eyes closed," intent upon conserving every sensation experienced.

"Taste my bull's blood, master," says Christophine, the Earth Mother, handing Rochester a cup of coffee, the brew of virility capable of initiating him into manhood (85). Conveyer of brute strength, the bull—for the Egyptians and Assyrians as well as for other ancient and contemporary peoples—was a tyrannical beast that also symbolized the perpetual struggle waged against the rule of the mother. The bull, in Crete, for example, helped constellate the primitive father archetype. For Rochester, this animal spells mystery; it contains the terrifying secrets of the Great Earth Mother.

Antoinette, too, is caught up in the wonder of carnal discoveries, and in Grandbois, which she loves "more than anywhere in the world. As if it were a person. More than a person." Grandbois is the locus for her newborn joy (89). Why, then, Rochester wonders, does his wife wear an expression of melancholia even during moments of ecstasy?

> "I am not used to happiness," she said. "It makes me afraid. . . . If I could die. Now, when I am happy. Would you do that? You wouldn't have to kill me. Say die and I will die. You don't believe me? Then try, try, say die and watch me die." (92)

And he does say "die"; and he observes her as she dies, symbolically: in sunlight, moonlight, candlelight, and shadowy abysses.

With the discovery of her sexuality, Antoinette knows the meaning of passion. She loves as she has never loved before—to the "extreme." But Rochester only *thirsts* for her, with raw, unbridled instinct accompanied neither by love nor any other tender feeling. When, for example, he sees her dress on the bed, he becomes "breathless," overcome by a "savage" desire for her. Outside of the sexual element, she means virtually nothing to him: She is an alien and a stranger—"a stranger who did not think or feel" as he did.

Rochester knows he has taken a dangerous, un-Christian course. Eve-like, Antoinette spells Evil for him. She must be punished for enticing him to commit the sin of the flesh. She is to blame. "Die then. Sleep. It is all that I can give you. . . . Desire, Hatred, Life, Death came very close in the darkness" (94). Their world together is now unsafe.

Rochester is revolted by Antoinette's awakening sexuality. That his wife should enjoy the fruits of love—of the body—is unacceptable to him: "She'll moan and cry and give herself as no sane woman would, *or could*."

The onset of tragedy approaches when Daniel Causway, the half-caste bastard son of Antoinette's father, writes Rochester a letter informing him of his wife's family secrets: Annette's insanity; the death of Pierre, the idiot brother; and facts about the reprobate father. Rochester uses this information to justify his newborn hatred for his wife. By heaping the blame on her, he experiences catharsis—pardon for himself.

Amélie, the black maid, taunts and mocks Antoinette, and tells her that her husband "must be tired of the sweet honeymoon," since everyone knows that the couple sleep in separate rooms. Stunned by the arrogance and the truth of the remark, Antoinette slaps Amélie's face. "I hit you back white cockroach," shouts the maid, and she does. Rochester enters to stop the fight, finding a way of further humiliating his wife by showing great tenderness to the maid. Amélie leaves the room delighted, singing, "The white cockroach she marry . . . The white cockroach she buy young man . . . " (101). Antoinette's rage is such that she grits her teeth, takes a pair of scissors, and cuts her bed sheet in half and again into quarters.

Christophine, distraught by the couple's behavior, has decided to leave. Before she goes, she gives Antoinette a piece of advice: "Get up, girl, and dress yourself. Woman must have spunks to live in this wicked world" (101). If she is to save herself, the *puella* must face reality; she must fight and struggle to win her man, and not merely play the passive game of eliciting pity and sorrow.

To try to evolve from a *puella* to a mature woman is beyond Antoinette's capabilities. Without identity, never having developed any inner resources, with no sense of belonging to any race, people, or family, she seems to float along, oblivious of what is happening. She is *marooned* in the true sense of the word. That she is called "white cockroach," as her mother had been, reinforces the identity/alienation syndrome she knew as a child—that deep-seated sense of isolation and rejection. The names themselves—Annette, Antoinette—with the same first and last syllables, further spell out the relationship.

One evening, after drinking himself into a stupor, Rochester awakens, looks at his wife's sleeping form through the open door, feels disturbed, and walks out of the house, as Antoinette had done in Part 1, into the "hostile" forest. He, too, stubs his foot on a stone, nearly falling in the process. He sees shadows peering at him from all corners: "I was lost and afraid among these enemy trees, so certain of danger that when I heard footsteps and a shout I did not answer" (105). Like Antoinette, Rochester is lost, psychologically, in his turbulent, chaotic, unchanneled unconscious. Although he discovers a lost road and the ruins of a house, he cannot see his way out of this labyrinth; the primitiveness and savageness of this overgrown area are a projection of his own unbridled nature.

Rochester's apparent indifference to his wife reaches such a point that, out of desperation, she visits Christophine. "I think he hates me," she tells her. "He always sleeps in his dressing-room and the servants know" (109). She asks Christophine to make a love potion she can give her husband. No potion, the Earth Mother answers, is capable of restoring love. She must leave her husband. She cannot, Antoinette answers. Her entire fortune belongs to him now. She clutches Christophine and begs her never to grow old: "You are the only friend I have, do not go away from me into being old" (114).

Rochester's further need to torment his wife is evident when he calls her Bertha, her mother's real name, instead of Antoinette, fueling the mother/daughter identification and even adding an incestuous twist. "You are trying to make me into someone else, calling me by another name," Antoinette remonstrates (147). A name is far more than an identification tag: On the human level, it links an individual to his soul and spirit; in the religious domain, it creates a mysterious identification between a mortal and God. By calling Antoinette Bertha, Rochester not only further disconcerts her, but he also devaluates her stature as an individual.

Antoinette's world founders. Everything about her annoys Rochester—even the fact that she holds her left wrist with her right hand. The image is significant: The left side, identified with the heart and associated with the feeling principle and the irrational sphere, is being held in check by the right hand, linked to the world of reason and thinking faculties. Antoinette, then, is trying to act reasonably and maturely. Her inability to do so, however, comes to the fore each time she tries to talk over her problems with her husband, when her voice grows "high and shrill" and almost hostile. Reason vanishes when emotion is involved. As she grows increasingly remote, Antoinette's hands become cold; she seems ill or asleep, and when Rochester makes a move to kiss her—out of pity perhaps—she draws away into the darkness which is her habitat.

Later, Antoinette pours two glasses of wine for herself and her husband.

Is this Christophine's libation? The reader is never sure. Or is this an aphrodisiac? a poison? He sleeps deeply and dreams a dream similar to the one Antoinette had as a child: "I was buried alive, and when I was awake the feeling of suffocation persisted. Something was lying across my mouth; hair with a sweet heavy smell. I threw it off but still I could not breathe. I shut my eyes and lay without moving for seconds" (137). Like Antoinette, he feels himself imprisoned and weighted down by a smothering force beyond his control. Some subliminal content within him is forcing him to face his unauthentic acts, his wayward behavior, the hypocrisy of his whole approach to marriage and to life. He is a criminal of sorts, having divested his wife of her fortune, and, more important, of the love he has kindled in her. These painful truths manifest themselves physically, arousing in him a terrible nausea. He begins retching and finally vomits. Has he been poisoned? he wonders. Or is it his own sinful nature he is regurgitating?

As Antoinette in childhood observed her mother's anguished brow when she was asleep, so Rochester sees a "frown between [Antoinette's] thick eyebrows, deep as if it had been cut with a knife" (138). Antoinette, however, had reacted out of love; Rochester responds with hate. His abhorrence of his wife stems from the fact that she has forced him to become conscious of his sexuality, as well as of his misdirected values. He cannot bear the weight of his own guilt and rushes out of the house into the forest once again. When he returns deep in the night, Amélie brings him food and drink. Moments later, he pulls her down beside him on the bed and makes love to her with anger in his heart. That only a thin partition divides his room from his wife's adds to the sadistic pleasure that comes with revenge.

Antoinette is traumatized by her husband's infidelity. Not even drink can assuage the physical and emotional pain his act has caused: "Her hair hung uncombed and dull into her eyes which were inflamed and staring, her face was very flushed and looked swollen" (146). The one she had loved, she now despises; the home which filled her with joy has been turned into a place of sorrow: "I used to think that if everything else went out of my life I would still have this, and now you have spoilt it."

As Antoinette lifts a bottle of rum to her mouth, Rochester tries to grab it from her: "I felt her teeth in my arm. . . . " Releasing his grip, she takes the bottle and smashes it against the wall, and she stands "with the broken glass in her hand and murder in her eyes" (148).

A marionette-like state takes possession of Antoinette, Rochester notes, as if some supradimensional force has thrust itself on her. And indeed, two invisible powers—Rochester and Christophine—are vying unconsciously for supremacy over Antoinette. Let us recall that marionettes or dolls, as used in Obeah, evoke energies intended for hexing purposes. During Rochester's stay in Dominica, he has begun reading works on Obeah, especially a section in *The Glittering Coronet of Isles* (107). He knows that when the practitioner of Obeah is concentrating upon a mental image, for evil or good reasons, an energy charge is transmitted from a doll to a living person, effecting an alteration of personality.

The living and breathing Antoinette has ceased to exist. Her ego, dismembered by Rochester's ruthlessness, has been transformed into a doll, an effigy, a regressive, infantile form, a will-less being, an object to be manipulated by any outside force. In Obeah, it is believed that puppets (made of wood or clay or other materials), taken over by life-giving or life-taking spirits, may, through transmission of thoughts or hypnosis, dominate flesh-and-blood individuals. To become a victim of foreign forces or wills may be termed, psychologically, a *doll complex*, in which an individual yields his autonomy and allows the ego to be taken over by an outer power—namely, contents in the collective unconscious. Antoinette's formerly reasonable nature has now been invaded by emotionally charged subliminal contents, which upset her already precarious psychic balance. She has become a girl possessed; her customarily functioning ego has been taken over by an inner rage which bursts upon her with tidal-wave force. Raw instinct responds to Rochester's attempts to placate her; clawing and biting are her way of dismembering her enemy, thereby rectifying the injustice done her.

Antoinette's face is blank and expressionless on the day she leaves with her husband for England. Not a tear is visible. As Rochester looks back at the house, he feels sadness for the first time in his life, and he "wasn't prepared for that" (167). As long as he could hate, he felt safe; such a catalyst churned his passion, making it virtually impossible to face his feeling-world. "Save me from destruction, ruin and desolation. Save me from the long slow death by ants" (167), he thinks as he looks at Antoinette "staring out to the distant sea. She was silence itself. . . . She lifted her eyes. Blank lovely eyes. Mad eyes. A mad girl." Her voice is also scarcely recognizable; it has "no warmth, no sweetness. The doll [has] a doll's voice, a breathless but curiously indifferent voice" (171).

"Who Am I?"

The third and shortest section of *Wide Sargasso Sea* takes us to Thornfield Hall, Rochester's estate in England. We learn that his father and brother have died, leaving him sole heir to their fortunes. His marriage and trip to the West Indies had been unnecessary. The irony of the living hell he now experiences is the cause of his intense "misery," which shows in his eyes, just as similar pain had once shown in Antoinette's.

Declared insane, an excruciatingly thin Antoinette is kept locked up in a wing of Thornfield Hall under the surveillance of Grace Poole. She "lives in her own darkness" as she sits "shivering" in her room day in and day out, but Antoinette has not lost her spirit. "She's still fierce," notes Grace Poole, and must be watched all the time (178).

Included in Part 3 are sequences written in Antoinette's hand during moments of lucidity. She wonders, for example, why she has been brought to such a mansion and locked up in a cold room, far from everyone. She probes the reasons for her new life, as fleeting images of the past in the West Indies are interwoven here and there. Why does her room have only one high window, which does not allow her to see out? Why is there no mirror in her quarters? She doesn't even know what she looks like."Who am I?" she questions; there "must be a reason" for being here. "What is it that I must do?" (179).

One day she takes out her red dress from the closet—the dress that had aroused Rochester's savage "thirst" for her, and later his sense of shame. As she holds it against her, it triggers words of a dead past: Rochester saying to her, "Infamous daughter of an infamous mother." Red symbolizes primordial energy, the masculine fertilizing power of nature, ecstasy, desire, raw passion—that bull's blood Christophine had mentioned with regard to coffee. As she stares at the red dress, "it was as if the fire had spread across the room. It was beautiful and it reminded me of something I must do" (187). Other memories take hold: scents of vertivert, frangipani, cinnamon, dust, and lime, but also confused and fragmented images, such as the fire at Coulibri, Tia, her nightmares, and the terrifying footsteps in the forest. Her life in England, in contrast to the spectacular luminosities of the West Indies, is dark brown and dismal, divested of light, sun, and flame. A sense of time is also lost to her: "Nights and days and days and nights, hundreds of them slipping through my fingers. But that does not matter. Time has no meaning. But something you can touch and hold like my red dress, that has meaning" (185).

Antoinette records her third and last dream, a reworking and reintegrating of the previous ones, as if the entire disparate tapestry has finally been fitted together, and order—her own—has been restored. Antoinette sees herself taking Mrs. Poole's keys and candle, letting herself out of her dungeon, walking down a flight of steps. She feels lighthearted, as if she were "flying," and as if she had finally discovered her *real* way. She visits a red-carpeted and curtained room with white walls; it seems "sad and cold and empty," she notes, "like a church without an altar." In the dream, she thinks she hears footsteps. Concerned, she holds her right wrist with her left hand, the opposite of the hand gesture in Part 2. Now her unconscious is holding her reason in check; the subliminal sphere dominates, while the rational factor has been forever buried. Walking out of the room with her candle in hand, she pauses in front of a looking glass and sees "the ghost," the "woman with the streaming hair . . . surrounded by a gilt frame" (189). So shocked is she by this figure she sees in the mirror—although there is virtually no self-recognition—that she drops the candle she is carrying and it sets fire to the tablecloth. Flames suddenly leap up. She calls Christophine for help. As the fire flares and she escapes from the heated areas into the cool ones of freedom, the dream is so real that she cries out in her sleep.

Mrs. Poole is awakened. She sees Antoinette sleeping soundly and assumes she has had a nightmare, so she returns to bed. Antoinette, however, is fully awake. She waits patiently until the older woman begins snoring; then she rises, takes her keys, and unlocks the door:

> I was outside holding my candle. Now at last I know why I was brought here and what I have to do. There must have been a draught for the flame flickered and I thought it was out. But I shielded it with my hand and it burned up again to light me along the dark passage. (189)

Flames, we assume, though Rhys never actually states it, destroy Thornfield the way Antoinette's passion had annihilated her reason.

Like Cybele, who punished her lover with castration when he thwarted her, Antoinette lit her sacramental fire, blinding her enemy in the process. Reminiscent of the eyes of Oedipus, which he tore out of their sockets as an act of contrition, Rochester's eyes would be burned out, forcing him to look within for the rest of his days, to face himself and his acts *plain*. Only then would he find redemption in Jane Eyre, the Victorian ideal woman, pure in soul and body.

No conflict exists in *Wide Sargasso Sea*, nor any development in the feminine characters. *Puellae*, such as Annette and Antoinette, seem to drift along with the tide of events, forever directed by those with whom they become involved. The mother/daughter identification of these hapless women brought about a spiritual and psychological sterility. The alienated and introverted Annette neither sustained her daughter nor guided her along a positive course. A duplicate of her mother, but without her beauty and her ability to attract men, Antoinette had a weakened ego that collapsed when faced with trauma.

For Rochester, Antoinette was not a woman, but rather a feminine nature spirit, a nonhuman force that reflected certain qualities which allowed him to carry out nature's deepest drives and learn its darkest secrets, which the puritan in him considered demonic. Just as husband and wife succumbed to the magical spell of sensuality, bewitched by their bodies, so they fell into hate with equal rapidity, each constellating upon the other those unhealed psychic wounds with which they could not cope.

Only one person of stature stands out in *Wide Sargasso Sea*: Christophine, the Great Mother. A figure of authority, a nurturer, she could have wielded a positive influence, but she had to yield her irrational power to Western rationalism. Obeah—the world of the spirit—was unable to function in an arid, logical, and solipsistic domain.

> Blot out the moon,
> Pull down the stars.
> Love in the dark, for we're for the dark
> So soon, so soon. (169)

7 Nathalie Sarraute's *Between Life and Death:* Androgyny and the Creative Process

Nathalie Sarraute's *Between Life and Death* (1968) deals with the creative process, from the uncreated work of art embedded in the *prima materia*—the great void—to its completion in the book. The Writer, the focus of Sarraute's attention, takes the reader through the multiple stages of his literary trajectory: the struggle involved in the transmutation of the amorphous word into the concrete glyph on the blank sheet of paper; the pain and anguish accompanying the birth of the created work, alluded to as the "thing" or the "object"; the attitude of the successful Writer, who postures and panders to his public; and the rebirth of the creative élan following an inner vision.

Like the ancient seer, or *Vates*, Sarraute's Writer is also a miracle worker or a magician, able to inject "life" into what has previously been "dead," or uncreated: the written word. How is such a sleight of hand accomplished? How does the course of words from the uncreated to concretion in the empirical world affect both the Writer and the reader during the happenings in *Between Life and Death*?

Nathalie Sarraute was born in 1900 in Ovanovo-Voznessensk, Russia. Her parents were divorced two years later. In 1905 she moved to Paris with her mother. Returning to Russia the following year, she spent her summers with her father in France and Switzerland. In 1908 she returned to Paris to live with her father, who had remarried. An excellent student at the Lycee Fenelon and at the Sorbonne, where she obtained a *licence* (1920), she studied for a B.A. at Oxford, then attended the Faculty of Letters in Berlin and the University of Paris Law School. She was admitted to the Paris bar in 1925, and that same year married Raymond Sarraute, a fellow student. *Tropisms* (composed in 1932 but not published until 1939) was a highly original volume which set the pace and style for her future creations, including *The Portrait of a Man Unknown* (1948), *Martereau* (1953), *Planetarium* (1959), *The Golden Fruits* (1963), and *Between Life and Death* and *Do You Hear Them?* (1972).

Descriptions of the creative process per se have been undertaken by many poets and novelists, including Nerval, Rimbaud, Goethe, Baudelaire, Woolf, Joyce, and Gide, to mention only a scattering of authors. Sarraute's approach is different. She concentrates on the word alone: the sensations, feelings, and ideations which make for its *livingness* or its *deadness*. She organizes, on a verbal, conscious level, what might be called polyphonic musical compositions, emerging from the interweaving of successive voices from the unconscious into single or double oft-repeated themes. Sarraute's images and vocal devices take on a fugal quality as they impose themselves—amplified or diminished—at various stages during the creative process, in keeping with her willed, disordered order.

The circular images achieved in Sarraute's fugal construct create a dizzying and disorienting effect upon the Writer, divesting him of any individuality he or the reader might wish to impose upon him. The Writer exists on a nonindividual level, as a collective or transpersonal figure. He is a stereotype to be sure—part of the common herd—but also quite different, in the way that every thumbprint is unique, or each concentric ripple created by a pebble thrown into a lake achieves its own form and depth. Spiraling, coiling, rounding, rotating, and revolving images occur and reoccur with Sarraute's frequent reference to the circle, associating this geometric form with the world of abstraction (idea), the sensate domain (circulation of the blood throughout the body), and the cosmic and mythic sphere which encapsulates all of nature in a space/time continuum.

The creative process, as viewed by Sarraute in *Between Life and Death*, transcends temporal philosophical, aesthetic, and sexual schemes. Values and demarcation lines have changed. Heretofore, the notion of giving birth—be it to an object or an infant—has almost always been linked to the Great Mother, since she is the bearer of life, the nourisher and devourer, and is identified with *Eros*, the relating principle which brings things together in nature and within the psyche. Spiritual and intellectual factors—*logos*—have usually been associated in the West with the male. Sarraute's Writer, however, exists in an archetypal dimension. Although alluded to as masculine, since the masculine personal pronoun (*il*) is used to identify him, he is neither male nor female. Androgynous, he is a component of both sexes, a complex of opposites, as is the creative spirit in general. He transcends polarities and reaches beyond the empirical into eternal realms. Pierre Teilhard de Chardin's remark with regard to the creative process is applicable to Sarraute's androgynous Writer: "Everything in the Universe is made by union and regeneration—by the coming together of elements that seek out one another, melt together two by two, and are born again in a third."[1]

Androgyny is archetypal. It is a universal and collective image that implies "unity-totality" emerging from primordial wholeness or nothingness into the empirical world as divided entities (man and woman). Androgyny has been alluded to in the Bible (Genesis 2:21), Plato's *Symposium*, the *Rig-Veda*, the *Tao te Ching*, and alchemical and Kabbalistic tracts, among other ancient texts. The notion of self-containment in the spiritually and psychologically androgynous being, if approached in a relatively objective manner, may pave the way for expanded consciousness and greater evaluation, development, and maturation. Once the potential for increase has been exhausted, however, death ensues—a return to the uncreated world of the absolute—to be followed by rebirth. Thus is the circle completed; thus does it pursue its course in endless gyrations. Androgyny should not be confused with hermaphroditism, which has always been considered "an aberration of Nature," writes Mircea Eliade; the former is "not an augmentation of anatomical organs," as found in hermaphrodites, "but symbolically, the union of the magico-religious powers belonging to both sexes."[2]

Not only is Sarraute's Writer androgynous; he is also physically unidentifiable. In fact, he is sexless and torsoless. Outside of a few appendages (hands, fingers which gesticulate and mime every now and then), he is all *head*. As a kinetic object dramatizing his emotional experience, he is forever distorting, foreshortening, expanding, rotating, and shifting spatial and sensorial illusions. Nor does this metaform convey much feeling; love, warmth, and tenderness are virtually banished in his non-relationships with others and even with himself. Interaction exists only on an intellectual and sensorial level—no other. *Thinking* is the Writer's dominant function. His rational capabilities enable him to structure and synthesize data via categories, concepts, abstractions, and generalizations. As a *sensation* type as well, he is able to perceive and adapt to external reality through his senses of sight, hearing, touch, taste, and smell. Introverted to the extreme, his world revolves around his creative output—and later, when he becomes famous, around the admiration his works elicit from his reading public. Like a hypersensitive instrument, the Writer is forever monitoring his internal environment via his mind, perceptions, and bodily sensations, which relay information concerning external situations to his inner world and thereby affect his entire system, including his nerve endings, or receptor-neurons. There is little that is human about the Writer. Like

Athena, he is all intellect, all mind, all thought; he knows how to develop good tactics during moments of conflict, think clearly when challenged, and avoid personal entanglements. Unlike Athena, he uses sensation as his catalyst.[3]

Although in *Between Life and Death* Sarraute depicts the Writer through three phases of his development, there is no chronological sequence in the events, since the flash-forward or the flash-backward devices, repetitions, and repositionings implicit in her technique prevent it. During the Writer's first phase, as a child of seven or eight, his chief occupation is playing word games, as attested to by his spectacular forays into *active imagination*. The second phase focuses on the young Writer just starting out in his chosen career. He is filled with turmoil as he struggles to transmute thought/sensations—those living and burning forces inside him—into their final form as words on the white page. The last sequence dramatizes the tribulations of the successful Writer who is adulated and feted by his readers. He has lost contact with that inner being that once motivated his creative élan, and no longer knows whether he exists as an individual in his own right or whether he is merely playing at being a role model, fulfilling the expectations and needs of his reading public. That he finally questions the validity and authenticity of his approach to writing, at the conclusion of the book, makes him realize that he has become a puppet whose strings are manipulated by the collective—those "others out there." No longer is his work actuated, as it had once been, in that unlimited realm of wonderment and enrichment existing inchoate within his depths. A panderer to his public, he is no longer master of his art. A renewal is in order.

The Archetypal Word

To understand the Writer's obsession with words, an explication of Sarraute's literary concepts will be offered prior to an analysis of *Between Life and Death*. For Sarraute, the word is of prime importance. She explores how it is born from the void (like the child emerging from the womb) and how it becomes humanized, taking on a personality and electric charge of its own. As in the alchemical process which transmutes primal matter into gold, Sarraute's words—which are like archetypes and are the foundation of her Writer's life and art—are constantly generating, degenerating, and regenerating. Sarraute's literary technique is based on an aesthetic she calls *tropisms*:

> They are undefinable movements which glide very rapidly to the limits of consciousness; they are at the root of our gestures, our words, of the feelings we manifest, which we believe we feel and which we can define. They seemed to me and still seem to me to constitute the secret source of our existence.
>
> When these movements are in the process of formation, they remain unexpressed—not one word emerges—not even in the words of an interior monologue; they develop within us and vanish with extreme rapidity, without our ever really perceiving them clearly; they produce within us frequently very intense, but brief, sensations; these can be communicated to the reader only through images, thereby giving them an equivalent and enabling them to feel analogous situations. These movements had to be decomposed and allowed to extend into the reader's conscious mind in the manner of a film in slow motion. Time was no longer experienced in terms of the workaday world, but rather in a distorted and aggrandized present.[4]

Time is reversible: Cyclical regeneration is a reality; the future may be looked upon as a prefiguration of the past.

Tropisms, experienced in single words or in images, as they are in *Between Life and Death*, become manifest "with the birth of consciousness before its transformation into rational thought."[5] Sarraute's visions are "protoplasmic," Sartre wrote, because they are delineated with utmost accuracy and finesse, with Cartesian precision and geometric method.[6] The clarity of her observation, with its emphasis on microscopic details, creates a series of eidetic images, each imposed and superimposed upon the other, as in a sequence of layers. These stratifications are never static; on the contrary, they are "amoeba-like" and are in a state of perpetual flux and reflux, altering in form and content, substance and point. Sarraute's tropisms are unlike Joycean interior monologues, which "flow through one's conscious mind." They are pre-conscious incisions, pre-interior monologues, clothed in a vocabulary as sensual as Proust's and as incisive as Beckett's.[7]

Unlike the conventional novel, Sarraute's fiction—and *Between Life and Death* is no exception—has no real plot. It centers on a controlled or contrived situation: in the Writer's case, the creative process. The essence of the work concerns words as individual entities or archetypal forces, as universal recurring images or patterns of behavior. One word interacts with another, affecting the Writer and his listeners or readers, and drawing energy and power to itself from other words, letters, or figures of speech. In the process, the pace slackens or increases, thereby altering the meaning, weight, emphasis, substance, rhythm, sensations, and impact of clauses, sentences, paragraphs, pages. This makes for the narration's sharp, frequently brutal, dramatic effects.

Sarraute, to be sure, is not the inventor of this kinetic literary technique based on the energetic power of the word. Nor is she the first to consider words and letters tantamount to God's creation of the world or to Prometheus's creation of the human race and to his theft of fire. Both notions go far back in history, to the *Sefer Yetsirah* (*The Book of Creation*), which predates the second century A.D., and to other mystical tracts. The *Sefer Yetsirah* describes cosmic creation and ways for humanity to share in it through ten "elementary" or "primordial" numbers (defined as God's Ten Emanations or the ten expressions of his "unfolding" into matter) and the twenty-two consonants of the Hebrew alphabet. The twenty-two letters are looked upon as composing the structural elements of the universe and are viewed, therefore, as the foundation of the world. It is through the infinite combinations and phonetic divisions inherent in these "basic letters" that the "roots of all things" exist. Each letter is thought to be charged with its own energy and to vary in power, meaning, sound, and image, depending on its placement in the sentence and on the page. Analogies to the three realms of creation—the human sphere, the celestial domain, and "the rhythmic flow of time through the course of the year"[8]—may also be drawn by means of a written character.

Just as every act of creation (animate or inanimate) occurs through combinations of letters, words, and numbers, as demonstrated in the *Sefer Yetsirah*, so, too, does Sarraute's kinetic literary technique bring the unactualized into being. Repetitions, flashbacks, reworkings of words and syntax, positional shiftings of clauses—all are used by Sarraute to create emotional experiences and to alter pitch, pace, and orientation, thereby affecting concentration, perception, and affect.

To bring forth the word from nothing, as Sarraute's Writer does, may be looked upon as paralleling a cosmogonic event. It arises from the Beginning, the Void, Chaos (psychologically speaking, from the deepest layers of the collective unconscious—the very source of creation and of reality); it then undergoes a transfiguration, from Nothingness to Something (or Being). The Kabbalists have illustrated this transformation linguistically, by means of the Hebrew words *ain*, which means "nothing," and *ani*, defined as "I." A mere rearrangement of the same letters alters their meaning. Such a change implies, symbolically, the passage from "a gap of existence," or the Void (Nothingness), to existence. It is this instant of transformation, and what leads up to and follows it, that Sarraute's Writer attempts to understand and to convey.[9]

Since some words and letters—emerging from the Writer's collective unconscious and considered the living creative matrix of "all of our unconscious and conscious functions"—are archetypal in dimension, they are endowed with substance, energy, rhythm, and patterns of behavior. They are "idea force"—a certain word or letter capable of fomenting a dynamic process, which puts into motion a feeling, an imagining, or an action. Once the letter(s) or word(s) is written, or even thought or sensed, it (they) takes on contour, becoming at once concretion and abstraction, sign and symbol; it (they) also has the potential to develop virtualities and possibilities in time and space.

Since certain words are archetypal in *Between Life and Death*, they may appear, disappear, and reappear, assuming not only the role of flesh-and-blood characters but of affects as well. Suprapersonal and nonindividual, their impacts are frequently inaccessible to conscious awareness. They appear or are sensed every so often as autonomous presences or tonal emanations which hover about for a bit, only to fall back into oblivion. At times, they reappear during other sequences as formless substances, as floating opacities, or as glistening crystallizations in an ever-dilating word/world.

Words in Sarraute's orchestrated prose achieve a scale of nuanced timbres, intonations, and amplitudes which at times triturate, lacerate, exacerbate, striate, bombard, and sear the Writer and reader both. Or they may work their charms on listeners by means of velvety, mellifluous, endearing, Siren-like harmonics, depending upon their connotations, their positionings in a sentence, and their juxtaposition with other words of the "tribe," as Sarraute calls them.

Cases in point are plentiful. When, for example, the Writer hears a woman at the next table in a restaurant say to her son, "Armand, if you continue, your father will prefer your sister" (78), the power of the words he has just heard affects him deeply; they cut and dig into his flesh, insidiously and mercilessly. On another occasion, the Writer's mother unabashedly accuses him of "ruminating," of literally and figuratively chewing his words, swallowing, masticating, pulverizing, regurgitating them, as he probes their origin, meaning, and effect upon him during his word-play sequences. She does not understand him—the artist in him—and for this reason is forever attempting to normalize him. She would like him to be just like the others. Once he has achieved fame, however, she makes a swift turnabout. She swells with pride—the pride of a mother who gave birth to a genius. He was "predestined" to become a great writer, she now claims. The minute he was brought to her in his swaddling clothes, "J'ai *su*," she states with authority—the way the Virgin *knew* the Annunciation, or the manner in which the priests instinctively chose the child who was to be the Dalai Lama (178). Words in this instance are premonitory signs of some sacred event in the offing; their numinosity transcends the event.

The Word: Gestural Language and Ritual

Between Life and Death begins as the Writer attempts to convey to his audiences the stages involved in the creation of his book. Sarraute's verbal and gestural language in the opening image is arresting: It offers the reader a reflection of the Writer's unconscious and conscious attitudes—a world of tropisms:

> He shakes his head, puckers his lids, his lips . . . "No, positively no, that won't do." He stretches out his arm, bends it again . . . "I tear out the page." He clenches his fist, then his arm drops, his hand relaxes . . . "I throw it away. I take another sheet. I write. On the typewriter. Always. I never write by hand. I reread . . . " His head moves from side to side. His lips are pouting . . . "No, no, and again no. I tear it out. I crumple it. I throw it away. And so, three, four, ten times I start over . . . " He puckers his lips, frowns, stretches his arm, bends it again, lets it drop, clenches his fist.[10]

Sarraute has drawn her Writer, verbally, in a series of studied poses. But are they really studied? Or are they spontaneous? Ambiguity and mystery lie at the core of Sarraute's figurations throughout *Between Life and Death*. Each time she repeats the above sequence in one form or another, repositioning certain words, omitting others or adding some new ones, drama is heightened, as is the acuteness of the pantomimic sequence.

Sarraute's Writer is unforgettable as we see him nodding, frowning, rising, sitting, extending his arm, then bending and lowering it, tearing a sheet of paper out of his typewriter, clenching his fist, opening his hand, grabbing another sheet of paper, inserting it into the machine, typing, reading what he has just written, deciding it's not quite right, tearing it out again, crumpling it up, throwing it away, and so forth. There are times, he remarks in another sequence, when he reaches such a peak of frustration—so preoccupied is he with finding the specific word that will evoke the right idea/sensation—that he leaves his study in a sweat, oblivious to all outside noises or presences. Then, for no apparent reason, the very word or letter he is searching for incarnates itself in his mind's eye; he transcribes it "on the white page and sentences form. Miracle. How do we do it? It's a great mystery" (2; 8).

The very mystery behind creation heightens the Writer's fascination with the transformatory process, from nothing to being. As he pursues his self-interrogation, even awakening at night in his continuous struggle to find the right word—that single power that will encapsulate meaning and sensation—his obsession imposes upon him a stinging torment. "Why my God, why?" he asks, as if experiencing excoriating martyrdom (8).

The Writer's continuous quest for *the word*, which he dredges up once he sinks into his unconscious, or which is ejaculated without any apparent rhyme or reason, may be considered a kind of transformation ritual. The gestural language used by Sarraute in the opening episode (quoted above) takes on a religious flavor, accompanied as it is by specific signs: punctuation, figures of speech, and other literary devices. (Religion here is to be understood in its original sense, derived from the Latin *religio*, meaning "link"—that which unites.) In keeping with the numinosity of the opening ceremony, its formality, increased each time it is repeated during the course of the narrative, discloses an ontological need on the Writer's part to repeat symbolically the original act of Creation.

The reactualization of a cosmogonic act serves several purposes. It regenerates time for the Writer, lending the entire novel a cyclical scheme and therefore a mythic dimension. In such a scheme, time is reversible and the Writer can regress to his childhood, becoming linked with events which have faded out of his consciousness and which he brings back to a present reality. The repeated transformations of the opening episode also commemorate for him the primordial conflict, the passage from Chaos to Cosmos, which parallels his struggle to articulate the Word and to give substance to the amorphous. In reexperiencing childhood and bringing forth language, the Writer experiences a sense of fulfillment and joy and a raison d'être. The written word—indeed, the entire creative process—acts as a compensatory device for the Writer. It takes him out of his world of unbearable loneliness, which is caused in part by his inability to relate to people on a human level. Later, when his readers describe his torment using the simplistic and banal term "unadaptable," they believe they have resolved the entire unresolvable problem. Mystery for them is an open book.

Examples of the Writer's extreme sensitivity to language and to the impact of meanings, rhythms, amplitudes, sensations, and variations of form and pronunciation are given early in the book. When he was a child, the verb *faire* (with many meanings, including "make," "do," "play a role," and "give the appearance of being") disoriented him completely. He recalls the time when he was in school and one of his teachers, noticing he was reading James Fenimore Cooper, questioned him: "Tiens vous 'faites' de l'anglais?" ("So you're doing English?"). The verb is used here idiomatically and actively, as when referring to someone doing the marketing, the ironing, and other chores (14). *Faire* is also used passively, as in "Je fais une pleuresie" ("I have pleurisy" or "I am having a heart attack"). The verb depicts character traits as well, such as in the description of the Writer: "Vous faites assez inadapté" (44).

The question remains as to why the young boy felt physically and emotionally bruised—even lacerated—by *faire*'s multiple uses. Why did he sense danger ahead for him? His reactions are not as outlandish as they might at first seem. The teacher's question (and the many examples of the use of *faire* given by Sarraute) aroused heretofore unknown sensations in the highly intuitive lad. The discovery that no one word had just one definition was like stepping into quicksand. He sensed that just as *faire* had many meanings and could be used in multiple ways, depending upon the context, so varied options and courses were open to him in the life experience which was his writing. The straight and narrow path was gone; barriers had vanished, and with them the security he thought existed in the empirical domain of words. Gone were the fixity and solidity—the very foundations—of his psyche and aesthetics. Everything existed in a state of flux; anything could become something else, transform, altering its own consistency and scope.

Only as he grew older and began to write literary works were the feelings which he had sensed as a lad understood consciously. He came to experience the truth that the very idea of security in general is an illusion—in the verbal domain first of all.

Psychologically, we may say that what had formerly been whole or *one* had become differentiated. The ego was emerging from the unconscious and had to weather the life experience itself, with all of its vagaries and tensions. The One had become Two. Choice and an unsteady course had superseded the fixed and facile way. But there is more to it than this. Like Proust's Narrator, Sarraute's Writer learns in time that he is not even *one* person, so to speak, but the sum total of all the people and events he has experienced, both passively and actively, during the course of his life. As Sarraute remarked in *L'ere du soupçon*, there is no single extreme bottom or depth in anyone; everyone is endowed with "multiple depths; and these rise tier upon tier to infinity." As the multiple selves inhabiting the Writer increase in dimension and scope, so, too, do his feelings of confusion, to the point that he sometimes wonders who he is. Today we label such anxieties as identity crises.

There is, however, a positive side to the Writer's anguish. The very notion of unlimited depths existing within each being may be viewed as an enrichment; like Aristotle's *entelechia*, human potential may be considered infinite. If this is true, so, too, are the Writer's possibilities. Within him, then, exists an inexhaustible source of creativity, which he has to learn to tap.

Technique is now called into play. Without discipline, innovative élan may be dissipated. To be able to sift the dross from the pure requires a highly tuned thinking function: the power to rationalize, to differentiate, to distinguish, and to evaluate the outflow of new contents emanating from the collective unconscious. The Writer's *eye*, one of the most powerful of perceptive instruments, must be turned into a tool. Inquisitive and discerning, it must be object and subject-observer and participant—wandering about in uncharted territories within his psyche, apprehending the psyche's unknown forces, then integrating them into what will become the work of art. Such a trajectory is arduous, for during moments of intense creativity the Writer must learn to cohabit, to coexist, and to cofunction with what may sometimes prove to be mephitic, insalubrious forces inhabiting him, as well as with sublime, opalescent sensations—each learning to nurture the other.

The Word and Active Imagination

As previously mentioned, words, for the seven-year-old child, were playthings—toys which he set in motion or immobilized whenever the spirit moved him. These treasures, which stimulated further verbal associations and incredible fantasy images, are presented by Sarraute in a spectacular bout of active imagination during a train trip the young boy takes with his mother.

As the train rolls through bleak and snowy countrysides, the lad turns inward, entertaining himself by pronouncing homonyms and homophones in rhythm to the sound of the turning wheels.[11] As each archetypal word comes into consciousness, heteroclite images form, removing him increasingly from his circumscribed and referential world and plunging him deeper into vaster, more nebulous spheres.

Active imagination can start with a fantasy, a dream, or an impression of a hypnagogic nature. Jung preferred the word "imagination" to "fantasy," considering the latter a kind of phantasm or fleeting impression. Imagination, on the other hand, he considered to be an "active, purposeful creation."[12] The images issuing forth into consciousness through the process of active imagination are endowed with both a life and a logic of their own. Jung described active imagination as "the only way toward a direct encounter with the reality of the unconscious without the intermediary use of tests or dream interpretation."[13]

The lad's starting points for his periods of active imagination were words which spurted forth homophonically and homonymically: "*Hérault, héraut, heros, aire haut, erre haut, R.O.*" Words and archetypal images hurtled forth almost simultaneously, and together they made up an entire story. The child's creative and pleasurable pastime in his mind's eye was forever being interrupted by his mother, seated in the same compartment, who criticized him for "ruminating." Not for one moment did she realize that her son was exploring the magical world of imagination—a domain where wholeness exists.

For the future Writer, active imagination "opened negotiations" with powers and forces in the unconscious which must have answered a specific need within him. Introverted and unhappy, living with a mother who had little if any understanding of her son's real nature, he used active imagination to help him escape into a land of warmth and comfort; but it also challenged and encouraged his creative élan. Unlike the dream, which is experienced passively, active imagination can be directed. The lad accomplished just that. The wanted or willed words he activated released images in his mind's eye, which in turn constellated clusters of sensations and feeling tones.

A whole world of secret desires and compensatory states of being emerged into existence. *Hérault* (the name of a department in France), herald, hero, an eagle's nest, a wanderer on high, and R. O. were, for the lad, archetypal in dimension. They evoked white landscapes, a lavender horn, a knight riding a richly caparisoned charger and followed by others, fog breaking out, dark skies lit by flickering stars. The *R* evoked a bulldog standing erect with his legs firmly set on the ground. The *O* symbolized the closed circle: "Everything closes and we start over again" (17; 29).

What do these images disclose about the child's needs and his personality? Does he see himself as Herald, Hero, or Wanderer? The words he uses imply aggressivity, power, and energy. He is struggling to be heard, to be understood, and to penetrate areas that will require of him a show of heroic strength. The charger that forges ahead into untraveled, snow-covered terrain will help him achieve his goal. A whole medieval atmosphere is conjured up as a spectacular battle scene unfolds before him: There are flags and horses; and men arrayed in brilliant tonalities, each bearing the heraldic symbol of his family or master, pursue their heated struggle. This is a violent, cruel, and electrifying action painting at its height.

This sequence of active imagination may also be viewed as a prefiguration of the Writer's future fight with words and his symbolical wanderings through opaque and dismally dark inner landscapes, illuminated only every now and then by scintillating stars. His projection onto a hero figure emphasizes his weakly structured ego, his inadequate or painful life experience, and his need to bring into existence what he lacks: strength, direction, and vision. Thus he removes himself from his circumscribed and individual frame of reference and plunges into the collective experience of timelessness.

The whites and purples daubed onto this same verbal canvas show the lad's feel for color and form and also inject a sense of tremulous excitement. Reminiscent in tone of some canvases by Monet, Cézanne, and Matisse, they ally the medieval to the modern in diachronic relational patterns, thereby linking, associating, and fusing past and present in a space/time continuum.

The *R*, associated with the growling bulldog, stands for strength, fortitude, willpower, attention, and feeling. This archetypal protector (the dog as man's best friend) may also be envisaged as a positive father image or the power that will prevent any harm from coming to the boy. The dog is power, but he is also caring. The *O*, following the *R*, is a semiotic device that stands for all of the Writer's work and the various stages and variants it has undergone. It also includes the techniques and tools—abstract and concrete—used in the actual writing process: lines, spirals, dichroisms, punctuation, sensations, and literary and aesthetic devices, all communicating with each other in a round. Psychologically, the *O* stands for the Self, the total psyche comprising both conscious and unconscious spheres.

The train in which the lad is riding is also a sign and symbol. As it speeds across the snow-covered landscape, activating his imagination, time expands and mythical time is born. The boy feels himself living in the medieval period; the charger in his imagination is festooned with colorful array, and the knight, strong and virile in his coat of mail, bears his heraldic symbols for all to see. Since the train represents the mechanistic world of objects, the boy is also part of the linear time scheme in a contemporary world, which functions scientifically and with the accuracy of an impeccable clock. Inflexible in its order, disciplined, controlled, and punctual to the extreme, the train is unconcerned with any human factor. It is a link in a complicated communicatory network that links a variety of areas and circadian cycles. Like a human artery, which carries the blood from one part of the body to another, it also functions as part of its own vast circulatory system, relocating travellers and merchandise in a continuous round. A train imposes its laws and rhythms on the human being physically and psychologically, since it determines the destinations of all those within its metal frame—both on an individual and collective basis. Another factor also comes into play with the train: Its circuit must be set well ahead of time. Such a situation implies the need to define one's course, thereby relying upon discipline and order. Any changes in scheduling or programming must be anticipated beforehand and carried out with precision and care.

Psychologically, the just-discussed sequence of active imagination implies an urge on the lad's part to precipitate the destruction of anything that might impede his course toward creativity or stifle his lunge for life—for creativity. It also suggests the opposite: his dependence upon the scheduled, rational function, the urge to plan ahead, to see to it that all factors in his world are linked, associated, and part of a cohesive whole.

At this stage of his life, the would-be Writer may be said to be symbolically charging and fighting his mother, rebelling against her demands that he return to reality. Over and over again, she suggests that he look out of the window at the scenery. But the speed of the train and the child's agitation blot out any definable shapes. Enjoying the freedom of his fantasies and mesmerized by the cadenced, rhythmic patterns issuing forth from the repeated archetypal images and the even-sounding wheels as they speed ahead on the tracks, he is endowed with a sense of continuity and contentment.

Although the woman in the train is the young boy's mother, she may also be looked upon as an *anima* figure: a negative, collective mother figure, with a decidedly disturbing, provocative, and irritating bent, that the Writer meets in various avatars in restaurants, at gatherings, and at lectures. As an interlocutor who never lets him rest in the serenity of his creative imaginings, she plays the role of devil's advocate, constantly challenging him at play and criticizing him for his laziness. She rebukes him for his futile meanderings, his overly introverted ways ("tourné en dedans, en train de ruminer"), his inability to see outside of himself, and his spasmodic span of attention. When the Writer later makes a name for himself, this same self-sacrificing and overly critical mother will gloat over what she considers to be her doing. He was "predestined" to become a great writer, she remarks, because as a child he played with words. Other anima figures appear at one of the Writer's lectures, including a faceless listener who questions him about his creative bent. The woman identifies with him, kowtows to him, blushes fleetingly as she talks to him, and then vanishes into the crowd of worshippers—into non-being—"un chainon anonyme" ("an anonymous link") (11). Whether mother, reader, or listener, anima figures highlight the Writer's hidden, shadowy, opposing, and conflicting side. The anima figure is that force that triggers discussion, provokes argumentation, compels analytical evaluation, and thereby increases the Writer's consciousness. It is the anima figure in part that invites the ego to come to terms with the polarities facing it in the differentiated realm—in the unfriendly world of contention.

The Successful Writer: Being and Appearing

When the Writer becomes successful, the schism corroding his psyche grows increasingly intense: *Being* and *appearing* are at odds. Questions of identity plague him. Who is he? How does he—a divided human being—function? Is he like the others—his readers, his audiences? No, certainly not, he responds. The Writer's feelings are ambivalent. He yearns to be part of the group, but he also wants to be unique. At times he feels like the romantic poet-martyr, a pariah whom no one really understands. His emotional crises are extreme: When he is criticized by his audiences, he cringes and bathes in humiliation; when he is complimented by them, he veers instead toward inflation. A Promethean and a demiurge now, he is convinced that what he writes is flawless and unequaled—the best. He disdains both the gullible, ignorant masses and the facile writer who yields to inspiration, impulse, and passion. Such stress transforms him into a heaving mass of pulsations, unable to capture the creative center that leads to greater understanding of his problems, both psychological and aesthetic.

How can the Writer *appear to be* and *be* at the same time? he wonders. Is he ever really himself when speaking to his audiences and readers—or even when writing? Or is he putting on an act, posing, posturing, incarnating a role, like the actor or mime? How can a creative individual, who scrutinizes and analyzes his every word—as each is ejaculated spontaneously from his unconscious—also exercise the discipline necessary to combine these two virtually antithetical experiences? How can he then set the fruit of his toil on paper in an ordered manner? The Writer sees himself as a divided individual, acting and acted upon, being and appearing, devoid of that wholeness needed to bring the real work of art to fruition. The word "individual" comes from the Latin *in*, meaning "not," and *dividere*, meaning "divide," which suggests something that cannot be divided, explicated, or reduced to its components. Like the Self or God, the individual transcends human understanding. As for the longed for wholeness the Writer seeks, it also implies a suprapersonal condition, which exists in the world of the absolute and is not to be enjoyed in the empirical domain. Both concepts exist as abstractions and ideals, unattainable in the real world.

Let us recall that, during the Writer's earlier struggles to liberate his ego from the womblike family atmosphere (participation mystique), he succeeded in detaching himself from the constrictions imposed upon him by withdrawing into his imaginary world. Struggling heroes came to mind, compensating for his lonely childhood; and, in his fantasies, he projected himself onto such figures. Now, however, the Writer really is attempting to become a hero. It is he who, at certain moments, seeks to be the innovator. Fearful and trembling, he is like Abraham, who listened to his inner voice and heard Jehovah say: "Get thee out of thy country, and from thy kindred, and from thy father's house, unto a land that I will show thee" (Genesis 12:1). So the Writer, in the literary field, will have to strike out on his own and earn the resentment and anger of all those who seek to prolong the status quo. Jesus also took an outward route, suffering the consequences of his revolutionary ideas. In both cases, conflict ensued, as it does during all birth and maturation processes. Whenever a new cultural canon comes into being, disruption and chaos result. The hero or innovator is usually rejected by the society to which he belongs and must find his own way, enduring hardships that may be seen symbolically as initiation rites preceding a higher sphere of development. Only when he has won his battle, when he has imposed his creative principle on family and society, does he attain the status of hero and earn the admiration of those around him.

The struggle to gain his independence, to become self-sufficient, and to renew the dialogue between the rational and irrational worlds is the drama the successful Writer must live out. For the creative individual, there is no fixed stage, no repose or serenity, no status quo. The *what is* must be reshuffled, renewed, and reborn to become the *what will be*, flowing in ever-expanding circles, in ever-deepening life cycles, in an eternal return from life to death and death to life.

Such a route is fraught with difficulty; it demands integrity and commitment on the part of the individual. The Writer is not yet prepared to deal with the prolonged years of self-questioning that creativity requires, nor with the utter loneliness and the vilifications that will be leveled at him by family, friends, and strangers. Such hardships and trials are the lot of the authentic Hero/Writer.

The successful Writer, also an aspect of Sarraute's creative spirit, is pulled in another direction. The need to be adulated, and the happiness admiration brings, fill the gaping chasm within him, which fears failure. How delightful it is to be applauded for one's novels, to rest on one's laurels, to be feted by a reading public. To surrender, however, has its price: the Writer's authenticity. He must begin to hide his real thoughts and feelings in order to write what the public demands. In so doing, his ego loses contact with his collective unconscious—that infinite source of riches which ejaculates into the Writer's consciousness its mobile forms and shapes and its tonal and rhythmic colorations and sensations. Adulation brings stratification, fixidity, and aridity.

The Writer is as yet unable to decide upon his course: whether to choose the hard route or the facile one, which requires that his work be polished, appealing, banal, and superficial. In language as visceral as any used by Sartre in *Nausea*, Sarraute discloses the real Writer's powerful emotions in his battle:

> Nothing must escape their watchful eyes. Upon all that moves in shadowy corners, wavers, trembles, slips away, . . . formless, flabby, vaguely disturbing, . . . into all that seeps, trickles, bleeds, palpitates, they hurl these words . . . they plant them in it . . . nothing revolts them, frightens them, they harpoon it and pull it towards them . . . they look at it, lying there . . . like a carrion, stretched out grotesquely on its back, with its belly open, its legs spread wide apart, like the blood-tinged, glistening, purplish skin of freshly flayed animals . . . it dries and hardens in the sun. (31; 49)

Then something happens to the Writer: A substance, a power, an amorphous entity, floats into his mind's eye. He seizes it, almost physically—ritualistically, as if undergoing a numinous experience:

> He takes it—a hard, pointed, sharp thing—and lets it fly, he closes his eyes so as not to see the living flesh into which the word has sunk and which is open, throbbing, bleeding, struggling . . . he pulls, but nothing comes, the word returns to him without having caught hold of anything: a coarse, hideous object, like the things you win in lotteries or at street fairs . . . he looks at it, perplexed, embarrassed, he doesn't know where to put it, what to do with it . . . He's blushing, he's too funny, look at him, he's perfect . . . really made to order. (32; 50)

Sarraute's extraordinary ability to humanize words and gestures, and her circular narrative technique, which allows for flashbacks and flash-forwards, take the reader into the heart of the matter: the conflict between the world of the callous and the snob, where her Writer plays out his roles as lecturer, performer, and mime; and the inner world, where the Writer probes the various facets of his prismatic personality and his artistic élan.

In sequences of stunning portraits, we see Sarraute's Writer's countenance altering as words act upon him, cutting and searing his sensibilities, and bruising his feelings and intellect. The mimed and dramatized sequences underline the poignancy of the Writer's struggle between being and appearing. Is the pain he describes as he searches for the right word real or superimposed? Are the gestures and emotions used to sway his audiences genuine or studied? In this regard, we return to the key word *faire*, used in the idiomatic expression *faire semblant* ("to make believe").

The ambiguity of the Writer's disclosures as he incarnates his role (or exteriorizes his real feelings) increases the acuteness of his trauma. When speaking to his audiences, he is not loath to disclose the ordeal of the creative process per se. He describes the choice of the exact word that will convey olfactorily, visually, sensually, metaphysically, and intellectually everything he wants to pour into it or force out of it. To create a word is an excoriating procedure, like the extraction of poisons from the body, or a tooth from the mouth. Flaubert depicted the writing process as an agony of the most abrasive type; so did Mallarmé, who, each time he faced the blank page, was shaken by his one great fear—the fear of artistic sterility. The delight the Writer takes in enacting these powerful emotions, however, serves to mystify him—and the reader. Is he consciously acting or unconsciously posturing?

Other problems plague the Writer in his quest to please his audiences and to serve that inner necessity which drives him on to create. His mind, like a machine (the train in the active-imagination episode), is always forging ahead, working, thinking, prying, focusing, absorbing, extracting, and sensitizing whatever comes into its orbit in the inner realm. The same occurs when observing the outer world: Images are frequently distorted and fragmented, as they were when the train sped through the countryside, blurring what could have been outlined in crystal-clear terms. The Writer questions the wisdom of his alacrity. A slower pace might allow him to better measure and think out the worth of his utterings. Banal conversations he overhears in lecture halls, gatherings, buses, streets, restaurants, and at home begin melding with his flesh and blood. Is he conscious of the transformation occurring within him? Is he aware that, trite as the conversations are, one cannot cut them out, because they are part of the living core of existence? Bombast and platitudes also have their place amid colorfully glazed and sculptured images. All forms of life must be incised in the work of art. The grotesque and the hideously ugly also contain their inward beauty.

Vowels and consonants are also to be probed. Like words, they are personified, since they represent livingness for Sarraute. Frequently they irritate the hypersensitive Writer, affecting his thoughts, feelings, and sensations. When mispronounced, they become disfigured, vulgarized, flabby, and flaccid, losing their ideal strength and power. The inclusion of gutless and seemingly impotent sounds in his work repulses the Writer, but to eject them limits the scope of his creative élan, distancing him still further from reality. Vowels possess their own viscosity and their own viscerality; they produce pleasurable or even hypnotic side effects:

> May the lazy, drawling vowels freely flourish . . . My vaalise . . . We must pass through them without stooping, leap over them without breathing, hold our noses, and look at what is there, behind them . . . Vacaaation . . . and there between the rocks are the emerald

> coves, the transparent water in which is trembling rippled virgin sand . . . the motionless peaks of pine trees, red suns, green rays . . . (33; 52)

Baudelaire allowed himself to be enthralled by the smooth and rounded sensuality of certain vowel sounds which corresponded in his mind's eye to the sultry and exotic dream. But the Writer grows annoyed by the way some people emphasize the *a* in "*vacaaances*," evoking feelings of satiny, golden, and copperlike tonalities for some; for others, gleaming transparencies, immobile sands, and blue-green waters. An ascetic at heart, the Writer castigates such hedonism: "The lazy, unctuous vowels stretch themselves, spread themselves, wallow over him . . . This vacaaation . . . the suhhn . . . the seeea . . . the stale-smelling liquid that they disgorge, sprinkles" (34). The disciplined artist must detach himself from words or parts of words, no matter how strong. The Writer and his double now begin their final struggle for supremacy. One part of him accepts the beauties of language, reacting passively to their endearing qualities. The artist in him, guided by that perceiving *eye* that refines, structures, scrapes, cuts, lacerates, sands, shapes, and reshapes over and over again, aggressively rejects the effete ways of the facile performer/Writer.

In time the Writer formulates his ethos, spasmodically and impulsively, still veering from the joy brought to him by success. He realizes, painfully, that he is merely repeating himself, as does a marionette, manipulated by outside forces. Yet these very polarities that trigger contraries within him also pave the way for the tensions necessary to pursue the inward process: the probing, questioning, and doubting of the work in process. The Writer finally becomes aware of the pitfalls awaiting him. Despite the absence of characters and conventional plot lines in his novel, he knows his readers will still try to situate the fleeing presences and opalescent forces which bob up here and there. Wasn't it true for Proust in *Remembrance of Things Past*? His readers were forever trying to find the key to his nonexistent creatures. Who were those flesh-and-blood people upon whom Proust modeled his characters? they asked over and over again. Sarraute's Writer—now without illusions—realizes that words alone people his literary universe; they form the topic, theme, locus, focus, and fabric of his book: "No longer need anyone. Words alone" (75). Unlike Balzac, the Writer needs no decors, furnishings, foods, clothes, or any other objects to identify things, beings, and sensations parading through the pages of his novel. Solitude alone is not expendable. The zone of emptiness that surrounds the Writer—a void from which he will draw his nourishment—is an obstacle necessary for his initiation into real authorship. Only within this sphere will he *know* vowels, consonants, words, language; only this sphere will endow him with the energy to transform the invisible and amorphous—or dead—object into living and vibrant forces on the sheet of paper.

The Writer again sinks into himself, withdrawing from the land of the living into the depersonalized realm, as Mallarmé had done when composing *Igitur*. In this unidentifiable, autonomous region, he loses all sense of himself as a person:

> From the soft substance with the insipid smell there trickled a sort of vapor, stream . . . it is condensing . . . the little drops of words mount in a thin jet, they shove one another, then fall down again. Others mount, and others still . . . Now the last jet has fallen. There's nothing left. (63; 91)

Like eruptions of lava flowing through him, exuding noxious fumes as well as glowingly spectacular sensations, the Writer experiences the extraordinary feelings provoked by the "chosen" words as they secrete themselves from his very essence and become living presences. Committing his gleanings to paper, he again grows anxious, fearful that he might never again know such an experience, one "that must absolutely happen again" (64).[14] And it does:

> It increases, spreads . . . it had the vigor, the untouched freshness of young shoots, of new grass, it is growing with the same restrained violence, propelling words before it . . . (64; 92)

Like an orchestra leader attentive to each of his instrumentalists, the Writer listens to the words, vowels, and consonants vibrating and resonating in unison or singly within him. And the "thing," the "object" which becomes the *work*, begins to surface. Words amplify, move about, displace each other; their music and chantings, their rhythms and arabesques, mount and descend, imbricating themselves in fleeting yet dense patternings. The Writer wanders through what seems to be inexhaustible avenues of endlessly oscillating vowels, consonants, and words; he palpates their contours, tastes and inhales their perfumed odors, fondles their ideations, and then detaches himself from the melee—as if exhaling the total experience. Again he plunges into the mass of fluid formlessness, catching, harpooning, grabbing more of these mobile forces, only to slacken his grip, guiding them gently to the surface, dizzy, even slightly nauseous from the strain of it all. As he examines his catch on the written page, he shakes his head once again. No, it's not just right. One more thrust into the void. Then, suddenly, "it moves, drags him, he is shaken" (103).

Fulgurating images ejaculate, triturate, bite, abrade, and pain the Writer as words leap onto the page. One by one he listens to them vibrate, pulsate, oscillate. Their intonations and accents rush forth, pounding out their litanies, dilating, diminishing, enriching, scorching, and deforming the very substance of his flesh and psyche.

The Writer has chosen his method. No self-indulgence; no sloppiness. He chooses structure, composition, rigor—the science of language—and imagination. Will his work attain immortality? Who is to judge, and who judges?

But then he has a change of heart. Although the Writer's yearning for perfection is strong, his will begins to slacken. Moments of hesitation intrude, even at this juncture. When again asked by his readers for his method, he surrenders to the sin of pride and the desire for approbation and glorification. Gone are the firm commitments to structure, composition, and authenticity. Thrilled at the thought of being accepted by the circle of admirers, the Writer comes forth as their guide, mentor, and deity; he is no longer a loner. But he vacillates. During a pause, he returns to himself: "I am alone. I have proof of it. I have nothing to do with you. Alone" (122). He longs for the anonymity he used to know: "to be nothing . . . formless slumped against a wall in a corner" (125). Only then can he maintain his independence and function with impunity.

As he listens to his audiences articulating even greater admiration ("excellent, remarkable"), the Writer regresses—this time to a virtually embryonic state. Feelings of infinite gratitude overwhelm him as his audiences raise him to the status of hero. Words, like unfurling flags, roll out before him in all of their colorful array. Like the child riding his charger, the Writer feels like running, prancing, and bounding about. No longer does he object to undefined and banal objects or to hackneyed terms bandied about by his readers: Symbolism, Surrealism, Impressionism, Rotationalism—paradigms of the meaninglessness of judgments of lay audiences and critics alike (143). Nevertheless, the Writer (and perhaps this is one of Sarraute's most brutal attacks on critics and readers) takes umbrage at those arbiters of taste—out there. How can critics possibly know how he feels and what words really mean to him? Their writings are tinged not only with ignorance but with the vacuity accompanying the arrogance of the blind and nonperceptive, those who have failed to achieve their goals as authors of fiction.

Over and over his audiences ask him how he creates his work, and each time he repeats the same sequence described at the outset of *Between Life and Death*, with variations in the alignment and distributions of the words. As he mimes that unforgettable sequence—rising, extending and bending his arm, nodding, shaking his head—sweat and blood pour off him. His gesturings, which mirror the agony of it all, are like a crucifixion. On the other hand, this same sequence has its ludicrous aspect: It relates a mechanistic saga, as the dichotomy between appearing and being increases. The Writer's countenance takes on the contours and colorations of a clown, a buffoon, or a kind of marionette, whose strings are moved not through inner necessity, but by an undetermined and whimsical reading public. Precision, definition, and dexterity mark his gestures, which he now makes without a moment of hesitation, with increasing amplitude and with a sense of achievement.

No longer the struggling Writer he once was, he has left authenticity by the wayside to become one of society's image makers, like those cardboard replicas featured in Genet's *Balcony*: posturing, pompous, pathetic consumer products pandering to obtuse, greedy, and possessive audiences. Enthroned in his own grandeur, venerated, lauded, feted, and virtually deified—there stands the Writer! No one budges as he explains the daily life-and-death struggle he wages with words to his breathless and ecstatic listeners.

Unlike the protagonists of Vauthier's *Character Against Himself* and Beckett's *Krapp's Last Tape*, who probed their youthful writings, attempting to understand the changes that had taken place in their styles (as they matured from fledglings to mechanical hacks), the Writer is increasingly caught up in the round of praise emanating from his audiences. Seated enthralled in a semicircle around him, they watch his every word and gesture with rapt attention as he raises his arm, clenches his fist, or tears the piece of paper from the machine. Is he a magus? some ask. A sage? A messiah? A prophet? A hypnotist? Others label him a procurer, unchaste and unclean.

Suddenly a woman seems to float forth like a cloud from within the semicircle of listeners. Unlike the mesmerized audience, she represents a negative presence. She criticizes his ways, questions his principles, and spreads confusion and doubt in his psyche. Has she seen through his game? his pandering? He feels depotentiated, as if all the hot air which had inflated his being had suddenly been let out; the balloon has been transformed into an empty vessel. Described as a "suction cup" and a "syringe," this anima figure is indeed the instrument used to suck out the poisons from the Writer's body.

Disoriented and uncertain, as the anima figure eats away at his self-confidence and bruises his arrogance, he is forced to reassess his approach to his work. The anima, really a mysterious and autonomous force within him, succeeds in draining him of those toxic compliments which served to distract him from his art and trample his creative élan by preventing him from facing his inner world, encouraging him to crawl, creep, scrape, and scrounge in order to maintain his image with his public.

Shock overcomes the Writer. He feels almost like the little boy in the train at the outset of *Between Life and Death*. Imagining himself riding his charger, brandishing his saber, and spurring his horse on to battle, he is suddenly deflated, called in by his nurse to take his bath.[15] Powerlessness and fear take possession of him. The mask crumbles. Suddenly he is aware of the fact that the real person—the authentic Writer—has died within him, and the Performer, the Mime, is presiding at a reception in his honor in a funeral home.

The dichotomy between what he *is* and what he *appears to be* shakes his equilibrium. Now he knows that there are times when he is ruled by a thirst for fame, when he renounces the pain and struggle needed to fashion the work of art—to shape, sculpt, sand, and polish it so as to create that seminal work which brings the unknown into the world. During these periods, he becomes an automaton—a bizarre, mechanical force. Like the train, which forged ahead but always went in the same direction, the Writer has followed the same course, never branching out into strange, mysterious, and dangerous territories. Suddenly, irritation takes possession of him. Without forewarning, he feels some arcane power digging into him, burrowing into his very soul and fiber:

> Here they are, the slow crawlings, the limp uncoilings, the tremblings, tiny particles become excited, whirl about, draw together, complicated forms appear and come apart . . . it's still there, the old fascination . . . in little drops of gray gelatine miniature worlds are gravitating . . . he yields to every touch, to every sticky contact, all repulsion disappears, all instinct of self-preservation . . . may he feel them crawl over his body, the better to follow the meanderings of their antlike processions, may bacteria circulate in him destroying the globules of his blood, he wants to feel again . . . further . . . to the very limit . . . he clings to them, he keeps them warm . . . (172; 239)

Harrowing feelings assail him as the very substance of creation is ejaculated from the deepest recesses within him, no longer to be cast aside. Real life is taking over—the life of the artist who apprehends raw reality in the work of art, imbricating every facet into its structured form. Direct experience culled from the empirical domain, no matter how banal or matter-of-fact it may seem, is now to be welded to that inner factor which stamps the work of art with its individuality. Only then can an edifice of worth come into being; only then does the puppet turn into the puppeteer and become both listener and questioner, thus fusing *appearing* and *being*. As the Writer looks at his audience, contemplating and examining each and all "from a distance," he realizes that there is only one way in the composing of a manuscript: "Is it alive. Is it dead" (78).

The Writer beckons to that primal material which he senses is becoming available to him. He cajoles it and digs for it, and as it rises before him, always "at a distance," he, as artist, captures the evanescent essence—his only friend and companion:

> Nearer to me, but not too near . . . a little to one side nevertheless . . . but rather far from all the others . . . at just the right distance . . . you my double, my witness . . . there, lean over with me . . . let's look together . . . does it emit, deposit . . . as on the mirror we hold before the mouth of the dying . . . a fine mist? (183; 254)

The Writer is no longer alone. As an androgynous principle, he is endowed with two selves: the traditionally "feminine" creative force and the traditionally "masculine" analytic force. And from these is born a third force: the work of art.

8 Pa Chin's *Family:* The Patriarchate Dismembered

Poetic interludes, pictorial qualities, and a transpersonal approach to nature and people invite the readers of Pa Chin's *Family* (1931) to go beyond the depiction of China's political, social, and economic ills. Images, symbols, and metaphors flesh out character and mood and disclose the meta-events occurring in a decadent regime. In a whole secret world, deeply introverted beings, taught from birth to repress emotions and feelings, live out their fantasies in a psychologically and intellectually circumscribed sphere. By paying homage to autocratic ways, some of the protagonists in *Family* are divested of that living and growing substance which is everybody's birthright.

What concerns us here most particularly are the root causes of the severe injustices perpetrated against women in China—women who are victims of a severely patriarchal regime. Why did such a rich cultural heritage, based on Confucianism and Lao-tzu's Taoism, foment such repression? How do the four young ladies in *Family*, whose lives we will probe, deal with such a harsh and restrictive environment?

Pa Chin, born Li Fei-kan in 1904 in Cheng-tu, capital of Szechuan Province in southwest China, came from a wealthy household that included fifty family members and forty-five servants. All were ruled by an unbending and unyielding grandfather. Only after this patriarch's death in 1917 (coincidentally, the year of the Russian Revolution) was Pa Chin given permission to leave his outdated school and enroll in a new and more modern one, in order to broaden and deepen his understanding of the volatile political situation in his country.

The overthrow of the Manchu dynasty in 1911, the proclamation of the

Republic, and the 1912 victory of the Kuomintang (Sun Yat-sen's Nationalist party) gave impetus to the formation of many different political, economic, and social groups, referred to in *Family*. The New Culture Movement (1911–22), for example, known also as the May 4th Movement, rejected China's traditional, strictly hierarchical family system—a codified ethical structure which treated children, outside of the oldest son, as virtual serfs. Also presented in *Family* are the anarchical views of Kropotkin, whom Pa Chin admired, and some of whose works he translated into Chinese. In 1927 Pa Chin left for a two-year visit to France and England. He joined forces with a Chinese anarchist group, siding with them against the Kuomintang (now led by Chiang Kai-shek), which had ordered a brutal massacre of countless Chinese Communists in Shanghai.

Although Pa Chin composed numerous political essays, he was most successful as a novelist. His fictional works include an autobiographical trilogy, *The Turbulent Years* (*Family* and *Spring*, 1939, and *Autumn*, 1940), and his patriotic works: *Fire* (1938–43), *Garden of Rest* (1944), *Ward Number Four* (1945), and *Cold Nights* (1946).

With the establishment of the People's Republic of China in 1949, Pa Chin adhered to the government's line for writers; he lived in comfort in Shanghai, married in 1944, and twice became a father. Feelings of dissatisfaction overcame him in 1961, however; he felt that government restrictions had hampered his free-flowing creative style. After he had advocated the writer's responsibility to speak the truth and to fight literary bureaucracy, the Red Guards looted his home, destroying many of his art objects and his fine library. He was taken to the People's Stadium in Shanghai and forced to kneel on broken glass and listen to the accusations of treason leveled at him by Mao's supporters. "You have your thoughts and I have mine," he replied. "This is the fact and you can't change it even if you kill me"[1] Kept under house arrest for a time, he was finally released, along with other intellectuals.

Philosophical/Religious Views

A glance at China's pantheon of gods and its philosophically oriented religious views based on Confucianism and Taoism may give us insights into the origins of the psychological problems plaguing the four female characters in *Family*.

That the celestial organization of deities is a mirror image of China's stratified and hierarchical society is an indication of the rigidity of this culture's governing archetypal image. All is structured, regulated, and ordered in heaven. Each deity has clearly defined powers; each performs the task of a government administrator, minister, or head of a family, reporting to his immediate superior, who, in turn, reports to his. Directives are issued to inferiors, censuring or praising them as the case warrants, always in keeping with the formalities required by the administrative code of ethics. The sovereign deity in China's spiritual construct is the August Personage of Jade. In divergence from Western religious views, he is not considered a creator god, but only the originator of the mandate from which ruling dynasties obtained their ordination. Chinese gods, in essence, are deified humans; they are not immutable in the Western sense and hence may be replaced by new deities in accordance with altering needs.[2] Because of the interconnectedness of heavenly and earthly spheres, it is believed that if disorder reigns on earth, it may also occur in heaven, thereby placing the entire universe in danger. Emphasis, therefore, is placed on the maintenance of strict regulations in the human sphere.

Translating this worldview into psychological terms, we may say that the rational function—the logical, causal, and reasoning process—is the dominant factor in Chinese society. Identified with the masculine principle, it guarantees a smoothly running society which will assure good fortune and happiness for rulers and people. There is no room in such a world for the nonrational, nonlogical, and noncausal factors identified with the feminine principle—factors which give rise to the unexpected and to the unknown and which therefore may create a dangerous situation in the empirical world.

Confucius (551–479 B.C.), who preached a family-style morality based on the ethical wisdom of "superior men," on character building, learning, virtue, filial piety, and ancestral piety, paid virtually no attention to women. For Confucius, "filial duty and fraternal duty" are "fundamental to Manhood-at-its-best."[3] In the *Canon of Filiality* (Hsiao Ching, third century B.C.), a collection of statements allegedly made by Confucius, we read:

> Filiality is the root of virtue, and that from which civilization derives . . . the body, the hair and skin, are received from our parents, and we dare not injure them: this is the beginning of filiality . . . filiality begins with the serving of our parents, continues with the serving of our prince, and is completed with the establishing of our own character.[4]

Because only the wisest and most honorable men were capable of governing society, moral integrity was stressed. A "gentleman" alone was capable of ruling China, and it was incumbent upon him to elevate those he governed by serving as an example, rather than by exercising autocratic control: "The virtue of the gentleman is like the wind; the virtue of the small man is like the grass. Let the wind blow over the grass and it is sure to bend."[5]

Civilization's continuity depended upon the moral fiber and rules of conduct of the central authority. In *The Great Learning* (Ta Hsueh, fourth century B.C.), we read:

> The men of old who wished to make their bright virtue shine throughout the world first put in order their own states. In order to put in order their own states they first regulated their own families; in order to regulate their own families they first disciplined their own selves. In order to discipline their own selves they first rectified their own minds (or, hearts); in order to rectify their minds they first resolved sincerely upon their goals; in order to resolve sincerely upon their goals they first broadened their understanding of things to the utmost. The broadening of understanding to the utmost was accomplished by studying the nature of things.[6]

The practice of paying homage to past generations—in China's case dating back to the wise kings of the Chou dynasty (1123–221 B.C.)—is implicit in most religions, as attested to in the Bible, the Egyptian and Tibetan Books of the Dead, and Hesiod's *Theogony*. Such a religious practice (*religio* is a linking back to the past) gives people a sense of continuity and security. A person does not have to feel cut off from his or her roots simply because a parent no longer walks the earth. Strength is drawn from the belief in a chain of generations. For the Chinese, such a belief took extreme proportions in the deification of mortals; though in the West similar beliefs prevailed, it was to a far lesser degree.[7]

Emphasis on genealogy, psychologically speaking, indicates the existence of a giant collective unconscious—an infinite ocean—within which everyone and everything exists in a space/time continuum. It is by means of the subliminal sphere, associated always with the feminine principle, that the collective patriarchal dominant can relate to that "nonrational" component of the psyche and feel *relatively* safe: It merely involves a sinking back into an *illo tempore*. Under such conditions, a communication between the living and the deceased is not only possible but is required. The proper rituals virtually insure the living from any danger. By returning to a space/time continuum, the ego (the center of consciousness), whose ability to recognize reality is limited to linear time schemes, is encouraged to tap deeper sources within the psyche in search of transpersonal dimensions which contain the image of all creation. To divest people (or an individual) of a past, be it on a collective or individual level, is to sever them from the instinctive basis of their personality and culture.[8]

Yet, when dwelling on the past is carried to the extreme, as it is paradigmatically in *Family*, negative components come to the fore: regression rather than progression; fixation instead of fluidity. Inordinate emphasis placed upon ancestor worship reveals an overly close psychological identification with the dead through projection, and a concomitant inability on the part of the person(s) making this identification to evaluate the validity of such a rapport. C. G. Jung writes:

> I use the term *identity* to denote a psychological conformity. It is always an unconscious phenomenon since a conscious conformity would necessarily involve a consciousness of two dissimilar things, and, consequently, a separation of subject and object, in which case the identity would already have been abolished. Psychological identity presupposes that it is unconscious. It is a characteristic of the primitive mentality and the real foundation of *participation mystique*, which is nothing but a relic of the original non-differentiation of subject and object, and hence of the primordial unconscious state. It is also a characteristic of the mental state of early infancy, and, finally, of the unconscious of the civilized adult, which in so far as it has not become a content of consciousness, remains in a permanent state of identity with objects. . . . It is not an *equation*, but an *a priori likeness* which was never the object of consciousness.[9]

Ancestor worship as practiced in the religious rituals depicted in Pa Chin's novel is divested of any conscious self-awareness with regard to the individual or to his society. The original projection always remains the model and constitutes the cognition of a process; but it is empty of any message, or of any real relationship with the reality of the land. No growth on the part of the ego, whose field of consciousness remains the same, can take place; only a static, rigid, fixated prolongation of the status quo is possible.

Taoism, unlike the hierarchical view of deity and the uniformity and regularity that marked Confucian society, approaches life in terms of a bipolar concept. Nature's cyclical processes (night and day, seasonal changes, growth and decline, etc.) indicate two factors at work in the universe: *yang* (masculine) and *yin* (feminine). Each contains its opposite: Within yang there is a dot of yin; and within yin, a dot of yang. One polarity, however, is not necessarily at war with the other; rather, it is viewed as complementary to its opposite.[10] These ordering principles, as yang and yin are frequently alluded to, interact eternally and constitute the only certainty in life—the continuously transforming elements in *Tao*.

While yang is identified with ethereality, light, spirituality, and the highest values, yin is equated with earth, moisture, darkness, and gross matter. It must be stressed that moral judgments are not to be assigned to these cosmic forces. As transpersonal powers, neither yang nor yin may be translated into empirical terms. Each has its destructive and constructive sides. A condition of aridity and sterility in a society may come to pass if that society overvalues the yang, or rational, function; if yang is properly diffused, illumination comes to pass, the thinking function becomes productive, and cosmos replaces chaos. So, too, may yin be nutritive, warm, and healing when applied to situations and individuals in a moderate manner, or death-dealing when used immoderately. When Tao is violated and the yang or yin principle becomes overpowering, one of the polarities is seen as *sinning* against the other. A reconciliation of the opposites is in order.[11]

Tao, viewed as a life principle (or breath of life), which circulates throughout the cosmos as yang and yin, was metaphorized by Lao-tzu (sixth century B.C.). He saw it as a perpetually flowing force like water, as the source of energy that vitalized nature, and as the "mother of all things." He writes in the *Tao Te Ching* (*Book of Lao-tzu*):

> The Tao that can be told of is not the eternal Tao;
> The name that can be named is not the eternal name.
> The Nameless is the origin of Heaven and Earth;
> The Named is the mother of all things.[12]

As an operative force meandering about the universe, Tao allows psychic energy to flow from patriarchal (yang) to matriarchal (yin) spheres. Since it is universal and eternal, activating and determining the path individuals and societies take, it may be said to be archetypal.

Since Tao is continuous interaction and perpetual renewal, life and death become part of a cosmic process of eternal transformation. Death, then, is not something to be feared. Rather, it must be looked upon as a natural occurrence implicit in the evolutionary nature of Tao. When the Taoist philosopher Chuang-tzu (365–290 B.C.) sought to depict the image of death, he did so analogically. He spoke as follows to a family in mourning: "Go, hush, get out of the day. Do not disturb the natural evolution. . . . Great is Nature! What will she make of you? Will she make you into the liver of a rat? Will she make you into the arm of an insect?"[13]

The abstract and philosophical concepts of Confucianism and Taoism appealed to the intelligentsia but not to the masses. The latter veered toward more pragmatic views; they believed that their forebears were alive and that their spiritual essences (or souls) existed on earth as shadows or demons—good or evil forces. Two types of spiritual essences (or souls) could become manifest: *shen*, or kindly yang souls, to be honored and praised by families; and *kuei*, or evil feminine souls, to be feared, avoided, and placated. (See page 163 below for psychological discussion of these parapsychological powers.) Around A.D. 300, the Buddhist notion of karma, or fate, was added to the belief in *shen* and *kuei*. Future existences were now thought to depend upon one's behavior in past lives. By the ninth century, Neo-Confucians had created an entire purgatorial organization along bureaucratic lines. Neatly organized rituals were programmed for the dead, including rewards for the good, and court trials, punishments, and tortures for the evil. That evil was identified with the feminine soul and good with the masculine soul furthered an already powerful negative identification with the nonrational sphere, representing the danger of what was impulsive and uncontrollable.[14]

Ethical speculative thought predominated throughout the centuries in China, with ancestral cults emphasized to such an extent that they took on a religious cast. Rituals of all types, designed to honor ancestors, burgeoned in the family clan system. Although the personal memory of the ancestor died, its outline remained encoded, we might say, like RNA, or the memory molecule, within its archetypal form (DNA structure) and thus lived on eternally.[15] Since the efficacy of the patrilineal structure of the clan rested on the power of the oldest male, and since many of those within the clan's compound were descended from a common ancestor, the family existed as a kind of religious corporation, each member being expected to act according to proper protocol, with no room for change.[16]

Such a patriarchal clan system, dating back to the Chou dynasty and reinforced by Confucian views which underscored the notion of male superiority, may be identified, psychologically speaking, with the conscious or rational sphere. Taoism, on the other hand, with its belief in the continuously fluid Tao—viewed as Nature or the Great Mother, feeding everything in the created and uncreated world with its inexhaustible supply of energy—is more in tune with the unconscious or irrational domain.[17] The polarities between the rational and nonrational worlds, varying in degree throughout Chinese history, may explain in part the deprivation and discrimination encountered by some of the women involved in the dramatic events depicted in *Family*.

Fulminating Archetypal Images

The Taoist animistic worldview is evident in Pa Chin's opening archetypal image of a storm:

> The wind was blowing hard; snowflakes, floating like cotton fluff from a ripped quilt, drifted down aimlessly. Layers of white were building up at the foot of the walls on both sides of the streets, providing broad borders for their dark muddy centres.
>
> Pedestrians and sedan-chair porters struggled against the wind and snow, but to no avail. They looked weary, and the snowfall was becoming heavier. Snow filled the sky, falling everywhere—on umbrellas, on the sedan-chairs, on the reed capes of the chair carriers, on the faces of the pedestrians.
>
> The wind buffeted the umbrellas in all directions; it blew one or two out of their owners' hands. Howling mournfully the wind joined with the sound of footsteps in the snow to form a strange, irritating music. This snowstorm will rule the world a long, long time; it seemed to warn the people on the streets, the bright warm sun of spring will never return again. (8)

Readers are immediately thrust into the very heart of a chaotic spatio-psychological complex. Just as Chinese landscape paintings place people in perspective with their environment, we see them in the above quotation as tiny observers of a vast universe, examples of humanity's helplessness and finitude. Because the Chinese live in close contact with nature, directed as it is by the Universal Spirit of Tao, they are receptive to its language; they are able to peer into its outer garments (clouds, lightning, storms, and wind) and experience its altering moods. A whole arcane realm is disclosed, subtly and sensorially, in the above physical description; colors, forms, and rhythms evoke feeling and thought.

The opening archetypal image not only sets the stage for the drama to come, but it also lays bare the emotions at stake. The locus is Cheng-tu. Although it isn't named, we know Pa Chin is alluding to his native city, one of the oldest and most beautiful in China, dating back to the "Spring and Autumn Annals" (A.D. 770). It is in an area that had been devastated by the Mongols under Kublai Khan, among other conquerors. The season is winter. Dark and heavy snows usher in white and gray tonalities that enshroud the atmosphere with a sense of bleakness and joylessness. That streets, walls, battlements, and gates are swept up in the powerful embrace of wind and snow suggests that yang forces rage out of control.

Pedestrians, normally so sedate, are hurled here and there with such ferocity that they are no longer responsible for their actions. The premonitory image of the storm—like a heaving volcano—is a projection of an inner emotional condition, and it particularizes the forces at stake. The collective world is in danger of destruction; and on an individual level, we may suggest that psychological instability is equally terrifying.

Wind, or *ch'i* (Cosmic Breath), an intermediary force between heaven and earth, is yang power. Such energy, viewed symbolically, suggests an enormous drive to sweep the area clean of any force that might endanger the reigning spiritual and psychological orientation. Let us mention in this regard the importance of the study of wind currents in China. Their patterns and energetic pulsations disclose empirical meanings for adepts. Why, then, we may ask, are these yang forces unleashing their negative powers? Why are they shoving humankind about so brutally? In keeping with the whims and fancies of an irrational patriarchal force, yang has become destroyer!

Archetypally speaking, the more extreme a patriarchate, the greater grows the dread of replacement by a matriarchate. To assure dominance, the male grows increasingly rigid in his thinking, thus maximizing his despotic ways. Imbalance is increased, catalyzing Nature's already volatile mood, as depicted in the storm image.

The whiteness of the snow, drifting by in massive clouds, masks deeper coruscating antitheses, revealed in such pragmatic metaphors as "a ripped quilt." The warm and comfortable image of the coverlet, and the homey atmosphere it conveys, are juxtaposed to the icy cold and death-dealing storm. The pedestrians and sedan-porters, representing the collective, are still intent upon maintaining order; they struggle against the wind, fight displacement, and refuse to be buffeted by yang forces. The personification of the wind, "howling mournfully," brings into focus an emotional frame of reference: pain and hurt, exacerbated by the "strange, irritating music" of footsteps, one of several auditory devices enhancing the mystery of the terrifying cosmic happening. The mood of distress and despair increases with the thought of Nature's cyclicality coming to an end: "The bright warm sun of spring will never return again" (8). Every rebellious force that might question yang supremacy is brutally eradicated. The yang order is repression.

Another archetypal image—the Dragon Dance, which takes place during the New Year's celebration—occurs midway through *Family*, marking a change in focus. Festive horns, drums, cymbals, and firecrackers, which the spectators carry around and use to the best of their ability, usher in a spectacular religious ritual:

> From head to tail, the dragon consisted of nine sections, made of paper pasted over bamboo frames and painted to resemble scales. Each section contained a lit candle, and was manipulated by a dancer who held it aloft by a bamboo handle. At the head of the dragon pranced a youth twirling a staff with a big ball of coloured

> paper streamers at one end. The dragon bounded after the ball, rolling on the ground, or wagging its tail or shaking its head as if in great satisfaction, leaping and cavorting like a real dragon, while the beat of cymbals and drums seemed to add to its awesomeness. (136)

For the Chinese, the dragon, like yin and yang, is both good and evil, male and female. According to Chuang-tzu, the dragon is a mysterious power that resolves nature's contraries. Unlike Westerners, whose goal is to kill this primordial force (cf. the myths surrounding Apollo, Perseus, Siegfried, St. George, St. Michael, St. Patrick), the Chinese view it as a cosmic power, emblematic of the rhythmic flow of life, and incorporating the highest spiritual values as well as their most inferior telluric counterparts. In that Celestial and King Dragons live in upper spheres, they are identified with fecundating forces such as thunder, lightning, and water; Guardian Dragons safeguard treasures; Flying Dragons represent hidden potential, or the nonactive turning into its opposite.[18] So powerful is the dragon archetype in China that its image is frequently embossed in gold thread on the Emperor's robe, his umbrella, and other objects identified with the power principle.

Because the dragon is androgynous, it is considered a complex of ambiguous forces which, when properly channeled, bring about a positive condition; when improperly directed, they destroy. How such a primordial power responds as it emerges from its hidden cavern deep in the earth, or from its tunnel in inaccessible mountain regions, or from its secret lair in the sea's unfathomable depths, depends upon its reaction to empirical conditions. The dragon may rise and unfold spasmodically, as in a storm, a cloud, or a whirlpool, its claws blazing in streaks of lightning, its scales taking root in pine trees, its voice bellowing with hurricane force, scattering people and things in its wake. It may also lull and calm, bringing with it the serenity of happier days, and of balanced ways. The dragon is mystery.[19]

The Dragon Dance described in *Family* is traumatic. As the animal begins its gyrations, swaying here and there in rhythmic beats, bystanders begin popping firecrackers and fire tubes close to it. The explosive noises anger it so much that its movements grow increasingly spasmodic and frenetic:

> A few sedan carriers who had been standing by, waiting with a powder-filled "fire tube," now ignited it and took turns spraying the flying sparks against the bare torsos of the dragon dancers. The maddened dragon rolled desperately on the ground, trembling

> from head to tail, trying to ward off the shower of hot sparks. People shouted, while the drums and cymbals crashed incessantly. The sedan-chair carriers laughed. The gentry on the grandstand laughed too, though in a much more refined way, of course. (137)

The relentless burning of the beast by fire tubes suggests the viciousness of the energetic forces at play. What is equally serious and damaging is the unfeeling nature of those perpetrating such an abrasive and painful act. We are no longer dealing with a symbolic religious ritual alone, but with nine real men being burned and others doing the burning. A sadomasochistic ceremony is taking place: The men being burned howl with pain, yet they resist. As for the young, progressively minded people who observe what they look upon as a ghastly ceremony, they leave in disgust. When, finally, the agony of scorching skin becomes unbearable, the men impersonating the dragon—sacrificial victims of sorts—run away in disarray. What had once been a single dragon has now been dismantled; its dismembered carcass may be viewed as the end of a projection.

The dragon, in this instance representing telluric power (a yin force, since prior to the dance it rested firmly on Mother Earth), has now been destroyed. What had once been a ceremony of religious dimension and majestic drama, leading to renewal, has become, for the younger members of the Kao compound (whose residents are protagonists in the novel), a travesty, a vacuous experience devoid of any spiritual message, and an excuse for a sadomasochistic round. No longer does it awaken an ancestral past and activate deeper layers of the psyche in a meaningful *rite d'entrée* and *rite de sortie*.[20]

In both archetypal images—the storm and the Dragon Dance—a sucking up, expulsion, and dispersion of energetic powers of cosmic proportion occur. Although combustion is awesome as a fulminating force, let us recall that destruction precedes construction: Death is the condition for renewal.

Fixated Archetypal Images

In contrast to the effulgent and coruscating archetypal images of the storm and Dragon Dance, we turn to a patriarchal compound, the residence of the Kao family, and a fixated condition. The architectural exactitude of the compound's layout—with its square or rectangular houses within mathematically demarcated framed spaces—may be viewed as a mirror image of a static approach to life. The stability and firmness of definition marking the Kao family's abodes are evident in the following description:

> A row of residential compounds, with large solid wood gates painted black, stood motionless in the icy gale. Pairs of eternally mute stone lions crouched outside their entrances—one on each side. Opened gates gave the appearance of the mouths of fantastic beasts. Within were dark caverns; what was inside of them, no one could see. (12)

Black, a noncolor or the sum of all colors, identified in China with yin power and associated with the Great Mother, represents obscure and abysmal forces. But just as the seed gestates in darkness, so blackness also stands for fertility. The blackness of the gates takes on archetypal dimension—a force to be feared by the patriarchate (since gates close and enclose). The feminine protects, but it also imprisons. Psychic energy (libido) contained within the "dark caverns," a clandestine sphere, hides a whole secret and self-contained world.

"Mute lions" are ready to pounce on anyone who dares intrude. Masters of the feline family, these fantastic beasts are guardians of the precincts, prepared to frighten away evil spirits or *kuei* (yin spiritual essences), which may take on different forms (animals, plants, insects, water, trees, ghosts) and cause melancholia, suicide, or other types of maleficent effects. If some wrong has been unwittingly perpetrated upon an ancestor (improper burial, neglect during mortal life, etc.), the vengeful *kuei* are ready to tear the wrongdoer to shreds, so as to rectify a misdeed. The most powerful antidote to these destructive forces is *shen* (yang spiritual power)—in this case, the lions.

The *kuei* may be looked upon as negative feminine principles or projections of the male anima; they are devouring mothers in a patriarchal society. As unconscious and unlived aspects of the psyche, the *kuei* spark fear in man. Repression is the way patriarchal consciousness deals with these threatening forces. Since the libido aroused in the male by the *kuei* (viewed by the male as a negative feminine force) is not brought to the light of consciousness, it festers and increases in intensity. Constellating outward, it is projected onto people, things, animals, or minerals—or it is perceived as *kuei*, that is, as parapsychological phenomena. With the eradication or temporary dislodgement of these projections, panic is momentarily eclipsed.

The *kuei* were born into the empirical world with the psychization of the feminine principle. Woman (in *Family* and, generally speaking, in China) is considered the breeder of inferior, nonrational, and dangerous characteristics. Whatever is associated with her is unacceptable and mephitic and must be devitalized. Yet, to suppress yin, according to Tao dicta, leads to cosmic imbalance—and to imbalance within the human personality. When a woman (or a man) is deprived of her (or his) basic rights through deprecation, subjugation, or cruelty, although control may be exercised for a time, an explosive situation is sooner or later built up—then unleashed.

By looking upon the feminine as a negative and threatening force, as is the case in *Family*, man divests himself of *eros*, that factor which encourages him to relate to woman and convey tenderness, love, and kindness. The seeming harmony in the Kao compound is deceptive: Stasis and a cold, unfeeling climate reign within the compound, as within the personalities of the inhabitants. Unrest, distress, and great pain prevail. Dictatorial rule over the emotions makes it inevitable that some of the protagonists will come to a violent end. For man not to take into account the feminine principle—the *anima*—is to belittle his own soul.[21]

The compound's black gates (embodying the Great Mother) stand guard, ready to swallow any outsider who enters the "sacred" precincts; and the patriarchal yang lions squat vigilant, ready to dismember anyone who commits an infraction. Irony is implicit in the motto inscribed in black ideographs on the red veneered plaques hanging vertically on either side of the compound's entrance: "Benevolent rulers, happy family; long life, good harvests" (13).

In keeping with the bipolarity of Taoist philosophy, there are also beautifully warm and flexible elements present in the Kao compound, such as a courtyard with pots of golden plum blossoms placed on either side of a flagstone path. The flowers and fruits of the plum trees are particularly meaningful in China: In *Family*, they are associated with young women, paradigms of malleability and softness; with winter, because of the snowy purity of their petals; and with longevity (blossoms appear on leafless and apparently lifeless branches until the plants reach a ripe old age).

"Coated with frosty white, the [plum] branches were like lovely jade," writes Pa Chin. That the flowers of this fruit are compared to jade, symbolizing the highest and purest effulgence of heaven, as well as the yang force, indicates a fusion of feminine (plum) and masculine (jade) principles. *The Book of Rites* (*Li Chi*), one of the most celebrated books in Confucian literature, states that "the superior Man competes in virtue with Jade."[22]

As we enter one of the houses in the compound, we see the members of a small family seated around a square table, each allotted his place in accordance with his status in the household, which is based on age, sex, and relationship to the patriarchal figure. After the completion of the dinner, the family files out, and the watchman sounds his gong. Darkness clothes the precinct:

> The night died, and with it the glow of the electric lights died too. Darkness ruled the big compound. The dismal cry the electric lamps

> uttered as they expired still quivered in the air. Although the sound was low, it penetrated everywhere; even the corners of the rooms seemed to echo with soft weeping. The time for happiness had passed. Now was the hour of tragic tears. (25)

The electric lamps, representing the spirit of clarity, have "died"; crushing darkness prevails, and a poignant premonitory image announces searing hurt, attested to by the personification of the lamps (their "dismal cry" as they "expired"). Not one corner of the room is spared blackness; nor does the land surrounding the compound fail to reap its harvest of tears. Does Pa Chin's framed visualization, with its photographic realism, foretell the end of an epoch?

A negative patriarchal figure rules the Kao compound, acting in complete disregard of the ethically oriented Confucian dicta. "First he sets the good example, then he invites others to follow it," Confucius wrote.[23] Unlike the wise and positive archetypal old man which China's great sage had in mind, the personage Pa Chin introduces us to is a stern, unfeeling, demanding, inaccessible, remote grandfather, Yeh-yeh. Depicted as white-haired, with a long and thin body, reclining most of the time on a chair or couch, and dozing frequently, he spells diminishing strength. Seldom does he exchange more than a few words with anyone: Only twice a day, morning and evening, when his family calls on him to pay their formal respects, does he utter a few words. Outside of these occasions, there is little or no contact between him and the other members of the group, and certainly not with the younger generation, which feels awkward and overawed in his presence. His two young grandsons, Chueh-hui and Chueh-min, in particular, resent what they look upon as his pious air and his outdated, crusty Confucian morality.

The patriarchal grandfather, Yeh-yeh, the antithesis of the Confucian ideal, suffocates everyone in the compound and destroys all attempts at spiritual and psychological renewal. He is shadow, not light; negative, not positive; limited, not universal. Nor, according to the younger members of the clan, does he comport himself with honor, integrity, or virtue—character traits Confucius emphasized in his *Analects*. On the contrary, Yeh-yeh rules through coercion, anger, and punishment. He commands not respect, but fear.

Yeh-yeh's sexual proclivities are equally offensive to his grandsons. That he wrote poems to singsong girls as a dashing youth is perfectly understandable to them. What is not, is that he has acquired a pious air and become the Confucian—or pseudo-Confucian—moralist, as he claims to be, and still invites female impersonators to his home. How can such a man take pride in his purity and integrity? (Let us recall, however, that at this time, to patronize the performers of the Peking Opera and other theatrical groups was considered a sign of refinement; it was also acceptable to the Confucian Moral Society, of which Yeh-yeh was a member.) That Yeh-yeh took a concubine, Mrs. Chen, after his wife's death was dimly viewed by the younger generation. The head of a family should be a guide—courteous and understanding—and generate "affection between father and son, and harmony among brothers."[24] Yeh-yeh's adherence to only the outer shell or empty effigy of Confucian doctrine invites perversion and decadence; and his constant references to the book *On Filial Piety and the Shunning of Lewdness* are the ultimate in hypocrisy.

Chueh-hui and Chueh-min refuse to accept Chinese customs with regard to women. They reject concubinage, a system existing in China for centuries whereby young, nubile girls were sold to the highest bidder; the frequent drowning of baby girls so as to alleviate financial burdens on their families; and the forced renunciation of all claim to her father's heritage by a married daughter. Nor are sexual customs, or Taoist philosophical and physiological views of sex, any more welcome to the young in *Family*. According to Taoist dicta, men are endowed with limited semen, whereas women have unlimited vital reserves. Because ejaculation leads to a depletion of yang forces, the male maintains his potency by absorbing yin essence, which is present in the vaginal secretions during a woman's orgasm. His goal is to arouse his sexual partner to a state of ecstasy by practicing *coitus reservatus*, thereby increasing his virility. If women were to discover the extent of their own power, they might suppress their orgasms, while stimulating men to states of rapture. Not only would they earn greater wisdom and spiritual energy for themselves, but they would be able to control men.[25] It is therefore considered important for men to have numerous concubines and to ejaculate infrequently, thus eliminating any possibility of impotence in old age.[26]

If the woman is the reservoir of infinite energy, as Taoists believe her to be, and can gain dominance over the man if this secret is revealed to her, it stands to reason that she is considered—at least unconsciously—a threatening power. In the *Tao Te Ching*, Lao-tzu wrote of the germinating seed and of life eternal as woman; it is understandable why man sees himself as dependent upon her for his very life principle:

> The Valley Spirit never dies.
> It is named the mysterious Female.
> And the Doorway of the Mysterious Female
> Is the base from which Heaven and Earth Sprang.
> It is there within us all the while;
> Draw upon it as you will, it never runs dry.[27]

Love is rarely, if ever, called into question between husband and wife in *Family*. Since the anima is that autonomous force within the psyche that fascinates, drives, lures, and encourages the male to be adventurous, to act and to create, and that "sets the personality in motion, produces change, and ultimately transformation," it is viewed, psychologically, as a constant threat to a smoothly running life course. To alter what *is* may disrupt what *was*.

But even the best-ordered life must be able to adapt to change, lest it become rigid or decadent. Yeh-yeh has not been able to change. Consequently, the younger generation in the Kao compound does not look up to him as the archetype of the wise old man—an archetype that has been considered since time immemorial in China as the vital and civilizing agent. Unable to adapt to new situations, resisting renewal, and succumbing to inertia, the wise old man figure has lost its value. Yeh-yeh's conscious outlook no longer corresponds to an inner process. Truths, once significant and substantive, are not applicable; they have worn thin. If the wise old man archetype were operative, opposites would work together in a fluid and nutritive interchange. Representative of an archaic and one-sided collective view, Yeh-yeh's negative anima has destroyed any possibility of bringing the victimized feminine image to consciousness. Like a withered branch, Yeh-yeh will eventually have to drop off the tree and return to the Great Mother.

Feminine Figures

The feminine figures in *Family* are fascinating as products of an incredibly underprivileged group. Confucian ethics, as we know, gave women a lower place than men: "Women and people of low birth are very hard to deal with. If you are friendly with them, they get out of hand, and if you keep your distance, they resent it."[28] A wife was duty-bound to obey her husband and his parents, to tend to the house, and to bear healthy male children. Separation of sexes in compounds was advocated in order to maintain purity in family life: "In the dwelling house, outside and inside are clearly divided; the man lives in the outer, the woman in the inner apartments." Nor should husband and wife use the same clothes rack, bathe together, share the same sleeping mat, or borrow each other's articles of dress. "When a woman goes out she shall veil her face.... Walking in the street the men shall keep to the right, the women to the left."[29] Only once a year, at New Year, is she free to go out into the world.

Not only did Confucius advocate stringent rules for women, but they themselves, judging from statements made by Lady Pan Chao (first century A.D.) in her book *Women's Precepts*, were intent upon following them:

> The Tao of husband and wife represents the harmonious blending of Yin and Yang, it establishes man's communion with the spirits, it reaffirms the vast significance of Heaven and Earth, and the great order of human relationships. . . . Yin and Yang are fundamentally different, hence man and woman differ in behaviour. Strength is the virtue of Yang, yielding constitutes the use of Yin. Man is honoured for his power, woman is praised for her weakness. . . . To be reverent and obedient, that is the golden rule of wifehood.[30]

The feminine characters to be analyzed in *Family* each depict a different approach to Confucian and Taoist ethics. Mei and Jui-chueh exist in a *participation mystique* with their environment. Living according to tradition, they have no sense of being individuals—no ego consciousness. Ming-feng, the bondmaid, is also submissive. She does have a clear understanding of her function and place in society, but her true feelings run counter to them. Chin represents the new way: not extremist in attitude, but willing to understand both polarities and integrate these into a new ideal—that of woman conscious of her own identity.

Mei: Anorexia Nervosa; Jui-chueh: Deadly Passivity

Mei, meaning "plum blossom," is in love with Chueh-hsin, and he with her. Yeh-yeh, however, has arranged that he marry Jui-chueh. Shortly thereafter, Mei is married off and sent to live with her husband's parents. Although they treat her ignominiously, she adheres to the rules set down by Lady Pan Chao:

> How must a wife gain the affection of her parents-in-law? There is no other way than complete obedience. If her mother-in-law says "It is not" while it is so, the wife must still obey her. . . . And in order to obtain the affection of her parents-in-law, she must first secure that of her brothers- and sisters-in-law.[31]

Mei's husband's premature demise, a year after her marriage, increases her in-laws' cruelty toward her to such an extent that she returns home to her widowed mother. Neither a loving nor a kind woman, the mother spends all her time playing mah-jong with the other women of the compound. No nurturing and cherishing feeling has ever existed between mother and daughter. Mei's father died when she was a little girl; as for her younger brother, he is too busy preparing for his exams to pay any attention to her.

Mei's isolation is deep; her melancholia adds to the pressures on a barely existent ego. She has no concept of herself as an individual; nor is she conscious of any polarities either within or outside her. Having acquiesced at all times to her husband's desires and his family's dictates, Mei has never experienced any conflict, living always in a *participation mystique*—an identification with the negative image of the feminine principle imposed upon women in the patriarchal society. She never thinks of agitating for any kind of independence, psychological or intellectual. She neither sees into the world nor makes any effort to arouse new ways of seeing or thinking. Thus her feelings are never mirrored, deflected, or reflected; they simply center on her unhappiness. Only if her present outlook is shattered will there be any important progress out of her depressed state. Mei's single interest is reading poetry. It makes her weep, as she thinks back to her one great love, Chueh-hsin, now married to Jui-chueh:

> I see fading flowers and I weep. The waning moon hurts my heart. Everything recalls unhappy memories. . . . There's a tree outside my window that I planted when I went away to be married. It was budding then but by the time I returned, its branches were bare. I often think that tree symbolizes me. (122)

Flowers, particularly the plum blossom identified with Mei's name, are usually joyful and exquisite images, but they are envisaged by Mei as "fading," colorless, and lusterless, replicating her inner despair. Usually symbolizing love and harmony when in bloom, for her they spell depletion—a wasting away of the breath or very spirit of life (*ch'i*). The moon, a body that owes its luminosity to reflected sunlight, is "waning" in her mind's eye; cold and unfeeling, its rays lacerate her heart, which is deprived of love and tenderness.

Trees, representing a world axis and a link between both heavenly and terrestrial spheres and yang and yin forces, no longer fill her with serenity or feelings of well-being. Although she enjoys a poetic appreciation of these natural forces (which the Chinese believe are inhabited by the souls of deities), they bring her pain. Their beauty, which once brought her happiness, now serves to reinforce the ugliness of her existence; their florescence and bouquet, her despair. The tree outside her window, once the bearer of life and joy, is now defoliated, excluding, symbolically, the possibility of any earthly joy or further psychological development.

Unrelated to empirical reality, unconscious of any duality within her own psyche, be it on a feeling or thinking level, Mei does not engage in life. Rather, she grows increasingly detached from the world and from the young people in her compound. That Mei has not developed any kind of relationship with her mother except on the most perfunctory level has not enhanced her sense of being a woman; that she has failed to create some kind of rapport with her in-laws further endangers her feelings about herself and her place in society. Her empty inner world is filled with compensatory fantasies, which encourage her to dwell more and more on that entirely unlived part of her life, exiling herself increasingly from the real world. Mei is a spiritually starved animal.

Chin, her cousin, advises her that to dwell on the past is to cut herself off from the present and from life, and to risk drying up and stunting her personality. But Mei is incapable of changing her passivity and introversion: "You know my disposition. I can never forget the past. It seems engraved upon my heart" (122). Her melancholia leads to increased depression and inertia: She has lost all appetite for life and literally eats virtually nothing, growing weaker and thinner from lack of nourishment. When she begins coughing blood, she hides her illness from her mother because she does not want any medicines that might prolong the agony which is her existence. "Every day she lives is another day of misery—she'd be better off dead," Chin states (267).

Emaciation of the body leads to the eradication of any viable relationship with the feminine contour. Unlike the Western anorexic, Mei does not look at her thin torso with pleasure, admiring it for its flatness, nor does she reflect upon or engage in any kind of real relationship with it. She sees it as eroding matter which is paving the way for her deliverance from continuous grief. While other young girls leave the adolescent state to assume the responsibilities of wifehood and motherhood, Mei has been essentially deprived of both. The possibility of her remarrying in the patriarchal system described in *Family* is virtually nil. She has no destiny, no direction, no future.[32]

Mei is psychologically ill. Her inherent morbidity, aggravated by the personal hardships she has undergone, indicates a spiritual as well as physical breakdown. She is incarcerated in a vision of herself that permits no change of condition: an unalterable life which will never vary from the sameness she knows. By depriving herself of food (anorexia nervosa), Mei encourages an already strong death wish, which she substantiates by her philosophical belief in karma: a predetermination of death by deprivation.[33]

Jui-chueh fares little better. Unlike Mei, however, she lives out her function as wife and mother. Early in her marriage to Chueh-hsin, she believes he shows her signs of affection. In time, she learns that it is Mei he loves, and not her. This discovery arouses love in her, rather than jealousy. She reasons that since Mei has been the object of her husband's passion, she must treat her as graciously and as kindly as possible. So she does. After Mei's death, Jui-chueh mourns her.

Jui-chueh's situation might have pursued its normal course had she not been expecting a second child shortly after Yeh-yeh's death. The Chinese of that time, who believed in the "curse of the bloodglow," felt that the large quantities of blood spilled during the birth process would attack corpses and cause them in turn to eject so much of this vital fluid that they would be unable to attain peace after death.

Jui-chueh, therefore, is not given permission to give birth in the Kao compound as long as Yeh-yeh's corpse remains in the precinct. Since the extremely intricate burial ceremonies take a long time to perform, Jui-chueh has to be sent away. Her husband, Chueh-hsin, does not have the courage to fight family tradition. Submissive always, he believes that to reject customary ways is a sign of filial disobedience. Dutiful and self-sacrificing, Jui-chueh never once complains when sent outside the city, across the bridge, to a damp and gloomy house, where she is to remain until her child is born. Chueh-hsin, who happens to be visiting at the time she is to deliver, hears "terrible screams. Cries hardly human . . . " (307). The boy is born; the mother dies.

To have exiled Jui-chueh from the family was to have deprived her of her sole sustaining force; her loneliness was too profound a divestiture for her to bear. Uprooted and displaced, she felt like a criminal—unworthy of being alive.

Both Mei and Jui-chueh were introverted, passive, and subservient types. Their egos were virtually nonexistent. Neither was aware of her situation or her identity; neither was capable of creating a life-style for herself. Subservient to the collective needs of a patriarchal society, Mei took out her repressed rage on herself by willing her death—as an anorexic. Jui-chueh, exiled from the only world capable of comforting her—husband and son—experienced an eclipse of consciousness and let herself die. These emotionally starved women viewed death as the only alternative to an unbearable existence.

Ming-feng: Suicide

Ming-feng, the sixteen-year-old bondmaid, has spent seven years in the Kao compound. Healthy and smiling, she goes about her work free of timidity and hesitation, although her face turns red when she is teased by the young masters of the house—Chueh-hui, in particular. It is with him that she falls in love. Nevertheless, she has no illusions as to her future. Accustomed to her employer's harsh words, as well as to those of Shu-hua, Chueh-hui's sister, who has learned the art of deprecating "inferiors" with great ease, she never answers back; nor does she grow angry or flustered: "Like the sea, she accepted everything, swallowed everything, without a sound" (20).

That Ming-feng should be identified with water images at the outset of the novel is significant. Water and wetness imply the transitory, continuous movement in life, as well as its indecisiveness and informality. Ming-feng's position in the Kao household is impermanent, like quicksand. Her employers have the right to send her back home, or marry her off to anyone they wish, or sell her as a concubine.

Only at night does Ming-feng reveal the other side of her nature. When all are asleep in the small cubicle of a room which she shares with other household servants, she allows her feelings to emerge undisturbed. She removes the mask—that pleasant smile frozen onto her flesh—she wears by day, unlocks "her mind," and "spreads out its secrets for her heart to see" (26).

That Ming-feng is conscious of wearing a mask (persona) indicates her ability to distinguish the moral and physical polarities which mark her life. She knows when and where to assume a public face so as to conform to the outer world and its expectations of her. Her persona is a mediating force between her and society; but it also acts as a shield, protecting her from the harsh realities of life.

Ming-feng has recourse to metaphors that reveal a whole feeling dimension: She "unlocks her mind," treating it as if it were a box containing repressed emotions. So unsure is she of how this aspect of her personality will react to given situations that she fears it might emerge impulsively, thereby toppling the image she seeks to maintain: that of the stable, subservient, yet joyful bondmaid. Only at night, when she is alone, is her heart allowed to hold office, and secrets permitted to be revealed. No longer dominated by her will, feelings and instincts open up like so many budding flowers. For the Chinese, the heart, along with the liver, stomach, kidneys, and lungs, represents the world of emotion and the irrational. A pragmatist, Ming-feng seeks to keep her vulnerable area closeted, lest her future be in jeopardy.

During moments of stress, Ming-feng, like Mei, draws on the Buddhist doctrine of karma, not to substantiate her weakness as Mei had done, but to steady her highly charged emotional world and to bring her back, paradoxically, to reality. For Ming-feng, "all that happened in the world was decreed by an omnipotent being." As long as her rational function holds sway, her persona and pragmatic approach to life dominate and she feels safe. When, however, she falls in love with Chueh-hui and he displays similar feelings for her, difficulties arise. Her heart has been awakened. The metaphor she used to describe the blossoming of her feeling world in her darkened room at night has not only taken on consistency, it has overwhelmed her; and she is unprepared to cope with such *foreign* emotions. Love awakens fascinating, titillating, and exciting feelings in her. She begins to fantasize: Perhaps her dreary and dull existence, so filled with desolation and distress, will now change? Her dream world, be it during waking or sleeping hours, increases in importance, conjuring up a hero—a counterforce to take her out of her dreary life of drudgery. Subliminal spheres set off a new dynamic not controlled by her will, which allows her emotions virtually free range, but which by the same token opens her up still further to the vagaries and fluctuations of optimism and pessimism.

The more she withdraws to her room, to its darkness and to her subliminal world, the more difficult it becomes for her to cope with reality. On one occasion, when she is listening to the howling wind outside her window, a young man appears in her mind's eye, and he smiles. Her heart "bursts into flower. Warmed again by a thread of hope, she prayed he would stretch forth his hand." Then, suddenly, "the face gradually floated away into the sky, higher and higher until it vanished" (29).

Pa Chin frequently associates Ming-feng with flowers—not with defoliated branches, as Mei, but with gorgeously healthy ones, revealing an inner capacity for joy. One afternoon, when her employer sends her out to pick some pink plum branches from the trees in the compound, Chueh-hui appears on the scene. Offering to break a branch heavily laden with blossoms, he shakes the tree. Ming-feng, who is standing under it, is inundated with a shower of perfumed petals.

The Chinese writer in general—a symbolist at heart—frequently chooses a natural force, like a flower, to describe a woman and her feelings, rather than drawing a person representationally. Skilled horticulturists, the Chinese believe that since Nature is life, any and all of its manifestations are paradigms of being; they say more about the human personality than can be stated verbally. The picture of Ming-feng burying her face in a shower of blossoms discloses a joy beyond expression—a lust for life. This very same picture also tells us that the rational principle is no longer strong and steady as once it had been, that Ming-feng's emotions have been touched and so have made her vulnerable. Although she warns Chueh-hui that they must not be seen together, when he asks her to walk with him along a small path to the plum groves, she acquiesces. Her words speak reason; her body follows her heart.

Together Ming-feng and Chueh-hui then make their way to the flower terraces, through a dark and straight tunnel leading to a small stone table at the edge of a lake. There they sit opposite one another and talk. When Chueh-hui informs her that he is going to tell her employer that he wants to marry her, Ming-feng puts her hand over his mouth. No, she cries, he is not fated to be the husband of a bondmaid. Then she tells him one of her dreams:

> Once I dreamed I was running through the mountains, chased by a pack of wild animals. Just as they almost caught me, someone rushed down the slope and drove them away. And who do you think it was? You, I've always thought of you as my saviour! (78)

Clearly, this dream and others depicted in *Family* state the feelings of panic and dread that haunt her subliminal world. Each time fantasy life takes over, empirical reality grows increasingly harsh, and Ming-feng feels as if her heart has been cut by a whip. Sensations of laceration overcome her, physically and emotionally. Melancholy thoughts are replicated metaphorically by the "lamp flame that was dimming." Illumination is withdrawn as her rationally oriented ego fails her at a crucial juncture in her life.

When Ming-feng's employer informs her that the patriarch of the compound has decided she is to be sent away to become an old man's concubine, she loses control. She begs and beseeches. To remain a bondmaid in the Kao compound is her only wish. But the patriarch must be obeyed; no alternative is possible. To become a concubine, for Ming-feng, a highly moral person, is to despoil her body. Such a life is unacceptable to her.

The days slip by, and no rescuer appears on the scene to save Ming-feng. Chueh-hui, who is oblivious to her fate, does nothing. Silence marks the victim's manner, as it did that of most Chinese women of the period. Her body must remain chaste and pure, Ming-feng believes—at all costs. The time has come for her to take matters into her own hands. With calm and determination, she walks toward the lake where she had spent such happy moments with Chueh-hui and peers into its calmness: "The crystal depths of the lake would give her refuge. She would die unsullied" (215). In this idyllic scene, Ming-feng realizes once again that a wall, a moat, a barrier of insurmountable dimensions, exists between her and her beloved. She is determined not to let Chueh-hui sacrifice himself for her; pronouncing his name with tenderness and sorrow, she plunges into the lake:

> The placid waters stirred violently, and a loud noise broke the stillness. Two or three tragic cries, although they were very low, echoed lingeringly in the night. After a few minutes of wild thrashing, the surface of the lake again became calm. Only the mournful cries still permeated the air, as if the entire garden were weeping softly. (217)

That Ming-feng takes her own life is to be expected in view of the premonitory introductory image that compared her to a sea, accepting and swallowing everything around her. The formless element—that virtual force which sees to the maintenance of purity and regeneration—would welcome her in its embrace.

As Chueh-hui's anima figure, Ming-feng stood for his *feeling* domain—that loving and warm side of his nature which was now to be eclipsed so as to allow his strongly aggressive masculine side to develop. As part of the new order, he would have to fight for his principles and learn to harden himself in the face of suffering. Although he felt he had neglected Ming-feng and reproached himself for her suicide, her act had motivated him to strike even harder at eradicating a social system that swallowed up its victims by the mouthful.

Unlike Mei and Jui-chueh, passive and introverted beings dominated by a sense of despair, the charming and charmed Ming-feng looked outward into life and pleasured in its excitement. Rather than attempting to strike at the social structure (which she believed would have little or no effect), she turned her anger upon herself, destroying that very power which she would no longer allow to suffer: her own being.

Chin: Thinking/Feeling

"A hamlet of ten homes will surely contain someone as loyal and reliable as I, but none to equal my love of learning," Confucius stated.[34] This statement serves to describe the young and beautiful Chin, who also lives in the Kao complex. Psychologically, she represents the integrated girl who feels, wants, understands, and also reasons. Endowed with a sense of proportion and responsibility, she has the gift of maintaining and deepening relationships—with her widowed mother and with her cousin Chueh-min, with whom she is in love—and of evolving intellectually despite the obstacles set in her path.

A student in the provincial Normal School for Girls, Chin is deeply interested in things of the mind, and most particularly in the liberation of women from their bondage. Clear-thinking and determined to create a life for herself, she rejects regressive ways, but not her feelings. Chin is respectful of her mother's desires and needs, though she knows she is far from being a bright woman. In her early forties, Mrs. Chang, like many women in the Kao compound, spends her time playing mah-jong; her days follow a dull routine. Unlike Mei's mother, Mrs. Chang loves her daughter and, in her own limited ways, relates to her.

Having been nurtured by her mother's love, Chin has been able to adapt to the workaday world and deal with its harshness as well as its beauty.

She also has a sense of herself: her worth, needs, and desires. Possessed of a strong ego, "the instrument of realization of all the different psychological, inborn dispositions of the human being," Chin looks out upon the world clearly, evaluating, whenever possible, personal and collective situations.[35]

Chin reads a great deal, but she supplements intellectual knowledge by listening to the conversations of her cousins Chueh-hui and Chueh-min and the other future political agitators in the compound. She absorbs their viewpoints and borrows their magazines: *New Youth*, published in Peking (1918–19), a very influential magazine concerned with political problems; the *Weekly Review*, the organ of the Kuomintang (1919–20); and *New Tide*, brought out by the students of Peking University (1919–22), one of the most powerful student magazines of the time. Chin uses every opportunity to enrich herself intellectually: For example, when her cousins discuss the policy of nonresistance as opposed to overt rebellion, she questions them about alternatives. Their conversations stimulate her. Unafraid to denigrate the feudal ideas of moralists who oppose women's education, she conveys her annoyance at having to study antiquated texts (seventeenth-century classical prose in Lin Hsiu-chung's *Selected Ancient Chinese Essays*), while her cousins read modern works written in the colloquial language.

Not only has her mother's love given her a sense of her own worth, but it has also developed her *eros*—her capacity for friendship with Chueh-min and his brother, as well as with other young men of the compound—counteracting, thereby, the negative feminine image which dominates the family. Chin's course is pragmatic, realistic and not idealistic. Her first priority is her examination. That she asks Chueh-min to help her prepare for it, however, is not strictly for rational reasons. Her heart as well dictates in this regard. She will try to convince her mother to let her take the exam in order to be eligible for transfer to a coeducational school. Her mother will side with her, she thinks. Hasn't she sent her to the provincial Normal School for Girls, thereby fighting against the ruling authority of the compound and her aunts as well, who are decidedly opposed to women's education? Haven't they done everything in their power to prevent her mother from letting Chin go out on the street alone? What will people say? they ask. But Mrs. Chang has always stood fast. She has also refused to have her daughter's feet bound. This, too, is a giant step toward modernism and enlightenment.

Chin realizes that she will have to sacrifice a great deal to continue her education. Sacrifice implies a separation from the rest of the world—a renunciation of old ways. Chin will have to give up the comfort and security of the compound. Such a sacrifice does not seem too harsh a price to pay for independence. The thought of living her own life arouses such spiritual and creative energy in Chin as to prod her on to grasp and reach out to life, though she knows that "the moment she stretched out her hand, people would hinder her" in every way possible (30). The metaphor used here is particularly apt: The *hand* conveys the notion of activity. As an aggressive force, it goes out into the world to snatch whatever can be of use to it. It is an instrument that paves the way for a transfer of energy and power.

During the period of nonaction prior to Chin's asking her mother for permission to continue her education, her moods alternate from gloom at the thought of her mother's refusal to happiness at the prospect of winning her fight. Yet, during this entire period of tension, she performs all of her obligations, to her mother in particular, with dispatch and feeling. When her mother returns home, for example, Chin accompanies her to her room, as is the custom, watches the maid change her mother's clothes, hangs them up herself in the closet, then sits and talks to her. All the while, of course, she attempts to enlighten her mother. She is powerfully motivated, since she does not want to follow in her mother's footsteps any more than she does in those of her grandmother, a woman who spends her days reading Buddhist scriptures. "A life with nothing to do is boring if it lasts too long," she says (31).

One afternoon, when taking some tea to her mother, Chin suddenly feels awkward and agitated. Unconsciously, she knows she must confront her mother to obtain permission to take the entrance exam that will admit her to a coeducational language school. As she talks, her voice trembles, her fingers play with the edge of her jacket, and her eyes are cast down. She informs her mother that three girls have already been admitted to universities in Peking, Nanking, and Shanghai, and then broaches the crucial point of her future studies. Mrs. Chang vetoes the entire plan: "When I was a girl, I never dreamed there'd be such things!" (32). Her mother's words strike Chin "like a gourd ladleful of cold water" (32). Chilled and dazed, she remains silent. That the word "gourd" is used in this metaphor indicates the enormous impact her mother's statement has upon her. Gourds were used in China for medicines, but most particularly by boat people to assist them in floating in water. Strength and durability are identified with the gourd, which not only prevents one from drowning but also possesses healing nutrients. The image discloses Chin's inner strength and her determination to struggle and fight rather than simply yield to defeat.

"Ma, times have changed," she answers; "girls are human beings the same as boys" (32). Mrs. Chang refuses to argue the merits of the case because she knows she cannot outtalk her daughter. "Let me go, Ma. You usually trust me. You've never refused me anything" (32). Although Mrs.

Chang wants to please her daughter, she feels that she no longer has the fortitude she once had to face her relatives.

Chin is on the verge of tears, yet she does not blame her mother for her unwillingness to send her to school. On the contrary, she understands her mother's predicament and is grateful to her for her continual affection. In this regard, Chin may be said to follow the traditional ways outlined by Mencius (390–305 B.C.), whose authority was second to Confucius: "Duty to parents is the greatest. . . . Among our many duties, the duty serving the parents is fundamental."[36]

What makes Chin's situation so difficult is her need to fulfill Confucian ethics and also to reach her own goal. She would violate neither principle. To reject China's ancestral cults would be tantamount to annihilating her own archetypal foundations, thus causing her great trauma.

Back in the privacy of her room, Chin picks up the *New Youth* she has borrowed from Chueh-hui and happens upon a quotation from Ibsen's *A Doll's House* which is, she thinks, particularly apropos to her situation:

> I believe that before anything else I am a human being just as much as you are—or at least that I should try to become one. . . . I can't be satisfied with what most people say. I must think things out for myself and try to get clear about them. (34)

The statement inspires her to write a letter to her friend Chien-ju, who also wants to take the exam: "I hope you're willing to take the plunge. We have to fight, no matter what the cost, to open a road for sisters who come after us" (33).

Chien-ju, a plump eighteen-year-old girl, does not have Chin's problems. Her mother, who had died young, had studied abroad; her father, who had attended university in Japan and had managed a revolutionary newspaper that had advocated the overthrow of the Manchus, now holds a post in the Bureau of Foreign Affairs of Szechuan Provincial Government. He has always encouraged his daughter to educate herself, as has the nursemaid who has cared for her since her mother's death. Deeply loved by both her nursemaid and her father, who want to see her fulfilled, Chien-ju has developed a strong ego and a clear goal in life. Unlike Chin, however, she has never known the meaning of struggle or of bondage.

Chien-ju, along with some of her friends, has taken a most drastic but "courageous" step: She has cut her hair—a sign of freedom and modernism and one more blow against discrimination against women. (Unmarried girls of this period usually wore their hair hanging down in long plaits; married women twisted it up toward the back of the head, ornamenting it with flowers, jewels, and bodkins.)

If Chin were to follow suit, she reasons, she might incur her mother's displeasure, which she does not want to do, both for emotional and pragmatic reasons (it might defeat her more important goal of furthering her education). Thinking and feeling are Chin's arbiters. She does not cut her hair, but she does take up the cudgel another way and writes an article for the *Weekly* concerning the positive reasons for cutting women's hair. Her pioneering spirit and "manly" courage are much admired by her friends, who feel strongly on this issue. Nevertheless, she feels ashamed for not cutting her hair. Will others interpret this lack of decisiveness as weakness on her part? Cowardice? Tears run down her cheeks at the thought. Clearly, Chin's battle revolves around her feelings for her mother and her own need for independence—a battle which she depicts in terms of light and darkness, yin and yang, each a duality, each with its positive and negative side: "I love my future, but I love my mother too. I love light, but for the sake of my mother, I would remain in darkness to keep her company" (197). The contrasts between light and dark, and subject and object, in the above quotation not only disclose her sensitivity and her understanding of her own feelings and those of her mother, but indicate her consciousness of the situation as a whole.

In the *I Ching* (*The Book of Changes*), one of the most significant works of the Confucian literati, polarities are not viewed as fixed, but rather as alternating forces. One passes into the other and transforms what seems incompatible into what is viewed as compatible. That Chin associates her emotional situation with the philosophical concept of polarities suggests a desire and an ability on her part to search for a proper attitude that will include both extremes and enable her to apply her findings empirically.[37]

Each time Chien-ju tries to convince Chin to cut her hair, she argues that her mother would be hurt, and that she does not want to be the cause of her mother's suffering. When Chien-ju suggests that she should not sacrifice a cause—the well-being of the multitude and her own future—for a single person, Chin understands her argument. On the other hand, Chin responds with an equally important point: "Your reason can conquer your feeling, but my reason is often conquered by feeling" (197).

Unable to counter her mother's wishes, she is not capable of seeing herself as the passive and yielding girl whose destiny it is to marry an "illiterate vulgar businessman or a good-for-nothing." Such wanton disposal of her body in marriage to a man she does not love is tantamount to prostitution. When Mrs. Chang informs her daughter that a match with a rich, handsome, but uneducated young man has been put to her, Chin's face grows pale and her eyes fill with tears; though her mother quickly adds that she has turned the offer down, the dread of such a possibility evokes the following image:

> Before her eyes there suddenly appeared a lengthy highway stretching to infinity, upon which were lain spreading corpses of young women. It became clear to her that this road was built thousands of years ago; the earth on the road was saturated with the blood and tears of those women. They were all tied and handcuffed and driven to this road, and made to kneel there, to soak the earth with their blood and tears, to satiate the sex desire of wild animals with their bodies. (201)

Chin has made up her mind. She refuses to take the well-trod road: "Like a man . . . I will take a new road" (203). In this regard, she is reminiscent of Kuan-yin, the most popular deity in China, goddess of mercy and compassion. Once a man—the Bodhisattva (Avalokitesvara), one of Buddha Amitabha's two assistants—he was transformed by the masses into a loving and kindly mother figure. Chin also has an androgynous psyche: She is masculine in her determination and feminine in her warmth of feeling. Like Kuan-yin, Chin has integrated her masculine and feminine sides. A strong ego engages her in life's struggles, but her deeply sensitive nature alerts her to the feeling world. Neither repressed nor depressed, she learns to work in harmony with both polarities of her instinctual domain, dealing with the objective facts of the workaday world with compassion and love.

Unlike Ming-feng's fatalism, or Mei's negativism, or Jui-chueh's passivity, Chin's psyche helps her maintain meaningful relationships while always retaining her own identity. Never unyielding or basking in extremes, Chin considers others and herself—not one without the other—before making decisions. She bides her time, and with Yeh-yeh's demise, the entire Kao compound is gradually released from the grip of the stultifying patriarchal forces that had been plaguing it. Sufficiently evolved, Chin is prepared to forge her own way in life.

During the course of the centuries, sophists and legalists, with their inflexible attitudes toward life, had not only defeated Confucius's enormous contributions to Chinese and world culture but had turned them into destructive forces. As for Taoism's approach toward adaptability and change within yin and yang, opposites struggling perpetually to create cosmic balance and harmony, it underwent a similar fate. Ossification of what had once been creative and fertile doctrines had taken place, with empty rituals codifying the prevailing vacuous worldview. "We must liberate ourselves from morality in order to be able to live morally," Nietzsche wrote. To codify morality is to fixate it and transform it into an absolute. If morality is looked upon as an end unto itself, it may become an evil.[38] Nietzsche's statement was paradigmatic: China had become a land of repression, degradation, and tyranny.

Decadence, in the form of an excessively patriarchal yang principle, prevailed in *Family*. With the exception of the young people in the Kao compound, notably Chin and her two cousins Chueh-min and Chueh-hui, the inhabitants lived according to worn-out structures and credos. Mei and Jui-chueh were victims of the old way; their weakly structured egos were unable to see beyond their own petty worlds. Ming-feng, although enjoying a capacity for joy, was imprisoned in the structure, and rather than use her strength to break loose, she destroyed herself. Chin was proud of her femininity, her intellect, and her individuality. *Logos* functioned in her psyche, as did *eros*. Taking the middle course, she did not reject past, present, or future without first evaluating her situation, consulting for guidance both her judgmental faculties and her feelings. Like Kuan-yin, the goddess of love and compassion, she functioned androgynously, adapting consciously to circumstances and to people, whenever possible. Chin is representative of Tao in her fluidity and malleability. Her sense of rectitude and her wisdom make her a true descendant of the Confucius who wrote: "Do not do to others what you would not desire yourself. Then you will have no enemies either in the state or in your own home."[39] An embodiment of China's great cultural past and its catalytic present, Chin is the paradigmatic woman of the future.

9 Fumiko Enchi's *Masks:* A Sacred Mystery

Masks (1958), by the Japanese novelist Fumiko Enchi, takes us into the heart of the feminine world: its mysteries, its sacred and profane rituals, its exorcisms, and its initiatory rites. For Enchi, the unexpressed is more important than the expressed: Silence has greater value than the spoken word; emptiness, than fullness; formlessness, than form. Behind each word, image, line, color, object, gesture, and protagonist, there lies a hidden realm tingling with excitement, which holds the reader enthralled.

Masks may be viewed in part as a modern reworking of ceremonies that took place when Japan was divided into small clan-based states regulated by shamanesses and priestesses. The Shrine of Ise, which was founded in 478, became one of the most important sanctuaries in the country. It was dedicated to the Sun Goddess, Amaterasu Omikami ("The Heaven-Shining-Deity"), progenitrix of the Japanese emperors and people, who was looked upon as the archetypal mother, protector, and nurturer of human and earthly forces.

Psychologically, we may say that it was she who safeguarded (and still safeguards) the embryonic psyche and saw to its growth and health. Since Amaterasu was born from the left eye of her father (Izanagi, the Sky God), she has a pronounced masculine side; in that she emerged from his eye, she represents consciousness and vision.[1] Her brother, the Moon God, Tsuki-yomi ("The Counter of the Months"), born from his father's right eye, represents darkened, nebulous spheres and irrational, intuitive domains. Solar consciousness, identified with Amaterasu, was and is the dominant archetype of consciousness in Japan—and is feminine.[2]

Shamanesses and their mediums, important elements in Japan's indigenous religion, Shinto, were and still are transmitters of messages from the world of Amaterasu. Such priestly offices, traditionally held by imperial princesses, also referred to as high priestesses, go way back in time, starting with Yamato-Hime, the daughter of Emperor Sujin (97–30 B.C.), and continuing to modern times.[3] To Amaterasu were offered the early fruits of the season, the early catch from the waters, and the first spoils of war. The preservation of humanity was Amaterasu's goal, but the accomplishment of this goal did not necessarily imply sexual satisfaction or gratification. On the contrary, women could be inadequately developed sexually or even frigid. The fertilization of the ovum was the sole concern.

We are dealing in *Masks* with a contemporary shamaness, Mieko, Amaterasu's earthly counterpart. Her sine qua non is the continuation of her family and, by implication, her own eternality. The issue is reproduction. Mieko's daughter-in-law, Yasuko, is the medium through which she will carry on her work. Both are widows. The man in such a matriarchal climate is viewed as a stud. No real personal relationship exists between male and female. Feelings are not involved. In such a context, sex becomes sinless and impersonal.[4]

Enchi interweaves expertly throughout her novel details of Japanese history, art, and literature, especially of the Heian period (794–1191), which brought a renaissance in women's letters to a society which had become rigidly patriarchal. Women were considered intellectually and socially inferior to men—their "handmaids." During Heian times, women excelled in the literary arts, writing novels, poems, essays, diaries, and letters. Court ladies frequently spent hours copying Buddha's *Lotus Sutra*, a favorite among them, since it preached salvation for both men and women. Lady Murasaki Shikibu's *Tale of Genji*, to which Enchi alludes frequently in *Masks*, was written at this time.

Heian, meaning "peace and tranquility" enjoyed by the courtly and refined aristocrats, also elicits sadness, stillness, reflection, and delicate blendings of colors and perfumes. Just as a hierarchy of values is suggested in the gracious language of the literary works produced during the Heian period (with their images of snow, trees, flowers, and a moon obscured by rain, and their evocations of the mystery of silence and the pathos of transient beings), so Enchi reproduces a similar panoply of sensations in her novel. In the feminine mode that dominates *Masks* lies a rich world of intimate thoughts and feelings—always secret and controlled.

Enchi's extraordinary insights into the psyches of Japanese women and her masterful writing style and method not only reflect in part her own personal views and experiences, but might also be said to have been influenced by Lady Murasaki's writing techniques as described in "The Art of the Novel," from *The Tale of Genji*:

> . . . an art so fitting each part of the narrative into the next that, though all is mere invention, the reader is persuaded that such things might easily have happened and is as deeply moved as though they were actually going on around him. We may know with one part of our minds that every incident has been invented for the express purposes of impressing us: but (if the plot is constructed with the requisite skill) we may all the while in another part of our minds be burning with indignation at the wrongs endured by some wholly imaginary princess. . . . I can assure you that for my part, when I read a story, I always accept it as an account of something that has really actually happened.[5]

Fumiko Enchi was born in Tokyo in 1905 to the daughter of a professor of linguistics. Although she lived in a world where the intellect played a considerable role, she nevertheless dropped out of high school and began to study drama—mainly Kabuki. Her first play was performed at Tsukiji Little Theatre in 1928. At the same time, she became committed to the proletarian literary movement and joined a Communist organization, subsequently withdrawing so as not to cause her father any problems. Rather than leave her family, as she had first planned, she took the less rebellious path and married in 1930 a young journalist, Yoshimatsu Enchi, whom she did not love. She remained with him until his death in 1974. They had one daughter.

Enchi gave up play-writing and turned to novels because they gave her, she felt, greater freedom of expression. Her novella "Starving Days," which won the Women Writers Prize, was followed by many successful short stories and novels, including *The Waiting Years* and *Masks.*

Masks is divided into three parts, each bearing the name of a specific feminine No mask. Since women were not allowed to partake in No theatre, a dramatic form which came into being in fourteenth-century Japan, they were impersonated by men (and still are today). Hence, the mask incarnates an unclear and undefined sex, as well as a personality. Once the male actor dons his feminine mask, he vanishes, and *it* takes over. The mask itself may be said to be archetypal: It exists in a universal and timeless domain; it also represents a pattern of behavior and forms the structural dominant of the psyche.

The first section of Enchi's novel is entitled *Ryo no onna*, referring to a mask representing the spirit of a woman tormented beyond the grave by unrequited love. The mask from which the second section takes its title, *Masugami*, is a metaphor for the madwoman. The third mask, *Fukai*, symbolizes the "deep woman," the "grief-laden," mature, middle-aged mother.[6] Because Enchi's use of the mask in her novel is archetypal in scope, it possesses a dynamism of its own, containing a numinosity and fascination which absorb the spirit and psyche of the protagonists affected by it, and the reader as well.

Ryo No Onna

Perceived to be unmodifiable, immutable, and unaffected by the world of contingencies, masks are used as accessories in ceremonies and rituals in Japan. They are also considered to be instruments of possession, capable of capturing and vitalizing—or destroying—what is human and inhuman in life.

Mieko Togano, the shamaness in Enchi's novel, is identified with the *Ryo no onna* mask: a transhuman vengeful spirit. Her outward expression—detached, meditative, and quietist—hides an inner world, the duplicate of the *Ryo no onna* mask, which spells torment and pain. A dichotomy exists between the empirical domain, which reveals a facade of complacency, and Mieko's inner climate, possessed by turbulent and repressed unconscious powers. The *Ryo no onna* mask alone knows the truth. As an archetypal power, it will dictate her pattern of behavior.

Mieko, a matriarchal force, has secreted everything personal in her life, rigidifying her ego in the process. Arrogating unto herself the collective powers of the high priestess, she has successfully dominated what could have proven to be troublesome unconscious contents within her, as well as the lives of those who are drawn into her orbit. Intellectually, she is a superior woman; she is the editor of a poetry magazine and a poet in her own right. She is equally well versed in matters of religion and is knowledgeable of spirit possession, among other things.

Yasuko, her daughter-in-law, mourning the untimely death of her husband, Akio, killed by an avalanche when climbing Mount Fuji, has chosen to live with Mieko rather than return to her own family. In accordance with Mieko's advice, she is continuing the research work begun by her husband on spirit possession during the Heian era, and is auditing classes on Japanese literature given at the University of Tokyo by Professor Ibuki, who had also been Akio's senior thesis director. That Ibuki is thirty-seven years old, married, and a father does not prevent him from being sensually attracted to Yasuko. His friend Mikame, a medical doctor and also a student of spirit possession, likewise has his eye on the attractive widow.

The opening scene, which takes place in a cafe in Kyoto, sets the climate for the novel. Kyoto, the capital of Japan during the Heian era, was and still is the seat of temples, gardens, parks, and imperial palaces known the world over for their beauty and mystery. That Enchi chose this city as the locus of the early scenes of her novel underscores the importance not only of religious rituals but also of the aristocratic elements in *Masks*.

The introductory images are significant for their symbolic ramifications. On the table around which Ibuki and Mikame are seated there are "a single white chrysanthemum and an ashtray piled high with cigarette butts."[7] Contemporary Japan is represented by the cafe, the ashtray, and the cigarette butts; its numinous and aesthetic past is identified with the white chrysanthemum.

The white chrysanthemum is an image of crucial importance. Its petals, disposed in a circular pattern, represent the earthly counterpart of the sun's rays—Amaterasu in all of her burgeoning purity, power, and eternality. Awesome yet friendly, the goddess in the guise of the chrysanthemum welcomes those who seek to be warmed by her glowing rays. The power of the flower's illumination—and, therefore, numinosity—has come to symbolize cosmic intelligence. The chrysanthemum becomes a mediating force between the universal and the personal, between the cyclical and the perennial, and between light and shadow.[8]

Ibuki and Mikame, friends since college days, believe themselves to be in full control of their lives, but by entering the world of spirit possession, which is traditionally a woman's area, they tread on dangerous ground. During their conversation, they mention a seance both had attended only a few weeks earlier. The medium, a woman who spoke in French in the voice of a male alpinist, told of his fatal fall into a crevasse while climbing the Matterhorn. Yasuko, who was present at the seance, was powerfully shaken by the experience, which recalled her husband's death on Mount Fuji. Ibuki and Mikame began discussing the incident scientifically: Did the medium have the power to "pick up the voices of real human beings from around the world, like a radio picking up air waves"? If so, the mind is comparable to a computer or word processor, possessing its own antennae, which are capable of tuning in and out of anything and everything, according to the length of the waves. An exciting and ambiguous world of imponderables emerges from this experience, a bit frightening even for these intellectually awakened men.

What also intrigues Ibuki and Mikame is the peculiar relationship between Mieko and Yasuko. The latter, they are convinced, is a medium figure, and the former, a shaman spirit: Yasuko is psychologically fettered to her mother-in-law, her very vitality fed and nurtured by the older woman; Mieko, an impassable and immutable force, by working her mysterious will, subdues the younger person.

That the name Mieko may be identified with *miko*, the Japanese word for a priestess presiding at a Shinto shrine, suggests that she is inhabited by some transhuman power.[9] Yasuko's unconscious identification with her mother-in-law prolongs the undeveloped nature of her childhood and her life as a young bride. To free herself from Mieko's influence would require a sacrifice of the archetypal mother, or the power represented by this force within her unconscious. Should such an amputation not take place, the younger woman would fall further under the domination of the older woman's personality and eventually become overpowered by it.[10]

Shamanesses and mediums, who figure so significantly in Enchi's novel, have for centuries played important roles in the ritual of Shinto ("The Way of the Gods"). Followers of this animistic religion with no official scriptures believe that a life force exists in all things, animate or inanimate, and that everything in the world of phenomena is endowed with a spirit. Shinto worship is based on the simple feeling of "awe" for nature: a waterfall, a flower, a stone, an insect, a mountain, snow, an ancestor, a hero, the emperor, the sun, the moon. Numinous forces such as these are called *kami*, which is translated as "god," "superior," or "above." Human beings approach *kami* in reverence and friendship, and without fear. Before doing so, however, they must purify themselves by washing and taking part in devotions, such as standing within a sacred enclosure (a quiet grove with a shrine) or before a particular stone or mountain. The high priestess or shamaness, who understands the language of the *kami*, interprets their will. The mediums transliterate the spiritual essence of what remains a mystery for others. It must also be noted that belief in spirit or demonic possession, necromancy, black magic, and witchcraft was and still is popular among the common folk of Japan.[11]

In ancient days, people spoke of being possessed by a spirit, demon, or ghost. Today, however, we talk of an archetype: an alien energy or a mana figure which releases its libido (psychic energy) into an individual. Like a demon or djinn, the archetype represented by the *Ryo no onna* mask has invaded Mieko's unconscious, spreading its poisons in the process. These, however, are closeted and invisible. Only Mieko's other side remains exposed—that of shamaness/priestess, direct descendant of Amaterasu. Wearing such a persona, Mieko is Sun, perception, the Great Progenitrix, and, as such, an awe-inspiring force for Yasuko—a *tremendum*.

Yasuko, the medium, is not only caught up in and dominated by her mother-in-law's grieving archetype; she is also catalyzed by her energetic Sun force. A woman medium, psychologically speaking, is one whose ego (center of consciousness) remains undeveloped and who is dominated by another's power, mood, or philosophy. So strong can this alien force (human or ideational) become that the medium woman unconsciously makes it her own. Yasuko, although somewhat aware of her identityless nature, does not realize to what extent she is being manipulated by her projection. She neither enjoys nor can she take advantage of her individuality or her life, her ego having yielded its authority to superior forces. That she may sometimes appear elusive, even secretive or subtle, simply indicates that she has no real identity, that she does not know who she is, and that she does not have any true understanding or recognition of her situation.

Confusion, annoyance, and a desire to free herself from what she senses to be her mother-in-law's domineering presence characterize Yasuko. She dreams of escaping into freedom, thereby attaining, she erroneously thinks, independence and fulfillment.

Yasuko, a shadow figure, as we have already suggested, does not necessarily live out her mother-in-law's inferior traits. She lives out her weaknesses, or those characteristics which the ego has not yet recognized. Because she lacks lucidity, it may be said that Yasuko roams around in darkened realms in a state of psychological myopia. Her dependence upon Mieko will increase rather than decrease, transforming her eventually into her spokeswoman and her tool.

Yasuko's nature is depicted from the very outset of *Masks*. When she makes her appearance at the cafe where Ibuki and Mikame are chatting, she is described as "a flame-red shadow" which "passed over the frosted glass window near their booth" (14). Yasuko will remain a reflection throughout the novel; she will never come into her own. Not necessarily negative, however, she will simply be unidentifiable, cloudy, and specterlike. In sharp contrast to her shadowy nature is the flame-red color of her coat, suggesting a fiery and passionate temperament as well as a highly charged and energetic personality. The incandescence she generates attracts men to her orbit. So, too, does the contrasting whiteness and iridescence of her skin tones. They arouse Mikame sensually, glowing as they do with "the internal life-force of spring's earliest buds unfolding naturally in the sun" (15). As a medium figure, Yasuko constellates, as already suggested, Mieko's springlike enthusiasm as well as her autumnal sadness. The younger woman is never separated from her entourage, and in that she blends into this entourage as well as reflects it, she may be said to be all things to all men.

The first direct contact with Mieko introduces the reader to the matriarchal sphere. She is seated in the back of a large car, which is to take Yasuko, Ibuki, and Mikame to a No master's home. Her voice, which emerges "gay and youthful" as it comes "floating toward them from the interior of the car," is our first point of contact with this shamaness. Its reverberations from within the car, which may be considered a symbolic womb, are impressive for their power and transhuman dimension.

For the Japanese, sound, word, and non-sound are of supreme significance. They exist prior to manifestation and long after dissemination into the invisible domain. They both fill and absorb the universe. Like a magical power, the tonalities and rhythms of Mieko's voice infiltrate the psyches of those present, effacing the barriers erected by consciousness and immersing their egos in her protective yet constricting sphere. Lying back "languorously deep in the cushions, nodding slowly or smiling in agreement with everything Yasuko said," Mieko gives the impression of a remote background figure, never acting overtly, but merely directing the events through her radiant energies. Yasuko, by contrast, is "alert and vivid." The two women complement each other; they live in a world that no man can penetrate. Nevertheless, Ibuki and Mikame will attempt to lift the veil behind which the shamaness and her votary hide.

Once at the No master's home, the visitors are shown a variety of female costumes. The beauty and artistry of these ancient garments, handed down from generation to generation, are breathtaking, as in, for example, a "gray figured satin, stamped with a heavy gold-leaf pattern, embroidered with large, drooping white lilies" (19). The range of brilliant and pastel colors may be looked upon as premonitory of the emotional patterns that will come into play during the course of the novel—a range of emotions stimulating and exciting, appeasing and serene, and destructive and cruel as well. A story is connected with one of the robes: A weaver worked so hard to complete a garment in time for the opening of *The Chrysanthemum Youth* that he died in the process, but his spirit, seated in the imperial box next to the emperor, appeared to the actor who was wearing the robe onstage. Although ghosts frequently return to life in the second act of No plays, Mieko and Yasuko realize that a whole *other* world exists in these costumes and that they contain life and breath.

Robes and weaving are significant for worshippers of Amaterasu. It is she and her followers who weave the garments of the gods. The gorgeous kimonos Mieko and Yasuko see in the No master's home are earthly counterparts of divine fabrics. As they cast their eyes upon them, they, too, begin spinning their webs—not concretely as yet, but figuratively. Caught up in the richness of the costumes' textures, designs, and colorations—manifold varieties of flowers, trees, and birds worked in brilliant and dark greens, blues, reds, and mauves—Mieko and Yasuko react affectively to this feast for the senses. Like the garments, which fuse disparate elements, they feel knit one to the other by unbreachable links, experiencing, in Ibuki's words, "a whole private worldless" domain.

The masks are brought out moments later. Yasuko is stunned most particularly by the expression worn by the *Zo no onna* mask:

> . . . the visage of a coldly beautiful woman, her cheeks tightly drawn. The sweep of the eyelids was long, and the red of the upper lip extended out to the corners of the mouth in an uneven and

> involved line, curving at the last into a smile of disdain. A haughty cruelty was frozen hard upon the face, encasing it like crystals of ice on a tree. (23)

Covering her eyes with her hands, Yasuko attempts to block out what she has just seen, thus rejecting the archetype imprinted in her mind's eye. Frozen cruelty, hardness, and iciness are the images she identifies with Akio's death. The shock of confrontation is so traumatic that she grows dizzy.

For No theatregoers (and Yasuko is conversant in this art) the mask not only severs the actor from the outer world, encouraging him to look inward, but it also takes on a numinosity of its own. For some, it embodies the spirit of an ancestor or the soul of a dead person paying a visit to the living. By implication, the mask is an entity capable of transcending barriers, of destroying obstacles, and of renewing ties between the living and the dead. In that it is archetypal, it is a unifying, determinate form, which is capable of coalescing opposites. It thereby precedes creation and every manifestation of ordered form.[12] The mask represents the primordial image of an aspect of the psyche that is nonperceptible but nevertheless filled with potential.

Usually made of cypress wood and covered with many layers of paint, the No mask is treated with utmost care and reverence by the actor. He does not merely place it on his face in a cavalier manner before going onstage; on the contrary, he follows precise rituals. After donning his costume, the actor goes to the "greenroom" behind the stage, looks at himself in the mirror, lifts up the mask he has chosen for the performance, bows to it in greeting, and places it on his face. At that moment it is endowed with life, and he actually becomes the character symbolized by the mask; he is the mask, and henceforth it sees and determines his performance.

Why does the *Zo no onna* mask take Yasuko's breath away? The livingness and vibrancy of the unconscious content represented by the mask, so powerfully enchained within Yasuko's subliminal realm until now, break out of their closeted domain with such violence that they cause a momentary eclipse of the ego. The impact of the displacement of energies is such that it also smothers her spirit/soul or breath in the process, cutting off the oxygen feeding the brain. Whatever equilibrium, or semblance of equilibrium, she has possessed until now is destroyed, bringing on a state of confusion and dizziness. Yasuko fears the sensations represented by the cold, cruel, hard, and frigid ceremonial mask because they remind her of her dead husband, but also because of what these same sensations represent within her own psyche. Does she perhaps feel a certain frigidity on her part, and has feeling been replaced in her world by icy impermeability? Can she still maintain a warm and deep relationship with a man?

If the *Zo no onna* mask takes its toll on Yasuko, the *Ryo no onna* mask, the next one brought out to view, frightens her even more. Its "utter tranquility" of expression and its "deeply inward" look remind her of Mieko:

> I think Japanese long ago must have had that look. And it seems to me she [Mieko] must be one of the last women who lives that way still—like the masks—with her deepest energies turned inward. (26)

It is clear to Yasuko at this point that she must break away from Mieko's influence. She will, of course, continue working as her secretary, devoting her time to the poetry magazine, and will also pursue her research on spirit possession. As for the rest, however, she has to find her own niche in life before it is too late. Otherwise, Ibuki's appraisal of her will be correct: She looks "like a woman wrapped in chains" (27). She decides that she will marry Mikame, though she does not love him. It is the easiest way of escaping from her mother-in-law's dominion.

To set a fixed course in life and follow the directives ordered by the intellect are not always possible. The irrational factors involved—in Yasuko's case, her fascination with Mieko's archetypal power—may prevent such a neat plan:

> She [Mieko] has a peculiar power to move events in whatever direction she pleases, while she stays motionless. She's like a quiet mountain lake whose waters are rushing beneath the surface towards a waterfall. She's like the face on a No mask, wrapped in her own secrets. (30)

Yasuko marvels at the "motionless" expression and the immobility marking Mieko's facial contours. Their inner strength derives from an inner power which has enabled her to overcome adversity, or at least to deal with it. The "quiet mountain lake," representing the persona—her mother-in-law's facade—exudes tranquility. Such a persona, however, is deceiving in that it is antipodal to the truth conveyed by the *Ryo no onna* mask, which concretizes the pain emanating from the surging waters of Mieko's subliminal world.

Mieko is a microcosm, a world unto herself, and a composite of opposites. As high priestess or shamaness, she is a paragon of strength in her dealings with outer events; she is also a superb puppeteer, a manipulator of marionettes and of those whose destinies she seeks to regulate. Like the oracles of old, the Sibyls and prophetesses, she is that force which links the disparate: The terrestrial, celestial, and infernal are bound by her into one energetic whole.

Yasuko senses the untold energies contained within Mieko's tightly sealed inner world. Aspects of these shimmering luminosities are forever constellating outward, radiating and catalyzing those who capture them. The stilled outer world of the *Ryo no onna* mask speaks its message loud and clearly, revealing the swollen oceans of suffering contained within Mieko, yet she has succeeded in living a fulfilling existence within the framework of the archetype which possesses and bewitches her. She works with that inner power, using it for what she considers to be her advantage.[13]

At the end of the visit to the No master's house, Yasuko and Ibuki take the train back to Tokyo. Mieko has informed them that she must remain in Nara. Only at this point do they realize that—somehow—they are being manipulated by her, ever so subtly and mysteriously. There is some "devious" plan she is putting to work, they think. Does she want to leave them alone so they may have an affair? An outside force has "taken over my mind and my body," Yasuko claims (31). As she questions herself, she grows increasingly troubled and unsure of what she thinks and feels; even when she believes she is acting on her own, she now senses Mieko's presence lurking in the background, always arranging things for her, scheming and planning—forever present in her darkness. She thinks about Mieko as follows:

> The secrets inside her mind are like flowers in a garden at nighttime, filling the darkness with perfume. . . . Next to that secret charm of hers, her talent as a poet is really only a sort of costume. (31)

That Yasuko should identify Mieko with flowers is significant. Whether in natural surroundings, in gardens, or in arrangements (*ikebana*), the flower may be looked upon as an evolving manifestation of a cyclical power implicit in a triadic universe: earthly, human, heavenly. In that the flowers in Yasuko's image are in a garden, indicating highly structured and purposeful configurations, we are given to believe that nothing in Mieko's world happens haphazardly; everything is arranged according to a specific order and code. Nevertheless—and this makes events all the more disconcerting and ambiguous—the secrets contained within the "garden [Mieko] at nighttime," which fill the air with perfume, usher in a sense of mystery. The unconscious reigns in this tenebrous region; the dream world dominates, elusive and perhaps beyond human comprehension, but also, like the flower, identifiable through its perpetually exuded amorphous sensations. Mieko is the flower—the transhuman shamaness.

As Yasuko and Ibuki continue their train ride, Mount Fuji looms in the distance, "swathed in deep red clouds, as if it had risen that very moment from the earth" (33). Mountains the world over and in all times have had special significance for humanity: Mount Meru for the Hindu, Mount Sinai for the Hebrew, the Mount of Olives for the Christian, Mount Kaf for the Muslim. Because of their verticality, they rise toward heaven, thus participating in transcendence. Volcanoes—those energies necessary for hierophanies and theophanies—may be hidden in their bellies.

Mount Fuji plays a very special role, religiously and psychologically, for the Japanese. They have always looked upon this sacred mountain, dotted with Shinto shrines and Zen temples and monasteries, as a spiritual ladder to be climbed. Each rung represents another stage in both a personal and collective evolution. Fuji's peak is usually hidden within a bed of white and graying clouds, which underscore its mystery, solitariness, and forlornness, as well as its pristine purity. Unlike the spiritual images the Japanese most frequently evoke when in the presence of Mount Fuji, or the mountain's inspirational force for artists such as Hokusai and Hiroshige or for poets like Saigyo and Jozan, the mountain's image, for Yasuko, is one of death. This mountain had cost her the life of her husband four years prior to the opening of the story, when Akio had been killed in an avalanche that followed a severe snowstorm. In spite of the search party's efforts to unearth the bodies of the victims, they remained interred deep beneath glistening white mounds. Yasuko had walked up the mountain daily, meditating as she awaited its oracular pronouncements. As she stared at it from afar—and even at close range—it seemed to take on the contours of a "snow goddess, clutching Akio tightly to her, and refusing to give him up." A *vagina dentata*, she froze, then paralyzed, her victims, and finally drained their blood.

This giant mountain force is feminine for Yasuko; a dominant power, perhaps it is a projection of Mieko. Powerful and rigid, as is her mother-in-law—her viselike strength being lethal in both terrestrial and supraterrestrial ways—Mount Fuji had clutched and devoured Akio, and now was menacing her. She wonders whether her husband had been aware of his mother's constricting nature; perhaps this was the reason he had wanted to climb Mount Fuji in the first place—to get on top of things, to prove his independence, his manliness, and his dominion over the mountain goddess. Had he wanted to stand above his mother? To reach great heights?

Other factors also suggest an identification between Mount Fuji and

Mieko. Hadn't she spent her married years in the deep north—in the snowiest and coldest of areas? Mieko had spoken so frequently of the benumbing cold she had had to endure, as well as of the brilliant whiteness of the landscape and the solitude and tranquility—perhaps the non-life she had been forced to experience during those years. The whiteness, or countercolor, emphasized so continuously in Enchi's novel reinforces the various motifs in *Masks*: death, absence, departure, and nocturnal-diurnal cyclical sequences. White absorbs everything around it—as does Mount Fuji, remote in its gleaming glaze and its frosted grandeur.

Akio's death should have encouraged Yasuko to go her own way. It had the opposite effect in that it reaffirmed her powerful bonds with Mieko. Is she in love with her mother-in-law? Ibuki wonders. Do they have lesbian relations? Not love, but admiration for Mieko's courage, assurance, vitality, strength, and calm attracts Yasuko to the older woman. Mieko has what Yasuko lacks. She is a woman in complete possession of herself. Still, there are aspects about her mother-in-law she does not understand: How do she and Ibuki fit into her scheme of things? are they pawns in her game? extraneous pieces of a puzzle of her manufacture? Whenever Yasuko thinks hard about these possibilities, she becomes almost paralyzed and feels as if she were choking.

Yasuko is fixated on Mieko—the archetypal mother. Only by increasing her consciousness of the undeveloped aspects of her inner world can she gain some semblance of independence. Her ego has stopped evolving, held down by the blanketing image of Mieko, that paragon of strength and fortitude. So deep is Yasuko's monomania, and so strong is her bond to this older woman, that in time she looks upon her as a virtual deity: Amaterasu. A suprapersonal presence, dictating her needs and wants, has infiltrated her being. No longer can she distinguish between her personal motivations and feelings and those belonging to the collective mother *imago*. Suddenly Yasuko feels helpless and will-less.[14]

In that Mieko's powers are archetypal—numinous—they are beyond her own comprehension. As the daughter of the head priest at a temple in Shinshu, she had certainly been indoctrinated into the world of spirits at an early age, and had been taught to communicate with the *kami*. Upon her marriage, her husband, of the upper samurai class, took her to live in the far north, in the Hokkaido area, virtually buried the year round in snow and ice. Shut off from the outside world, deep in the heartland of the Ainu people, Mieko learned about the culture of this indigenous race, which had been influenced by the Ural-Altaic populations from eastern Siberia and by the Sino-Mongolians from China and Korea. She was taught firsthand the secrets of shamanism and ancestral totemism. The Ainus revered mountains and volcanoes, considering them the central axis of the world, linking the three planes of the cosmos in a continuous process of regeneration. Mieko likewise looked upon them as sacred forces, symbolizing ever-recurring life.[15] These natural wonders permitted her to communicate with the world at large, on a deeper, inward level. No longer was she dependent upon her husband for feelings of well-being; she had learned to look within—to expand her consciousness.

Mieko had married at the age of nineteen. Unprepared for the harsh realities of life, for a time she bathed in the warm and serene seas of illusion. When Mieko became pregnant, her joy knew no bounds. A strange accident occurring in her third month of pregnancy put a halt to her euphoria. Her kimono had caught on a protruding nail, causing her to trip and fall down a flight of stairs. A miscarriage followed. Her trauma became particularly acute when she discovered that the housemaid, who stood erect at the foot of the stairway during Mieko's fall, had "planted [the nail] strategically on the staircase" (87). Only later did she understand the reasons for and the power of the maid's hatred for her and for her unborn child: Mieko's husband had impregnated the maid prior to his marriage and again shortly afterward, so that she had been forced to have abortions. The incident left Mieko with deep emotional scars, which neither vanished nor emerged into the light of day. They remained hermetically sealed within her depths. It was at this juncture that she created her persona. Her indomitable will and her rational principle now dictated her actions, and an ambiguous smile of seeming placidity was engraved upon her face. A moat existed henceforth between her inner, impenetrable world and the outer, accessible domain.

To the world outside, Mieko and her husband appeared to have resumed a normal relationship. Some years later she gave birth to twins: Akio, a boy, and Harume, a retarded girl. Her husband's family, believing multiple births to be a sign of misfortune, forced her to give up one of the twins. Harume was registered as the daughter of a widowed aunt and sent to live far from home. No one saw the child again until after Akio's death.

That Mieko's in-laws were fearful of the birth of twins is an expression of Japanese cognizance of polarities. Sun and moon, and, by extension, the light and dark side of the human personality, came to represent twins. Akio, the male, stood for the solar force (the ego); healthy and vigorous, he may be likened to Amaterasu. His sister, like Tsuki-yomi, the Moon God (the shadow), was doomed to spend her life in the darkened regions of the mind. Harume's family sent her away to live, which is tantamount, psychologically, to exiling or rejecting one's shadow. In this case, the shadow is an unconscious content associated with something defective within the psyche, something people fear for lack of understanding. People prefer to dwell in sunlight and in the known, logical sphere.[16]

Mieko's ordeals have strengthened her ego and hardened her persona. As a result, she is highly organized and motivated and always acts with a sense of equity and justice. Never, however, has anyone succeeded in peering beyond her persona. Yasuko, Mikame, and Ibuki have no inkling of where they stand with her, but all three are fascinated, intrigued, and mesmerized by this incredible being.

In time, Yasuko and Ibuki begin a liaison, and he grows passionately fond of her. At the same time, Mikame desires to marry Yasuko. All three seem to be functioning mechanically, according to some preconceived, mysterious plan. Only when Mikame picks up by chance an old issue of *Clear Stream*, a magazine in which appears Mieko's essay "The Shrine in the Fields," is some light shed on that eerie secret domain of hers. The essay deals with a Shinto shrine located at Sagano. It is a holy sanctuary where unmarried daughters of aristocrats and emperors went to undergo purification rituals, thereby making them worthy to serve as high priestesses at the Grand Shrine of Ise. Mieko's investigations center on the fate of Lady Rokujo, one of Emperor Genji's favorites (depicted in detail by Lady Murasaki in *The Tale of Genji*, and, later, in the No play *The Shrine in the Fields*).

Mieko's essay, written in 1937 at the outbreak of the Sino-Japanese war, is more than an investigation of Lady Rokujo's life. It is a psychological study of this historical and literary figure upon whom Mieko projects, and an exploration into the meaning and rituals involved in spirit possession.

Lady Rokujo came to court at the age of sixteen and married the crown prince. She was euphoric at the thought of one day becoming empress and commanding homage. Shortly after the birth of a daughter, her husband abdicated and decided to live the life of a wealthy nobleman. He died a few years later. Unable to remain at the Heian court unless she consented to be one of the emperor's concubines, Lady Rokujo decided to leave the court and spend the rest of her days with her daughter in an elegant home not far from the capital. There she would spend her time writing poetry and practicing calligraphy. Such gracious living, surrounded by friends and refined attendants, would have been her destiny had Prince Genji not entered her life. Fascinated by her wit, beauty, and "cool dignity and reserve," he courted her unceasingly (50). Only after she yielded to his advances did his ardor flag. Unlike Genji's other paramours, however, Lady Rokujo had enormous energy and a strong ego. She refused to give up either her individuality or her dignity. Haunted by an indomitable spirit of revenge, however, she took up the practice of spirit possession. Evil karma was aimed at all of her rivals. Genji's wife was the first to die; his paramours succumbed to illness successively. Lady Rokujo's curses were so efficacious and so ferocious that she herself was aghast at the power of her violence. In time, she and her daughter withdrew to the Shrine in the Fields, where Genji bid her farewell, writing a poem to commemorate the occasion; she responded in kind. Genji later attempted to rectify a wrong—to assuage his guilt—by giving her daughter in marriage to the Reizei Emperor. Satisfied by this success, Lady Rokujo believed she had emerged victorious from the relationship. She had been the only female in Genji's entourage to have maintained her calm and strength in the face of adversity. She had succeeded in channeling her inner rage and using this energy to do battle with forces that might otherwise have crushed her. Mieko explains:

> Rokujo lady is instead a Ryo no onna: one who chafes at her inability to sublimate her strong ego in deference to any man but who can carry out her will only by forcing it upon others—and that indirectly, through the possessive capacity of her spirit. (53)

Since most shamanesses in Japan are married to their tutelary gods and goddesses, it may be said that Lady Rokujo had identified with the masculine side of Amaterasu, and that Mieko, in turn, idealized Genji's paramour, attempting to emulate her enormous energy and drive. Never passive, she would attack those she despised in the subtlest of ways, not by making them ill, but by forcing them into complicity and by learning to manipulate everyone within her orbit. After experiencing torment and emotional divestiture, she learned to deal positively with what could have been detrimental factors. Like her mentor, she became an intellectual pragmatist, turning to poetic creation to express her surging and pulsating feelings. Like Lady Rokujo, she developed a strong ego, which allowed her to remain firmly rooted to the ground while delving into the nebulous, mystical climes of spirit possession.

Mieko and Lady Rokujo may both be said to have worn the *Ryo no onna* mask—a concrete manifestation of an inner dimension—while functioning superbly in the outer realm. Like Amaterasu, Lady Rokujo and Mieko used their masculine sides when confronting an enemy. Let us recall that Amaterasu was armed like a warrior when called upon to defy and challenge those who sought to destroy or demean her. She was her father's daughter, as already mentioned; her virility and strength were inborn.[17]

Mieko concluded her essay on the Shrine in the Fields with the following fascinating statement:

> Just as there is an archetype of woman as the object of man's eternal love, so there must be an archetype of her as the object of

> his eternal fear, representing, perhaps, the shadow of his own evil actions. The Rokujo lady is an embodiment of this archetype. (57)

What ancient and medieval peoples alluded to as "spirit possession," "apparitions," or "ghosts" may also be alluded to as a kind of hysteria, in which a portion (large or small) of the psyche is taken over by some unknown factor or content living out its existence unabetted.[18] Charcot, Janet, Bernheim, Freud, and Breuer were the first to approach the question of hysteria from a clinical point of view. Freud, describing the etiology of this disease, claimed that it resulted from a trauma, or "psychic wound," in childhood and was usually due to repressed sexuality. He later broadened his views concerning the disease. Fantasies which could have been traumata, he said, aroused excitement that would have been discharged under normal circumstances. With the hysterical patient, however, the release of affective fantasies was not possible. The "retention of the excitation" or the "blocking" or "repression" of the affect did not permit the psychic energy to be released. Hence it was transformed into a physical system. The goal of the psychiatrist was to liberate this pent-up energy and, in so doing, channel it into some positive direction.[19]

Mieko and Lady Rokujo had blocked their abrasive love experiences. The repression of such content gave rise to the accumulation of so much excitation that it finally split off into a complex: "a miniature self-contained psyche which develops a peculiar fantasy-life of its own."[20] In time, the complex gained extreme dynamism, becoming virtually autonomous. The resulting fantasies assumed abnormal proportions, so that the entire psyche fell under its dominion. Almost everything Mieko (or Lady Rokujo) thought or felt centered on this electric charge, distorting her views, her perspective, and her power drive. This autonomous complex attracted to itself energy that properly belonged to the entire psyche and was supposed to nourish the psyche as a whole. The more vigorous the complex, the greater was the aridity of the rest of the psyche—which was starving and atrophying. The volcanic pain of the complex remained buried within the psyche's geological folds; the *Ryo no onna* mask alone captured its meaning.

Masugami

The second part of Enchi's novel opens as Yasuko is awakening, terrified, from a nightmare. Stunned by the power of her dream and the unresolved unconscious energies which suddenly burst forth in a series of glazed images focusing on a mutilated Akio, Yasuko rushes into Mieko's room, then into her bed. Trembling in fits and starts, she tells her mother-in-law that she actually saw Akio dug up from under the snow. Mieko holds her tightly in her arms, cradling her as a mother does a child, soothing and comforting her as best she can.

Yasuko's dream is a reliving in part of a real incident. When she had joined the search party and had gone up Mount Fuji, she had been given a long rod to poke about in the snow. She hesitated before using it, fearing she might stab Akio by mistake and hurt him in some way. Finally, she acquiesced, thrust the rod down into the snow, and in so doing observed "a tiny deep hole of a blue that was so pure, so clear, so beautiful" it took her breath away (63).

Her dream was quite different. She actually did stab Akio with her rod: "I stabbed his dead face straight in the eye" (63). In reality, when his body had been recovered five months after his death, either because he had been dragged along by the avalanche or for some unknown reason, one side of his face was in perfect condition, with not a scratch, while the flesh on the other side had been torn away. "Beneath his left cheekbone his upper jaw had been fully exposed, revealing a line of white teeth," and on his forehead there was something "like a stab wound" (64).

As Yasuko continues to relive her dream, Mieko continues to reassure her, telling her she was not at fault. As she speaks, her voice grows distant, and her expression, "blurred into an even more indistinct white," becomes increasingly ambiguous. Mieko's mental suffering, aroused by the vision of her son, is rapidly repressed. The indestructible and timeless persona once again takes over. In sharp contrast are Yasuko's "deep self-destructive urges" and her uncontained guilt and anguish: "I killed Akio again myself. I lost the power to keep him and him alone, alive inside me. That's the reason. That's what made me dream I stabbed him in the eye with that rod" (64).

That the eye is focused upon here yields some insights into Yasuko's projection. It was not Akio's eye she had stabbed, but her own—her spirit and intuitive powers, or that sight which enables one to look deep and openly within. By maiming his vision in her dream, she had, in effect, cut herself off from her real problem, blinding herself and her consciousness. Important, too, in the dream are the feelings of guilt which emerge. Her affair with Ibuki is now experienced in a new light—as a violation of her husband's memory. Akio's real death by an avalanche had been viewed as a collective event; therefore, she assumed no responsibility for it. Her dream, however, pointed to her as the murderess and the blinder, guilty of having killed him a second time.

The entire stabbing incident may also be viewed as the maiming or destruction of Yasuko's *animus* (the masculine principle existing within her unconscious). Akio's death, then, is a premonitory image of the demise of her own subliminal maleness. Henceforth, Yasuko will yield completely to the woman's world—the matriarchate.

The dream marks a turning point in Yasuko's actions. She no longer really feels anything for Ibuki. Nor does she enjoy any kind of communication or relationship with him. Sex for her has become a completely impersonal act; it simply fulfills a need. Becoming more and more Mieko's "puppet," she lives out the *shadowy* destiny allotted to her by her archetypal mother. She even asks Mieko's advice as to whether she should marry. Yes is the answer; she should not live on memories alone, and, by the same token, she should complete her work on spirit possession. Mieko also feels a change: "You are my real daughter," she tells Yasuko; "the woman in me that I tried, but failed to pass on to Harume has found new life in you" (68).

As a daughter substitute, Yasuko continues to live out her shadow existence as Mieko's sensual aspect, which has long since withered in the older woman. Mieko is the head; Yasuko, the body. The traditionally hereditary role of shamaness, passed on to Mieko by her father, is to be bequeathed to Yasuko, her substitute daughter. As Mieko's appendage—the bearer of the shadow—she is to become *actor* and carry out her will. Together they will work, as Amaterasu had with her weavers, transliterating their heavenly designs into earthly dimensions.

Yasuko's admiration for Mieko is unparalleled, as is the mystery which surrounds her immobile—and sacred—countenance. Elusive in her quiet resignation, she is described as "a woman whose heart was as secretive as a garden of flowers at night; the mingled scent of unseen blossoms trailed from her every gesture" (93).

In time, Mieko reveals a crucial confidence to Yasuko. The essay she had kept so well concealed all these years, "The Shrine in the Fields," was written for the man she loved deeply, the father of her twins, who was killed on a tour of duty in China. Only after the death of her son did Mieko decide to bring Harume home to live with her. Since that time she has devoted most of her energies, emotions, and attention to this arrestingly beautiful but brain-damaged girl.

Harume is compared to "a large white flower bathed in light, magnificent in her isolation"—both physical and mental (39). As "she blinked slowly, moving her lashes like a dark butterfly beating its wings in time with its respirations, she resembled the Zo no onna mask," that of the "coldly beautiful woman" of exalted rank (41). Like her mother, she has an impassable and fixed expression, existing as she does in a different dimension—the transpersonal sphere. Unlike her mother, however, she is unable to return to the rational domain and communicate with others in a normal and logical way:

> Against the pallor of her face, lusterless and empty as a blank white wall, her big dark eyes and heavy eyebrows stood out exactly like those of an ukiyo-e style beauty drawn in india ink on fine white Chinese paper. There was something vaguely disturbing about her face, a sort of incoherence, as though the pitiable slumber of her mind had disconnected each vivid feature from the other. (70)

Mieko's plans for Harume are maturing; the religious ritual she has resolved to carry out, with the help of Yasuko, can now proceed as scheduled. Yasuko sets a rendezvous with Ibuki, at his insistence. The locus of the meeting has been predetermined by her, as has the time: nine o'clock in the evening, in what used to be her husband's study, where she now carries on her work on spirit possession. No one but she has been allowed in the room since Akio's demise. A dark, cavelike area, enclosed and warm like a mother's womb, it could be conceived now, symbolically speaking, as a receptacle for hidden energy. Alchemical mixtures could be cooked within this protected dwelling; magical forces could enact an initiation ritual.

Mieko has prepared Harume for the sacred phallic ritual. She has bathed, perfumed, and oiled her body most carefully; combed her long raven hair with loving tenderness; and colored her lips in bright camellia tones, so as to bring out her ripening sensuality. When all is in readiness and the purification procedure is complete, Yasuko takes Harume by the hand and leads her to the study, the *temenos* for the enactment of the sacred mystery. The room glows pink from the lamp, as if it were the dawn of a new day and of a new life. Still, it is night, for in the garden the late moon sends "dark pine shadows across the frozen ground" (103).

That the Moon God, Tsuki-yomi, rather than Amaterasu, should reign emphasizes the importance of darkness, blackness, night, and the unconscious in the transformation ritual. Tsuki-yomi is the force in Japan which sees to vegetation and fertility rituals and which regulates the growing process in a realm deprived of light. An unconscious force, Tsuki-yomi represents passivity and receptivity—indirect rather than direct experience and knowledge. His power will make its way unnoticed into Harume's unconscious. Like the moon, a reflection of the sun's rays, Harume is deprived of light and is a passive recipient in the sacrificial mystery about to take place.

The Japanese have always been moon lovers. The eerie and mysterious light which emanates from this body suggests a dim, insinuating, shaded world, never brilliant, and rather remote. Objects lit by moonlight are not individualized but blend into the environment, hazy and essentially obscure. The soft light of the moon's rays, moving about in complex designs and forms, times the modulations occurring in the secret world of gestation.

Night is sacred to the acolyte, about to begin the phallic ritual. Ibuki steps into the dimly lit study, where Yasuko has already placed wine and curaçao. Like the mediums of old, and contemporary ones as well, she has provided her acolyte with spirits and drugs to increase his sensibility and diminish his level of consciousness, thus altering his body chemistry and affecting his nervous system. Ibuki imbibes magic brews.

The sacred space has now been sanctified. Ibuki holds Yasuko close and then feels himself dreaming, "transported into another realm"—spellbound:

> Giving himself over to her, he fell into the bed in the shadow of the curtain, his body enmeshed with hers . . . after closing his eyes in comfortable exhaustion, having been drawn again and again into dream after blinding dream, he started suddenly at the coldness of the hair on his arm in the dark. He pushed back the curtain by his pillow, and the fading light of the moon flowed in, illuminating in soft gray beams a woman's face of snowy whiteness, the heavy brows and thick downswept lashes alone black, as if drawn with a brush: Harume. (110)

Stunned, Ibuki pulls away. Harume opens her eyes. She lies there exquisitely, in utter stillness, her face wearing the expression of the *Masugami*, the young madwoman. Has he been drugged? Ibuki wonders. Has he been dreaming? He drops off into another profound sleep, only to awaken later and find Yasuko next to him in bed. Has she been with him all night? he asks. Yes, certainly. Or has it been Harume? No. She has her own room, Yasuko tells him emphatically. Ibuki is perplexed and tells her: "But in the night you changed into her, I'm sure of it. . . . Did you come I wonder, or was it I who went? . . . In the hands of someone like you, a man is destined to become a fool" (112).

Ibuki, the male consort, has followed the dictates of the Great Mother with the help of Yasuko, her votary. His role in the grand scheme of things has been to fertilize the Mother through the Maiden, to nourish and fructify her as well as the family, the race, and the nation. Subservient to the Great Mother, he becomes a follower, not an innovator. Under subdued rays of the moon, that universal gauge whose function it is to govern the cycles of nature, Ibuki fertilizes the woman, in keeping with his karma. Acting in the world of shadows—in the subliminal sphere—he is no longer responsible for his actions. Confusion has set in. He is a being who has not come into his own, an unenlightened force, a funnel for transpersonal energies, and a vehicle of the shamaness's will.

The Maiden becomes Mother; death is transformed into life.

Fukai

Ibuki continues his trysts with Yasuko in Akio's study. Only once more does the No *Masugami* mask appear to him in his dreams. Difficulties arise, however. Ibuki's wife, Sadako, who has hired a detective to follow her husband, learns that Ibuki is entering a "witches' den" in the evenings and that Harume is going to have a baby.

What is a witch that such power has been attributed to this kind of woman for so many centuries and in so many lands? Witches may be looked upon in part as materializations of the shadow. If what they represent is incompatible with the ego, they may be incarnated as hideous and destructive forces. Such are Mieko and Yasuko for Sadako: evil and dangerous beings representing the basest of instinctual drives. Man-stealers, festering forces living in an airless and insalubrious terrain, they carry out their unregenerate practices on the most primitive of levels—by the light of the moon—like the Lamias, the Harpies, and the Hecates of the West.

Time passes. Mieko takes Harume to the doctor. She is in her third month of pregnancy, but because of a retroflexed womb and her mental retardation, the doctor suggests an abortion. Should she go through with the pregnancy, he warns, she might die. But Mieko has no intention of allowing the pregnancy to be terminated.

When she had heard her daughter was going to have a baby, her "expression remained mistily vague and impalpable," but she had descended into another level of being, where her joy could be experienced in the silence of solitude. Yasuko was entranced by the daring nature of Mieko's scheme and joyful over the part she had played in its coming to fruition. The thought of a baby with Akio's blood flowing in its veins tantalized; Akio would be resurrected in the baby. The matriarchate was functioning to fulfill itself. Yasuko tells Mieko: "You and I are accomplices, aren't we, in a dreadful crime—a crime that only women could commit. Having a part to play in this scheme of yours, Mother, means more to me than the love of any man" (126).

Mieko has suddenly become more aware of the meaning of "the deep and turbid male strength within her"—that power which had guided her through her ordeals and her years of emotional wanderings. Like Amaterasu, she is her father's daughter; archetypal, she is mystery. Sleek, smooth, her mask tightly placed upon her face, she has become what her lover had called her years back, "gracious as a goddess"—an object of worship with whom even he, the father of her children, could not relate. In a letter from China, he wrote: "You appear infinitely generous, but you are a woman of infinite passion, in hate as well as in love. Therefore, I have at times feared you and even tried to get away from you" (105).

Mieko thinks deeply of the infant gestating in Harume's belly, and she has a vision

> of an ancient goddess lying stretched out in the underworld, a prey of death. Her flesh was putrid and swarming with maggots, her decaying form covered with all manner of festering sores that smoldered and gave off black sparks. The luridness of the sight sent the goddess' lover fleeing in horror, and the moment that he turned and ran, she arose and swept after him in fury, all the love she had borne him transformed utterly into blinding hatred. A woman's love is quick to turn into a passion for revenge—an obsession that becomes an endless river of blood, flowing on from generation to generation. (127)

Further comparisons between Amaterasu and Mieko are fitting. Hadn't the heart of Amaterasu's father, Izanagi, been virtually broken when his wife, Izanami, died in childbirth? Hadn't he followed her to the underworld kingdom of Yomi to bring her back? When he finally arrived there, he saw that her body had rotted away. "What a hideous and polluted land I have come to unaware," he thought as he fled in horror and haste, lest the Ugly Women of Yomi restrain him and prevent him from leaving.[21]

As in the case of Izanami, aspects of Mieko died after she had given birth, after the discovery of her husband's betrayal with the maid, and after the receipt of her lover's letter conveying his less than powerful love for her. Her years of ordeal had strengthened her, but they had also rigidified her. Her obsessive hatred had led to a condition of stasis and to virtual victimization by this irrational condition. What had died from disuse—her healthy outlook upon life—had become putrescent and transformed (as the dream indicated) into maggots. With the birth to be, however, a change takes place within her psyche: The heretofore gangrenous elements are turning into living and healthy flesh. A symbol of futurity and continuity has awakened her creative and maternal urge, and, with it, love is being resurrected. Ebullient, violent, and all-encompassing, love, which had withered so long ago, is emerging anew. She will be a woman fulfilled. Warmth and radiance glow in her face; the persona is fluidifying, as communication between unconscious and conscious spheres resumes. The moat has been breached. Sensing the meaning of the change occurring within her, she allows a "faint tear," which contains "all the anguish of which she never spoke," to trickle from her eye. Lady Rokujo, her mentor, that violent and deprived side of her, has resolved. No longer living in exile, she and her shadow are ready to join the real world.

Ibuki happens to visit a place called Arashiyama a few months later. He wanders idly into the "Shrine in the Fields," the temple compound which Mieko had written about, where Heian emperors used to go for excursions, and where Harume is staying during her pregnancy. Despite its condition of abandonment, the beauty of the locale deeply moves him. The pines mingle with cherry trees dotting the precinct around the Jikoji temple; the stone lantern, representing deity, the torii gate, the purification fonts, the chestnut trees, and the golden flowers with cream-colored corollas, which Mieko had described, are all there. Then, as if from nowhere, Ibuki hears a voice—low and toneless—singing a children's snow song:

> Snow is falling,
> snow is falling;
> the lane is gone,
> buried in white . . .
> alas, alas,
> the way to my sweetheart's house,
> vanished from sight. (135)

Although he has never heard Harume's voice, he guesses it is she who is singing the Kanazawa snow song. Non-color accentuates her own features, increasing their stillness. Ibuki looks through the fence at Harume's stomach, swollen with child. He wonders whether her retardation will appear ugly to him:

> But in her blank and fair-skinned face, the dark eyes brimming with melancholy shadows like those of a handsome cat, he was relieved to find beauty so great that its lack of vivacity was all the more moving—a beauty that turned fear into pity. (136)

He looks in reverence at this beautiful feminine form which contains the mystery of life.

The baby is born. Harume dies of heart failure. As Izanami had sacrificed her life when giving birth to the deity of fire, thereby regenerating new cycles at different levels, so Harume has returned to her primordial condition, in order to bring forth the new.

Yu, the old nurse, holding the newborn in her arms, looks at it with the greatest love and tenderness: It is the image of Akio and Harume. No sooner has Yasuko taken the baby from Yu than she knows she loves it as her own. And when Mieko gazes upon its face, she feels herself peering into "the vast, mysterious depths" within her and suddenly realizes she is eternal.

The child is the beginning and the end: the *renatus in novam infantiam*. Fruit of a shamaness's powerful will and longing, this child is Mieko's creation. Its gestation had taken place in the temple precinct where Harume had been brought up, and where she returned for her pregnancy. Hence it may be said that the infant had received the blessings of the *kami* and of Amaterasu, indicating the collective nature of this sacred creation born to a family—and to the World of the Mothers.

Some months later, the *Fukai* mask is brought to Mieko by the No master's daughter. Its numinosity and its sadness move Mieko to her very depths. She gazes at

> the carved image [which] lay quietly with the yellowish hardness of a death mask. The long, conical slope of the eyelids, the melancholy, sunken cheeks, and the subdued red of the mouth with its blackened teeth—all conveyed the somber and grief-laden look of a woman long past the age of sensuality. (138)

The *Fukai* mask, displaying the features of a middle-aged mother, mature in understanding and in years—the living image of strength and courage—has allowed Mieko to rise above adversity and to bring forth new life amid the debris of an old and decaying world. She takes the mask in her hands and studies its "sunken-cheeked, sorrow-stricken face." Its loneliness and solemnity had once mirrored her inner world. Now, as she looks at it with veneration "in the lingering daylight like twin blossoms on a single branch," it spells the intensity of her grief at the loss of her children, and her bitterness and loneliness in a world devoid of love. Suddenly, however, when she has heard the crying of the newborn, "the mask dropped from her grasp as if struck down by an invisible hand" (41). She is "as if in a trance"; then, seemingly ordered to do so by some supernatural power, she "reached out and covered the face of the mask with her hand." The *Fukai* has been shed and is replaced by another: love in the form of the child.

Bathed in the gentle light of her titulary deity, Amaterasu, Mieko has become Universal Mother—the giver of life and the guardian of childbirth. Yasuko, the agent of her power, Ibuki, the inseminator, and Harume, the virgin, have fulfilled destiny in the enactment of a sacred mystery.

10 Anita Desai's *Fire on the Mountain:* A Rite of Exit

Anita Desai's novel *Fire on the Mountain* (1977) dramatizes the ordeals of an initiatory experience: the rite of exit from life. The world "initiation" comes from the Latin *in ire*, meaning "to go within," or to reconstruct one's knowledge of life. Nanda Kaul, a great-grandmother and the protagonist of *Fire on the Mountain*, undertakes just such a discipline, which alters and amplifies her existential and religious outlook. She becomes *another*, fully prepared for the rite of exit.

Nanda Kaul, an earthly replica of certain Hindu deities, is archetypal in stature: a complex of opposites, both mortal and immortal, individual and universal. Like the Shiva/Parvati couple, she is psychologically androgynous: feminine and masculine, passive and active. In the manner of *shakti*, that vital energy which moves throughout nature, Nanda Kaul's inner currents course through her, in nuanced or violent tempos. Identifiable also with Kali, her destructive/dark side sometimes predominates, when circumstances require a balancing of irregularities.

Desai's archetypal Old Woman is sign and countersign—the repository of filled and unfulfilled needs and feelings which the reader discovers and slowly sorts out during the course of the narrative. At the outset of the novel, Nanda Kaul gives the impression of enjoying harmony of being. The prototypal Indian woman, she has been both wife and mother. Her formerly active empirical existence justifies her present withdrawal on a mountaintop in the Punjab region. She has chosen to live out her remaining years in this *topos*—which is really an *a-topos*, a non-place—in serenity and repose. Here, too, will her initiation be completed; and, psychologically, an ex-centering or de-centering of her ego will take place.

The impediments to the achievement of Nanda's goal, when viewed symbolically, must be seen as obstacles purposefully set on her path, forcing her to struggle with troublesome adversities. Her combat will compel her to come to terms with factors she had either rejected or overlooked during her active years as mother and wife. The *agonia* she encounters in the process of gaining awareness arouses contents within her subliminal realm that might otherwise have lain dormant. Once energized and brought to consciousness, her view of life broadens. New orientations have expanded and enriched her vision, allowing her to pass from an ego-centered, limited domain to a supraindividual, cosmic sphere (the Absolute or *atman*), to become multiple and also One.

That Nanda must go through an initiatory process in order to reconstruct her knowledge of life is in keeping with Hindu dicta. The real world, it is believed, is the inner one. The exterior realm—Maya (Cosmic Illusion)—is a deception which remains impenetrable until an individual's blindness gives way to sight. Psychologically, Nanda's ordeal dramatizes a dispersion of the ego (center of consciousness) into the Self (total psyche).

Anita Desai, born in 1937, is the daughter of a Bengali father and a German mother. Educated in Delhi, and a graduate of Delhi University, she has been writing short stories and novels since she was a child. *Fire on the Mountain* won for her the National Academy of Letters Award and other prestigious accolades. The mother of four children, Desai makes her home in Bombay.

The Archetypal Old Woman

Nanda Kaul, tall, thin, and stately, is the archetypal Old Woman par excellence. Representative of a structural dominant of the psyche, she is a product of both her primordial past and of her own individuality.[1] Her name alone takes us back to both a historical and mythical past, to a powerful dynasty reigning in India at the time of Alexander the Great, and to Nanda, Lord Krishna's foster father. Like her great Vedic Aryan ancestors who inhabited the mountaintops near the Himalayas, so Nanda also has chosen to live close to nature, bathing in its vastness and brilliance as well as in its aridity and shadow.

Nanda's retreat is located at Carignano, near Kasauli, a hill station 1,900 meters above the Punjab plains and accessible only by footpath. Kasauli could boast of a Pasteur Institute, a mountain market, and tribesmen with Nepalese and Tibetan features, as well as a glorious historical and mythical past. Archaeological excavations undertaken at Kasauli and its environs yielded artifacts dating back to 3000 B.C. It was here, too, that Sikh Guru (Gobind Singh, 1666–1708) lived for twenty-five years struggling against the Mughals. This highland area of the Punjab—"The Land of Snow-capped Mountains"—is also associated with Valmiki, the alleged author of the *Ramayana*, one of India's great religious works.

Nanda is first glimpsed pausing under a pine tree near her small hilltop house. Her eyes, looking down onto the valleys below and up toward the jagged cliffs in the distance, seem to be ferreting out the mysteries hidden amid and beyond the seemingly endless slopes, ridges, and gorges. Nanda's eye, like Shiva's organ of perception and intuition, takes in both the world of appearances and that which lies beyond the sensate domain. It grasps the multiple and the disparate, the articulated and the unarticulated, and transforms these into a single unified principle.

Conscious of the law of devolution—old age and a concomitant decrease in active participation in life's work—Nanda looks forward to the slowing-down process. Virtually alone among the pines (symbols of immortality, since they remain green all year), she lives cut off from the outside world. Animals and insects are her only companions, and she has made their languages her own. As for their vibrations—their music—they parallel her heartbeat, as though she has become one with *shakti*. Nevertheless, from the very outset, we note that not everything within her psyche runs smoothly: Here and there, irregularities and smarting sensations surge.

The music emanating from animals and insects infiltrates Nanda's world: It speaks to her in several notes at times, or in but a single tone, conveying both emotion and spirituality. The "scented sibilance" of the cicadas, for example, replicates the stridulations of life's duality and, by extension, her own. Nature's silences and sounds are a complementary couple, presences that befriend or alienate her. The cuckoo as it flutters by and the eagle soaring toward the sun make their songs heard. The wind floating through the pines sends out its spiritual message in natural orchestrations. Such pure intensities become vehicles for subtle modal systems in Desai's text and also add a religious flavor to it. The wind, for the Hindu, ushers in the presence of Indra, the great Vedic atmospheric god responsible for rain and thunder, so vital to life in India. It is he as well who assures the crucial connection between heaven and earth. He, like Nanda, has made his home on a mountaintop—the fabulous Mount Meru, purportedly the center of the earth, somewhere to the north of the Himalayas.

Nanda, in the manner of a goddess, stands tall and erect, her dark sari emphasizing the austerity and sparseness of her life, in tune with the stark rocks that surround her. She constitutes a law unto herself, living, as did Lord Shiva, the fashioner of the world, outside of linear space and time. Resembling Shiva's consort, Parvati, the "Daughter of the Himalaya Mountain,"[2] Nanda, too, embodies feminine creative energy. Let us recall that it was Parvati who provided Shiva with *shakti* power, described as follows in a Tantric text:

> Never can She be known
> in Her perfect completeness,
> and Her omnipotence is in all
> that She continually does.
> Do they not say
> that even Shiva is unable to stir,
> lies as a corpse,
> until She grants him Her energies?[3]

As Nanda stands rooted to the ground—stark against a sun-drenched sky—she seems withered, severed, unrealized. Although she feeds, spiritually and psychologically, on the world around her—trees, grass, mountains, gorges, and cliffs—the nourishment gained from these natural elements is insufficient to sustain her and to give her the force necessary to perform her exit ritual.

Like the traditional Indian mother, who dedicates herself wholly to caring for husband and children, Nanda has fulfilled her obligations, but without joy or love. Disillusioned early in life, for reasons we discover only at the end of the narrative, Nanda's emotional universe has been relatively empty.

As she observes the large spaces that lie before her, colors, representing emotional states, are woven into the narrative by the wind-driven branches of the trees which shed dark and luminous shadows over the scene. The antithetical hues which emerge may be regarded as a projection of Nanda's own zones of conflict: feelings of disapproval and dissatisfaction existing within her, but remaining invisible on the surface. As her gaze rests on the irises or the apricot trees close to the house, or on the hoopoe bird which "struck down at it [the apricot] and tore at its bright flesh then flew off with a lump in its beak," she understands that this giant organism we call nature eats of itself to survive and that she, too, is nourished by it. The bird which ate of the apricot may be identified with those mentioned in the *Upanishad* which eat of the fruit and represent individual souls. Those birds which merely observe without partaking of the nourishment stand for universal souls.

To gain the tranquility she so desperately yearns for, Nanda has learned to peer into nature, perhaps unconsciously, using her field of vision as a meditative device—a *mandala*—enabling her to transcend the phenomenal world. Flower, tree, and cliff permit her to indwell, to center her gaze on a point in real space, thereby escaping the world of human suffering, where she has neither loved nor been loved. The mysterious power that seems to be tearing at her soul/psyche may be likened to the bird that had ripped the flesh from the apricot. The force within her that has remained unacceptable and unresolved is yet to be discovered.

Nanda withdraws into her house—her figurative and literal *temenos*. A sanctuary for meditation and for indwelling, it is a further protection from the medley of disturbances which the outer world thrusts upon her. Within its walls, she feels she can reach down into her center, stand firm without experiencing the pull and tug of the tension of opposites in the empirical world. When returning outside, however, and much to her dismay, she sees her cook and the mailman down the path, chatting. The latter's appearance she considers to be an unmitigated intrusion. He must be carrying a letter for her, she reasons, and her annoyance mounts. Whether due to the play of the sun's rays or to her own inner readings of the scene, she sees both figures "going up in flames with their arms outstretched, charred, too, about the trunks" (12). The fire image, representative of psychic energy, acts as a catalyst for Nanda, evidently forcing into consciousness some unwanted level of being—something unwilled. Rather than bringing her the condition of quietude for which she longs, the mailman's presence—and the letter he is to deliver—paves the way for an ominous and eruptive condition.

To offset her anger at the violation of her peace of mind, a whole floral world suddenly caresses her eye: marigolds, irises, yellow roses, pink and blue carnations, fuchsias. Cuplike receptacles and celestial containers, flowers stand for life's ephemerality, the rapid passage of all that is beautiful in the telluric domain. By means of these concretions, Nanda peers more forcefully into nature, penetrating its subdued and brash luminosities as well as its dispositions and signs. Her feelings, working in conjunction with the shapes and colorations which are the object of her attention, arouse certain patterns of behavior within her unconscious, which in turn trigger corresponding emotional states.

Nanda sits down on her veranda to read the letter the mailman has just handed her, and here Desai halts the pace of her narrative, thus arousing tension. Descriptions follow of geraniums, fuchsias, apricot trees, bul-buls, and birds of all types, vibrating, inhaling and exhaling the aromas of all living things. The musical tones of the bird songs, refined and dematerialized as they make their way to Nanda's ear, are received as carefully structured compositions. Like a *mantra*—the *OM*—an auditory perception which reaches various levels of a person's consciousness, so nature's noises, when concentrated upon, become carrier waves of universal tone, evoking feelings and relationships between sound and psyche in the process.[4]

Nanda is forced to cut off her *mantra*-like meditation by a butterfly—a creature symbolizing flightiness, transience, and inconstancy, and suggesting the illusory nature of human preoccupations. The butterfly puts an end to Nanda's rapturous vision of life as she would like to lead it. In the *Bhagavad Gita*, we read that "humans rush to their end like [the] butterfly hovers around [a] brilliant flame."[5] Nanda is likewise affected by the hustle and bustle of peripheral existence, by Maya/Illusion, the "Mother of the World." Despite the fact that she seeks to repulse duality, she is, nevertheless, continuously caught up in its complexities. She is unaware of the fact that only through existence in the concrete world (and not through escape from it) will feelings of opposition within her surface and antagonistic sensations be activated, confronted, coped with, and perhaps eventually integrated within her psyche.

The letter, which Nanda finally opens, is from her daughter, Asha. The least favored of her progeny, Asha had spent all of her days beautifying herself instead of devoting herself to her daughter, Tara. As a result, Tara married a diplomat who drank and brutalized her. After several breakdowns, she decides to go to Switzerland with her husband to try once again to put her life with him in order. Raka, their daughter, who has just recovered from a serious bout with typhoid, is too thin and frail to stand such a journey. The mountain air at Carignano and her great-grandmother's good food would—they have decided—put flesh onto her bones.

As Nanda's eyes "floated" over her daughter's letter "bloated with self-confidence," her anger flares (16). She resents that such a decision was made without consulting her; she also takes umbrage at Raka's presence, which she regards as an unwanted intrusion. As she sits back on her chair and muses, a whole personal past infiltrates her present; she thinks back to her role as a model wife to her husband, vice-chancellor of a small university in the Punjab, and all the colleagues and friends she used to entertain. Everything she did for her family was always perfect. Everyone said so. The servants were well trained and obedient; the children, brought up according to tradition, were a source of pride to the parents. How fortunate the vice-chancellor was to have her as a wife, people used to say. The perceptive individual, however, could detect a strange expression in Nanda's eyes, mirroring a distaste for her position and function: "like a pair of black blades, wanting to cut them, despising them, crawling grey bugs about her fastidious feet" (18). Nevertheless, she bore secretly all of her spiritual, physical, and emotional deprivations.

Nanda's reaction to her condition as wife and mother is not unique in India. A basic conflict—the ascetic versus the erotic—pervades Indian culture in general and the woman in particular. The Shiva Puranas teach the devout that Shiva was an ascetic, invulnerable to desire. Yet, because of his very detachment and remoteness, he caused his wife, Parvati, to want him all the more. While ruling out the call of the flesh, Shiva was, paradoxically, the householder and therefore a lover. Let us recall that Shiva was the one who destroyed Kama, the god of love. To do away with this deity served only, psychologically speaking, to increase love's power over the world.[6]

Nanda is an ascetic. In this regard, she is Shiva-like. Although the mother of many children, her sexuality had remained untouched, barren, and cold. Never having developed any real sexual or feeling relationship with her husband, she viewed the whole birth process with distaste. In the "small filthy missionary-run hospital," nurses were forever flitting around her but never helping her in any way. As for her children, they had always been a burden and an imposition—impostors of sorts. Drudgery, resentment, and despair stalked her at home, where she never really felt she belonged.

As readers follow Nanda in her repeated flashbacks, regressing further and further into a past that was anathema to her, they are exposed to increasingly turbulent vibrations and fiery innervations, as images of children at play emerge in her mind's eye: one falling from the swing, another stung by a wasp, a third wailing inconsolably. Clutter, noise, and toil mount in intensity. As the pace heightens, sparks fly; signs and de-signs explode like so many incendiary bombs, searing and charring an already troubled inner climate.

Some readers might label Nanda unfeeling or hardhearted since she is unwilling to receive her great-granddaughter. She feels, however, that she has earned the right to lead the life she wants, attempting to justify her decision to remain unburdened by petty daily details. As Nanda sits in thought, she again peers into the distance, observing the "bloodred gorge" dropping down from a cliff and the eagle flying about. How she longs to become one with the eagle as it glides freely before her in a seemingly unlimited expanse of sky!

The eagle, identified with celestial realms, stands in opposition to the matter-bound serpent, an animal of great importance in India and one which Desai will mention later in her narrative. As the eagle mounts from realm to realm—or, psychologically, from one level of consciousness to the next—it leaves the ego-centered sphere and merges with the transpersonal domains. Birds in general, and the eagle is no exception, are messengers between heaven and earth. Paradigms of liberation, they represent lightness and the soul escaping from the body—the condition Nanda would like to *know*. Nanda shuts her eyes in order to follow inwardly the eagle's circular flight, penetrating deeper dimensions while also, paradoxically, drawing her out of herself. By closing her eyes, she also indicates her desperate need to exclude the phenomenal domain and everything that spells strife and tension.

Mention must also be made of the cuckoo that flies by her moments later and sings out its musical message in a soft tonal language. In Vedic tradition, the cuckoo symbolizes the human soul prior to and after incarnation. Its nest stands for the body—the palace where the soul has placed itself for a period of time. Hence, it represents domesticity. Two contrary forces, then, are pulling at Nanda: the eagle and spatial flight (the body attempting to escape into ecstatic liberation); and the cuckoo, the homey bird calling her back to the workaday world, with its problems and hardships.

Nanda yearns to experience the *moksa* stage of life. As conveyed in the "Four Ends of Man" of the Hindu tradition, *brachmacharya*, *artha*, *kama*, and *moksa* are the four periods in a person's earthly sojourn. Although conceived of for men only, some women may also follow the pattern if impelled by an inner necessity. *Brachmacharya* refers to the student years, when one is initiated into Vedic studies and lives in an ashram; *artha*, to the period spent acquiring material wealth; *kama*, to the years when love and pleasure become important factors in life; and *moksa* (from the root *muc*, "to loose, set free, release, liberate"), to old age, when energies are turned inward and spiritual matters become all-encompassing, preparing the individual for his final release from the cycle of transmigrations. Of crucial importance in these four stages is the concept of *dharma*, from the root *dhr*, "to sustain." In the *Ramayana* we read: "From dharma issue profit and pleasure; one attains everything by dharma, which is the essence and strength of the world."[7]

Nanda seeks the quietist ideals to which the Hindu aspires: a withdrawal from or renunciation of life's activities. *Moksa* is identified with the flowering of a successful and fulfilled existence, the last human adventure.[8]

Nanda's need for isolation on her mountaintop retreat is, however, an escape from commitment and from the pain of life's dualities. Any intrusion, therefore, into her willed solitude, even the ring of the telephone, is considered offensive to her. The call from her friend Ila Das shortly after Nanda's receipt of the letter sounds more shrill to her ear than normal, and her friend's "hideous" and "screeching" voice grates on her nerves. No, she explains, she cannot visit her at this time since her great-granddaughter is coming to stay with her and she will be too busy.

Society—in any way or form—is a vise for Nanda. The more she thinks of Raka's visit, the greater is her sense of frustration, which Desai transmutes physically in hot, gluey, and insect-filled images:

> Flies, too lazy for flight, were caught in its midway web and buzzed languorously, voluptuously, slowly unsticking their feet and crawling across the ceilings, the window panes, the varnished furniture. Inside, the flies. Outside, the cicadas. Everything hummed, shrilled, buzzed and fiddled till the strange rasping music seemed to materialize out of the air itself or the heat. (22)

The continuously moving, grinding, buzzing flies and insects, their clamminess and gumminess, and the heat enfolding her and its stickiness create an unpleasant visceral condition mirroring Nanda's psychological attitude. She is glued to her flighty, insectlike world, not yet liberated. *Moksa* is not hers, despite her outwardly ascetic ways and her withdrawal into her hilltop *temenos*.

Still, she does her utmost to offset her involvement in earthly matters. In the afternoon, for example, when looking at the sun (considered a symbol of the heightening of perception and cognition), Nanda closets herself in her room, psychologically shutting out the conscious sphere and allowing free access to her subliminal domain. There she lies on her bed, closes her eyes, and withdraws into her darkness, visualizing in her mind's eye the sun's colorful orbs transforming themselves into *mandalas*. To this meditative device she adds the ritual of gesture (*mudra*).

Mudra, like *mantra* and *mandala*, is a meditative device which permits its practitioner to enter into communion with the collective sphere. Designed to harness disparate emotions, *mudra* is used, as a kind of self-hypnosis provoked by physical means, to prolong concentration and to take an individual, psychologically speaking, from ego-consciousness to Self-consciousness.

Placing her hands in a special position on her chest, Nanda lies immobile, like a "charred tree trunk in the forest" or a "broken pillar of marble in the desert" (23). Both images depict energy being broken and cut off from her, leaving her listless and virtually lifeless on her bed of despair.

During these periods of withdrawal, Nanda's thoughts again wander back to her youth and to her motherhood. She remembers how she used to steal an afternoon here and there from her family to rest, rising rapidly at teatime to serve the milk and sandwiches. Only at night did she know some semblance of repose: The coldness of the moon felt so refreshing to her as she stepped out onto the lawn in its "ghostly light" (25). As she thinks back upon her husband's death, and her children who had helped her move to Carignano, she remembers the pleasure she took when she gave them nearly everything she owned. She wants nothing for herself and luxuriates in the bare empty space which is her new home. Her devolution as great-grandmother—the archetypal Old Woman—has detached her from the material sphere. Even the garden outside her house at Carignano is sparse and spare. It, too, is going through a process of aging, of withering away and limitation.

Will Raka distract her from the great serenity she feels is her due? Will she disturb her privacy? As Nanda makes her way out of her darkened room, she bumps her knee on her bedpost and bruises it—a physical indication of the pain which Raka's arrival holds in store.

Raka: The Moon

That Raka's name means "moon" indicates the role she will play in Desai's narrative. Unlike the celestial body, however, the young girl's face is neither round, calm, nor radiant. She looks like one of "those dark crickets that leap up in fright but do not sing" (39). Raka is thin, her head is shorn, and she shuffles as she walks up the hill. When greeting her great-grandmother, "there was a sound of bones colliding" (40).

The word "collide" conveys both the psychological and physical impact Raka's presence is to have on Nanda. The contact between two bony bodies expresses the violence of clashing generations and conflicting life-styles. Raka, the archetypal child, is emerging in all of her innocence as if from the collective womb of nature, whereas the aged woman is preparing to return to the earth/tomb. The collision of these two forces and the hurt that is to ensue will prepare Nanda for the painful illumination preceding the completion of her initiation ritual.

Psychologically, Raka is a shadow figure. She represents the unlived aspects in Nanda's unconscious, elements the older woman has kept hidden in some dismal corner of her subliminal world, cast aside because they were deemed unusable by her ego. Like the moon, which shines only when the sun's rays focus upon it, Raka is a reflective force: She is consciousness illumined by her unconscious. Deprived of her own light, Raka is depicted only through Nanda's perception of her. Indeed, we may even look upon her as her great-grandmother's creation, or as an incarnation of Nanda as a little girl, before she was forced to conform to India's social structure. Prior to Nanda's becoming a role model for Indian women, she had not been the disconnected, disoriented, deprived, and identityless human being she later became.

Like the Moon God, Chandra, who measures time, is the bearer of nectar (*soma*), and is said to foster thought and ideas, Raka represents a period in Nanda's life. Contained within her being is that all-vital nectar which nourishes the gods; and because of the subdued light which encapsulates the moon on certain nights, she fosters indirect knowledge. As the moon is responsible for bringing water onto a parched earth and nourishing it, so Raka will fecundate Nanda's inner world, allowing her to articulate, to conceptualize, and then to assimilate those primordial waters which give birth to a fresh approach to life. With increasing consciousness, Nanda will be able to integrate the Raka factor—those chthonian forces—into her psyche, thereby helping her dilate her life experience, and enabling her to pass into death.

Raka, a reflection of Nanda as she used to be, is free, provocative, and essentially naive. We see her in many stances: trudging up and down the path, rushing about the fields, climbing the cliffs, and descending into the gullies and gorges. More and more she comes to stand for undisciplined nature—that irresponsible life force that seeks to participate in primitive substance. Raka, like Nanda, is silent and uncommunicative; yet, renewing herself continuously in accordance with nature's rhythmic cycles, everything she feels, perceives, and intuits is lived inwardly. She shares nothing with other human beings; her libido is forever driven into that secret realm which, like the moon's, remains enveloped in darkness. Raka is mystery; she is secret. So, too, is Nanda. She does not know herself *plain*; she will have to learn to see through that network of hidden matter if she wants to experience harmony.

Raka's reactions as she enters Nanda's house for the first time are described as follows:

> She felt over the room with her bare feet. She walked about as the newly caged, the newly tamed wild ones do, sliding from wall to wall on silent, investigating pads. She patted a cheek of wood here, smoothed a ridge of plaster there. She met a spider that groomed its hairs in a corner, saw lizard's eye blinking out of a dark groove. She probed the depth of dust on shelves and ledges, licked a window pane to cool her tongue-tip. (41)

Raka palpates, touches, senses, *feels* into life. The visceral and not the rational is her approach. Everything she investigates within and outside the house, as we shall see, she does with hands and feet—appendages which allow her to relate to the living world in silence, through body language. When she "sagged across the bed on her stomach," she feels its softness, hardness, and its contours (41). Later, rather than walk out of the house through the door, Raka slips one leg over the window frame to climb to freedom. At another time, she grabs fistfuls of hairy ferns, then strolls up the knoll rising behind the kitchen, inhales and exhales the odors of the giant deodar tree, grips and climbs it, and slides down its smooth bark, after which she rubs her hands on the rich earth with its gleaming pebbles.

What part of nature attracts Raka most? Not the garden and its flowers. They are too tame. As representatives of society and social consciousness, they are overly ordered. Structured ways have little allure for her. Cliffs and gorges, nature's dangerous features, hypnotize her. The wild, disheveled, frenetic powers beyond her reach lure her on. "The tip of the cliff and the sudden drop down the red, rock-spattered ravine to the plain"—that whole segment of life that she has not yet discovered and wants to *know*—fascinate her (41).

Nanda has never delved into these primal segments of her psyche, the very ones that "collided" with what was expected of her as mother and wife. She had been forced to adopt the facade of role model. Raka, in opposition, stands outside the pale, representing that whole unfulfilled universe.

As the days pass, Nanda realizes that, although Raka's presence is "irksome" to her, she becomes concerned if she is absent too long. When Raka becomes aware of Nanda's solicitude, she grows annoyed; she rejects her great-grandmother's observing eye, which she feels limits her freedom to bathe in the wholesomeness of nature. Yet, the two are alike: Both enjoy reclusion, although in opposite ways. Raka's approach to nature is visceral, whereas Nanda's is thought out, cerebral, viewed from a distance. Nanda never participates. She reasons. Her emotions are nevertheless involved, but they are angry and vengeful, inspired by the years of servitude forced upon her. Raka, on the other hand, lives her existence in full abandon, aware of nothing but joyful relatedness with an ever-nourishing nature.

What do cliffs represent, that Raka climbs their steep sides with such unabated joy and, reaching the top, bathes her body in the fresh and healthful wind-swept climes? Because of their hardness, cliffs represent durability and continuity. Unlike stones, however, which may be smooth and round, cliffs can be dangerous—jagged, sharp, and steep. One false move and Raka could fall to her death in the ravine. Careful as she mounts toward vertiginous heights, she is sure-footed, for her instincts guide her unhesitatingly every step of the way. Magnetized by the beauty of the Himalayan hills, Raka sees nature as a sign of her rapturous love for all that sprouts, grows, and generates life.

In contrast to the beauties of nature is the ugliness of the modern world. Shock rocks her being as Raka learns of the Pasteur Institute and its scientific experiments on animals. The cook warns her not to look through the bones of the dead animals that scientists have thrown into the ravine after completing their experiments: "It's a bad place." Jackals come to the ravine at night and chew up the bones; snakes make their home there, as do ghosts. Raka, however, is undaunted. Nothing frightens her. How could it? She is darkness. She symbolizes a whole chthonian realm representative of the unconscious.

The more Nanda observes Raka's wildness, the more set she is in refusing to be "drawn into a child's world again"; yet she feels a pull toward this moon force. Excitement, perhaps anxiety as well, spells life. Nanda notices "the child had a gift for *disappearance*," emerging and vanishing from the deep, as if paralleling Nanda's own instinctual trajectories. She is fascinated by Raka's cliff-climbing escapades: "scrambling up a stony hillside . . . wandering down a lane," stopping to examine an insect, "then dropping from the lip of a cliff" and passing out of sight only to show up moments later "from the dark like a soundless moth" that had visited "strange lands and seen fantastic" things (46). That Nanda associates her with a moth, a night-flying winged creature, parallels the butterfly image at the outset of Desai's novel. The moth and the butterfly both have antennae and sense organs. The former, devoid of color, is frequently indistinguishable from its background, existing in a participation mystique with the world at large, as does Raka.

Although Nanda is concerned each time Raka climbs to the top of a cliff, she cannot help but admire her fearlessness and openness. Projecting herself onto Raka activates her whole feeling world for the first time. She sees herself in this child, and feelings of tenderness and warmth replace those of coldness and austerity. Raka is Nanda at that age—a living presence who has aroused something within the older woman which had remained dormant within her for so many years.

The ravine, like the cliffs, also plays a role in Nanda's growing awareness and understanding of her spiritual and psychological condition. Raka, and Nanda through projection, is drawn to this long, deep hollow in the earth's surface; she wants to investigate this area worn down by the action of a body of water. Lower than other regions in the district, it can be considered the earth's receptacle for primordial vibrations—a cavelike, uterine area. For the Hindu, it may be likened to the "womb house" or *yoni*, the female counterpart to Shiva's "sacred phallus" (*lingam*), symbol of the male energetic factor inhabiting the world. Dating back to pre-Vedic times (2000 B.C.), *lingams* were placed in the holiest of areas in temples or caves. Combined with female energy, or *yoni*, they stood for the creative union that made for the procreation and sustenance of life. Shiva (*lingam*) and Parvati (*yoni*) are humankind's archetypal parents: Father and Mother of the world.[9] The ravine, then, is *yoni*—female energy—where water, moisture, and earth become active and the transformatory process goes on.

As Raka peers into the ravine, what she sees makes her forget the terrible heat and her physical discomfort:

> Her eye was on the heart of the agaves, that central dagger guarded by a ring of curved spikes, on the contortions of the charred pin trunks and the paralysed attitudes of the rocks. (48)

The ravine, or gorge, contains refuse and putrescent matter. For the alchemist, this rejected stuff spelled *nigredo* (*necro* in Old French), charred and blackened primordial matter. Not necessarily negative, this rich, rotting material contains the very substance that gives birth to new elements. Likewise, the unconscious—that dark shadow factor, that unformed, unlived substance—when investigated and palpated, can usher new and vaster visions into the world.

In the Hindu religion, the deity Kali is depicted in sculptures and paintings as a black woman with two dead bodies for earrings, a necklace made of skulls, and a girdle of dead men's hands. A gruesome hag with bony fingers, protruding teeth, red eyes, and breasts smeared with blood, she is always hungry and obsessively voracious. Kali worship may seem surprising at first for the Westerner, particularly when contrasting it to the Christian ideal of the immaculate Virgin Mary. For the Hindu and the Gnostic, however, to be "uncontaminated by the darker principle" in life is to reject the *shadow* on a psychological level. Just as good is implicit in life and in deity, so, too, is evil for the Hindu, and for mystics in general throughout the world. India's Mother Kali, then, is a "caressing-murdering symbolization of the totality of the world creating-destroying eating-eaten one."[10] She is the all-producing, all-annihilating factor in the existing and non-existing process which is life. The *Skanda Puranas* reads:

> Black as the petal of a blue lotus at night,
> black as the night touched by the light of the moon,
> Kali is the essence of Night,
> She who is called Sleep.
> She who is named Dream,
> She who is the joyous dancer of the cremation ground,
> She who chooses from among the corpses
> which souls shall be released
> from the bonds of existence—
> to know eternal bliss.[11]

Kali means time: the time it takes to grow and die, to give birth and to take back into the womb/tomb. Her blackness may be looked upon as a countercolor, representative of undifferentiated matter, the original tenebrous void, and the chthonian, passive, virtually inert, deathlike state. Like the Great Mother goddesses—the black Aphrodite, for example—who make their homes in obscure areas, operating in subdued, virtually unseen darkness, transforming the inert into the active matter, charred into flaming fire, so the uncreated becomes incarnated.

Psychologically, black Kali stands for the primitive, unconscious level within the psyche: the *prima materia*, the original chaos, the hermetic *nigredo*—initial obscurity before it has been brought to consciousness. Now that Raka has entered the physical domain and Nanda has penetrated it visually, the transformation ritual can commence: Stasis gives way to activity; the unlived to the lived.

That Raka sees a sleeping snake during one of her forays in the ravine is also of great significance. A personification of *naga*, the great serpent that directs terrestrial waters (lakes, ponds, rivers, and oceans), it represents the keeper of life's energy, the guardian of the riches in the sea. That it makes its presence known to Raka indicates, psychologically, that Nanda, through projection, is becoming aware of the immense power her shadow/Raka has encountered—a fecundating force in its own right. Although Raka has been warned not to explore the ravine, she disregards the advice, indicating her extreme need to see things through to the end, no matter what the dangers involved. And much to her joy, she even boasts that the snake she saw in the ravine did not bite her, that she welcomed its presence—a symbol of inner strength which rises from the earth and may some day, under proper circumstances, become sublimated and spiritualized.

The ravine, then, with its primal matter, its Kali blackness, its corpses, snakes, stray dogs, and other detritus/riches, is coupled with another image, that of fire, also aimed at enlightening Nanda.

As Raka stands staring out the window into distant space, she sees a storm brewing: dust, clouds, fire. Trees have been set ablaze, perhaps by lightning or due to the sun's intensity. Outside the house, disordered and disarranged powers are raging out of control; within the inner space, the *temenos*, action, both physical and verbal, is arrested. Raka is disappointed when she learns that the flames she saw were those of a small brush fire and not a full-fledged conflagration.

It must be noted that, for the Hindu, the fire principle and the Fire God, Agni, are of crucial importance. He represents the warmer of the unborn, the digestive fire within human beings, the household fire in the hearth, lightning in its atmospheric form, and the celestial fire in the sun's rays. As the swift messenger god in his capacity as fire, Agni connects earth and heaven. Since he exists in two pieces of wood but manifests himself only when these are rubbed together, he is considered a miracle worker.[12] In the *Rig-Veda* (I, 1) it is written:

> I extol Agni, the household priest, the divine minister of the sacrifice, the chief priest, the bestower of blessings.

> May that Agni, who is to be extolled by ancient and modern seers, conduct gods here.
>
> Through Agni may one gain day by day wealth and welfare which is glorious and replete with heroic sons.
>
> Agni, the sacrifice and ritual which you encompass on every side, that indeed goes to the gods.
>
> May Agni, the chief priest, who possesses the insight of a sage, who is truthful, widely renowned, and divine, come here with the gods.[13]

Raka's longing to see fire and flame indicates that she needs heat: psychologically, she has to be libidinized.[14] The moon or shadow qualities symbolized by Raka have to be given expression and have to be fluidified, vitalized, and electrified in order for Nanda to experience them transferentially. Libido arouses fire and force; psychologically, it helps the ego develop gradually out of the unconscious and experience its identity in a space-time continuum. It is that power that encourages the ego to connect with the unconscious contents.[15]

The psychic energy Agni brings into things, which obsesses Raka, and Nanda through projection, is that power that will help transform an undirected, unchanneled, and unredeemed force into an active, warm, loving, and creative power. No longer viewed merely as an external image, Agni/fire will have taken on an inner, psychic meaning.

Not long after the first brush fire, a real forest fire breaks out:

> The little pin-pricks of light went up in the black mass of the hill. They exploded here and there, ran up and down in lines, burnt clearly as the sky darkened, the glow reddened. . . . shivers ran through her, zigzag, leaving streams of sweat in their wake. Hugging herself with bone-thin arms, she stood on one leg, then the other, waiting. It was far away, across the valley, they could neither smell the burning pine trees nor hear the crackling and hissing. It was like a fire in a dream—silent, swift, threatening. (74)

Raka remains transfixed at the window as she gazes out, mesmerized by the sight. Agni is there, blazing in full glory, destroying and devouring, yet nourishing the earth and filling the universe with his infinite energies.

In time, the external fire is extinguished. Not, however, the inner blaze. Nanda tries to keep Raka within the *temenos*, to hold her attention by telling her tales about her childhood. She relates that her father had visited

Tibet and brought back exotic animals, Buddha figures, and other spectacular objects. Raka, however, "could no longer bear to be confined to the old lady's fantasy world when the reality outside appealed so strongly" (100). She escapes outside. Nanda remains within, moving "from one window to the other, mournfully" looking for Raka, annoyed by her own solicitude. A new feeling, with which she is not yet comfortable and with which she cannot yet cope, has taken flame within her. Nanda has begun to love the little girl tenderly and is moved by her wistfulness. Psychologically, Nanda has begun loving that part of herself that Raka represents. She has warmed up to her own qualities—to her shadow forces. What had formerly been cast out is now returning, integrating itself into her life.

The Exit Ritual

Raka/Moon/Shadow has made Nanda conscious of the aspects of her nature which she had repressed for so many years. No longer does she look out on life through her eyes alone. A whole visceral, feeling, sensate dimension has awakened into being. Perception through the mind is now accompanied by understanding via the body. So that *moksa* may be experienced, plenitude and balance are necessary to prepare for the exit ritual—to die to life and be reborn in the cosmic sphere.

Ila Das, Nanda's girlhood friend, is in the vicinity. She telephones Nanda, who, though she despises the idea, cannot *not* ask her to tea. Grotesque in appearance, Ila represents all that is awkward and old-fashioned in society. She is depicted as "proceeding towards Carignano with her uneven, rushing step, in her ancient white court shoes, prodding the tip of her great brown umbrella into the dust with an air of faked determination" (107). Young urchins jeer at her as she walks up the path, mocking "her little grey top-knot that wobbled on top of her head," her "spectacles that slipped down to the tip of her nose and were only prevented from falling off by an ancient purple ribbon looped over her ears," and the "grey rag of the petticoat that gaped dismally beneath the lace hem of her sari" (108).

Ila is a spectacle. A remnant of a defunct way of life and civilization, she is not by any means passive. She answers the jeering boys back, threatening to tell their teacher, and, in desperation, opens up her umbrella and charges at them. Ila is out of harmony with the world; she is retrograde, stilted, static, and unevolved. Contention and strife are "the motif of her life" (111). Her life is "contradiction" incarnate: disparate, fragmented, "simply not all of a piece" (110). Nanda now realizes that Ila "was that last little broken bit of a crazy life, fluttering up over the gravel like a bit of crumpled paper" (112). As for her voice, it is shrill, strained, jarring, cackling, screeching, and agitated. Even when Nanda and Ila were in school together, teachers and playmates had tried to soften that harsh, grating voice of hers—to no avail.

When Ila takes Raka's hand in greeting, as abruptly and rashly as she does everything else, she says to her: "My dear, you and I are simply bound to be friends, you know, *bound* to be" (114). She is unaware that in Raka's domain no binding or constraint is possible. Although she sits for a bit with the two old ladies as they reminisce, Raka "wilted" and could not participate in "that game of old-age—that reconstructing, block by gilded block, of the castle of childhood, so ramshackle and precarious" (116).

Ila's strident voice repulses Raka. Her insensitive manner annoys her, as do her tomboyish ways and her legs, "an inch or two above the ground" and swinging "to and fro, happily, as if five years old and at a party once more" (115). Then, amid the reminiscing, Ila begins singing "Darling, I am growing o-o-old," her voice more repulsive than ever. Desai writes:

> Nanda Kaul froze into a state of pale concrete. The entire weight of the overloaded past seemed to pour onto her like liquid cement that immediately set solid, incarcerating her in its stiff gloom. She sat with her lips tightly set and her eyes wide open, hardly able to believe in this raucous apparition now ripping into Honeysuckle Rose in a voice like an arrow that pierced Nanda Kaul's temple and penetrated her jaws, setting her teeth tingling. (118)

Ila is a *puella*, a girl who has remained an adolescent and never matured in any way. Added to her fundamental naivete are her staid and old-fashioned traits, her hypocrisy, her lack of taste and refinement, and her insensitivity. True, her life has been a series of misfortunes: Her father had died when she was young; her mother had remained an invalid for many years; and her brothers, in keeping with Indian tradition, had inherited the family's fortune, squandering it on drink and horses. Nanda and her husband had rescued Ila many times from penury by finding teaching and government posts for her. She failed in these posts, as she did in the piano and French lessons she gave. She had no attention span but thought she was "doing her duty" by fighting against child marriage and struggling for medical reform; but she alienated people at the same time.

When Ila finally leaves, walking down the hill "as jerky and crazy as an old puppet," Nanda sees her as "doomed" and "menaced" (133). How has she survived all these years? Nanda wonders. Hours pass. Suddenly, the telephone rings shrilly. Nanda picks up the receiver: Ila has been found raped and strangled. She must go to the police station to identify the body.

Nanda's shock is great—not because she loved Ila, but because Ila represented a segment of her past, even though it stood for all that was repugnant to her. Now it is dead, and with it the sham and facade that had been Ila's life. A woman who had never learned to face herself and had never grown up, Ila was no longer there to concoct lies and to share her little stories with Nanda. Her death means the end of illusion and of the sharing of lies.

This last wrenching away, this cutting out of part of her own flesh, forces the truth out of Nanda. She cries out to Raka, perhaps in desperation, that everything she had told her about her happy childhood, her wonderful parents, and her marvelous marriage had been an untruth. All had been a fabrication—fantasies that helped her sleep at night and stories that dulled the pain of her life. Nanda's father had been a traveling salesman; he had never been to Tibet. Her home as a child had never been filled with exotic animals, but merely with overfed dogs. As for her husband, he had neither loved nor cherished her. He had carried on a lifelong affair with the mathematics teacher in the school. He would have married her had she not been Christian. As for Nanda's children, they were "alien to her nature." She neither understood nor loved them. Nor had she chosen to live out the rest of her life at Carignano. Her children had forced it upon her for lack of anything better. Because her life has been so painful to her, Nanda cannot even mourn Ila's passing and the end of a world that had been so utterly barren and untenanted.

Strangely enough, Nanda's distress is such that Raka had left the house unnoticed, reappearing some time later as if from nowhere. Happiness radiates from her face. Why? Unbeknown to Nanda or the cook, Raka had taken a box of matches and had set fire to the grasses and trees. "Look, Nani," she says with extreme satisfaction, "I have set the forest on fire. Look, Nani, look—the forest is on fire." Nanda sits still on the stool. "Down in the ravine, the flames spat and crackled around the dirty wood and through the dry grass, and black smoke spiralled up over the mountain" (145).

Agni, the Purifier, has come to destroy Nanda's greatest illusion—that of life. With Ila's death, the last vestige of murkiness and inauthenticity has been wrenched from Nanda. Now that she is able to see beyond the ordinary world and the little impurities which have helped her make life bearable, love has taken over. Her joy in Raka, the Moon, her shadow factor, has made it possible for Nanda, the observer, the remote rationalist, the perfect wife and mother—the role model—to reconnect with her world of instinct, to feel into things, to experience *eros*. Accepted by the little Raka whom she had feared and rejected in the beginning, Nanda has been awakened to a new feeling dimension.

The presence of the Fire God, Agni, paves the way for the great liberation. Having experienced the meaning of love in Raka, an aspect of herself, Nanda is prepared to fulfill her potential: to experience the exit ritual. A correspondence between spirit and body has come into being. Past and present, mortal and immortal, fuse; Nanda Kaul is now one with herself and the Cosmos.

The great sacred fire which serves as a funnel between heaven and earth, and between humankind and divinity, heats the living cell, generates the living sparks of continuous activity, mixes and fluidifies the diverse, transmutes the formed into the formless.

The primeval sacrifice which gave birth to the Cosmic Being, according to Vedic scriptures, required self-immolation. Likewise, Nanda passes into living coals, thereby blending with Agni, deity's flame, and penetrating the "essence of fire"—the substance of eternal life. As written in the *Bhagavad Gita*:

> Both he who thinks that *this* can kill
> And he who thinks that *this* is killed,
> have neither truly understood,
> *this* does not kill, is never killed.
> He never dies and never born is he,
> came not to being and never comes to be,
> primeval, in the body's death unslain,
> unborn, eternal, everlastingly.
>
> Eternal and indestructible,
> this is unborn and unchangeable,
> and when a man knows this how may
> he kill, whom will he cause to slay? . . .
>
> 'Tis never cut and never burnt
> not ever wet or ever dry,
> eternal, ever-present, firm,
> this primal one, immovably.[16]

Fire, the purifier and regenerator, the devourer and illuminator, terminates Nanda Kaul's life, thereby breaking down the barriers of flesh and illusion. No longer does obstruction lie in the way of enlightenment. Energized and liquefied, the different planes of her psyche and consciousness allow an immanent or higher Self to be born. Like the Great God Shiva, who created the world as he danced the circular Nataraja—unifying space and time within evolution and surrounding himself by flames incarnating eternal energy—so Nanda is divested of dross. Her adamantine essence sparkles in all of its purity, beauty, and eternality.

Conclusion

"Our times, characterized as they are by an almost total disorientation in regard to the ends of human existence, stand in need, above all else, of a vast amount of psychological knowledge," Jung wrote. The creative process is one way of gaining access to the unfathomable and infinite sphere of knowledge.

What interests us in *Women in Twentieth-Century Literature: A Jungian View* are the disclosures—through sign and symbol—made by the ten authors whose works we have chosen to explore. Literary techniques reveal in part the authors' inner climates, moods, and glyphs—in sum, their psychological condition. What stereotypes, abstractions, or prescriptions are they intent upon abolishing or strengthening? What hidden factors lie dormant—*in potentia*—in the psyches of the female characters in the ten works discussed, and, by extension, in the psyches of women in general? Which ones need to be expressed and lived out in the real world as they have been in the literary domain?

Perhaps the reader of this book may be encouraged to go beyond the general categories in which the fictional characters have been placed, in order to probe the psychic parameters that motivate their behavior. The characters should not be viewed merely as passive or dictatorial, as good or evil, as modern or old-fashioned. Nuances and variegated perceptions may be added. Regardless of characteristics, every personage is unique and is an individual in the process of growing, discovering, and enriching or diminishing his or her being.

Speaking in general, we may say that making conscious certain factors involved in projection can help in the discovery and in the building of one's identity. What images or characteristics, for example, does one individual attribute to another? What do such contents indicate in terms of one's identification with that other person? How does she (or he) view that other person? As a threat? As an aid? And why? How did Elizabeth Bowen's teenager outgrow her projection in *The Death of the Heart*? Did Natalia Ginzburg's types in *All Our Yesterdays* ever learn to recognize their problems? If not, why not?

To understand the roles society or family has assigned to women, and to become aware of the virtues they must uphold and/or the qualities they must integrate (or not) within their personalities, are merely the first steps in the nurturing process. The *act* must follow. Whatever the steps, a decrease in self-repression or in social oppression allows women to discover their own ground-bed. No longer denied their due, they can reject the role of scapegoat. Women must learn to connect with pain as well as with joy. Let readers not fall into the same pattern as previous generations, allowing new polarized roles or fresh stereotypes to crystallize. Such would encourage barrenness, as in Yerma's case in García Lorca's play; or an eclipse of consciousness, such as the protagonist experiences in Jean Rhys's *Wide Sargasso Sea*. To revise and to renew with lucidity and openness of mind are the goals of the psychoanalytic process.

To explore the psyches of fictional creatures, as they live in the novels, tales, or plays of Sarraute, O'Connor, Dinesen, Lorca, Pa Chin, Enchi, Desai, Ginzburg, Bowen, and Rhys, is to encourage revelation—illumination—in the reader. Light may be shed upon what lies carefully hidden or dormant in their psyches, beyond the visible world. Glimpses into the subliminal spheres of others, even though they may be fictional beings, can pave the way for greater self-discernment and increased perception, thereby leading to a new birth for the reader. Just as an infant—the product of a *conjunctio*—needs nurturing and love, so characteristics, born from the deep, need attention to become strong and viable forces within an integrated personality. Relating to the psyche as a whole, and not compartmentalizing or secreting contents, paves the way for inner harmony and balance. The goal is to fluidify and not fixate, energize and not paralyze, feed and not starve the newly emerging and basically creative forces within each being.

Not everyone creates verbally, or dances, or sings, or performs. Nor are we all scientists capable of finding what Goethe termed the *Urpflanzen*. Yet, within each person exists an inner chamber where polarities fuse, conception occurs, and an embryo forms. Each one of us can fashion a labor room to facilitate the coming into the world of the new, the revolutionary, and the never before experienced. To give birth, as Lorca, Bowen, Dinesen, Ginzburg, O'Connor, Rhys, Sarraute, Pa Chin, Enchi, and Desai have done in their fiction, is to pave the way for confrontation, contestation, and praxis. It forces into the open what had remained hidden, shearing off the many protective layers which had been created to avoid life's struggles.

The ten writers whose works we have attempted to flesh out have revealed themselves plain via the creative genres most suitable to their talents. So, too, may the reader discover her or his own means of building a bridge to the outer world, and the wisdom necessary to convey unconscious and conscious feelings, values, archaic images, pulsations, and introjected opinions—energies crucial to the construction of a bridge leading within.

> *Forsake her not, and she shall preserve thee: love her, and she shall keep thee.*
>
> *Wisdom is the principal thing; therefore get wisdom: and with all thy getting get understanding.*
>
> *Proverbs 4:6–7*

Notes

Introduction

1. C. G. Jung, *The Visions Seminars*, 2, p. 414.
2. Edward Edinger, *Melville's Moby-Dick*, pp. 147–50.
3. Edward Edinger, "An Outline of Analytical Psychology," pp. 1–11.
4. Ibid.
5. Ibid.
6. Ibid.
7. Claire Douglas, "Analytical Psychology and the Feminine: A Historical and Critical Analysis," pp. 157ff.
8. Ibid., pp. 198ff.
9. Harold Stewart, *A Net of Fireflies*, p. 35.

Chapter 1

1. Federico García Lorca, *Tragedies*.
2. Rupert C. Allen, "Psyche and Symbol in the Theater of Federico García Lorca," in *Lorca: A Collection of Critical Essays*, ed. Manuel Duran, pp. 133–40.
3. Edward Edinger, "An Outline of Analytical Psychology," pp. 1–11.
4. Marion Woodman, *The Pregnant Virgin*, p. 81.
5. Marie Louise von Franz, *Apuleius' Golden Ass*, 2, p. xi.
6. Marina Werner, *Alone of All Her Sex*, p. 251.
7. Edward Edinger, "An Outline of Analytical Psychology," p. 9.
8. C. G. Jung, *Collected Works*, 5, pp. 100–101.
9. Lyn Cowan, *Masochism: A Jungian View*, p. 24.
10. Erich Neumann, *The Great Mother*, p. 99.
11. Liliane Frey-Rohn, "Evil from the Psychological Point of View," in *Evil*, p. 156.

Chapter 2

1. Edward Edinger, *Melville's Moby-Dick*, pp. 148–49.
2. See Allan E. Austin, *Elizabeth Bowen*, and Victoria Glendinning, *Elizabeth Bowen*.

3. Elizabeth Bowen, *The Death of the Heart*, p. 3. All quotations come from this edition.
4. Barbara Kirksey, "Hestia: A Background of Psychological Focusing," in *Facing the Gods*, pp. 101–12.
5. C. G. Jung and C. Kerenyi, *Essays on a Science of Mythology*, p. 80.
6. Erich Neumann, *The Child*, pp. 29–30.
7. Esther Harding, *The Parental Image*, p. 57.
8. Jung and Kerenyi, p. 87.
9. Edward Edinger, *Ego and Archetype*, p. 50.
10. Rivkah Scharf Kluger, *Satan in the Old Testament*, pp. 25–27.

Chapter 3

1. See Bettina Knapp, *Theatre and Alchemy*.
2. C. G. Jung, *Collected Works*, 13, p. 148.
3. Isak Dinesen, *Winter's Tales*.
4. *New Larousse Encyclopedia of Mythology*, pp. 256–57.
5. Esther Harding, *The I and the Not I*, p. 113; H. R. Ellis Davidson, *Scandinavian Mythology*, p. 42.
6. C. G. Jung, *Collected Works*, 6, p. 545.
7. Davidson, pp. 42–45.
8. Ibid., p. 92.
9. Frank Chapin Bray, *University Dictionary of Mythology*, p. 23.
10. James Graham-Campbell and Dafydd Kidd, *The Vikings*, pp. 25–32.
11. Emma Jung, *Animus and Anima*, pp. 54–55.
12. Birgitte Debusigne, "Karen Blixen's Literary Technique in *Out of Africa*," p. 2.

Chapter 4

1. Natalia Ginzburg, *All Our Yesterdays*. All quotations are taken from this edition.
2. Mario Jacoby, *Longing for Paradise*, p. 130.
3. Edward Edinger, *Ego and Archetype*, p. 18.
4. Esther Harding, *The Parental Image*, pp. 133–35.
5. Esther Harding, *The Way of All Women*, pp. 12–18.
6. Erich Neumann, *The Child*, p. 78.
7. Esther Harding, *Psychic Energy*, p. 219.
8. Erich Neumann, *Depth Psychology and a New Ethic*, p. 55.
9. C. G. Jung, *Collected Works*, 11, p. 76.
10. Neumann, *The Child*, p. 78.
11. Lyn Cowan, *Masochism: A Jungian View*, pp. 19–20.
12. Ibid., p. 70.
13. Ibid., pp. 59–60.
14. C. G. Jung, *Collected Works*, 9^1, p. 231.
15. Marie Louise von Franz, *Shadow and Evil in Fairy Tales*, pp. 213–15.
16. C. G. Jung, *Collected Works*, 8, p. 510.
17. Ibid., p. 349.
18. H. G. Baynes, *Mythology of the Soul*, p. 704.
19. Harding, *Psychic Energy*, p. 38.
20. Ibid., p. 45. From Richard Wilhelm, *The Secret of the Golden Flower*, p. 47.

Chapter 5

1. Flannery O'Connor, *Everything That Rises Must Converge*, Introduction by Robert Fitzgerald, p. viii.

2. All quotations come from the above edition.
3. *The New Columbia Encyclopedia*.
4. Esther Harding, *Woman's Mysteries*, p. 153.
5. George Ferguson, *Signs and Symbols in Christian Art*, p. 152.
6. Carol Schloss, *Flannery O'Connor's Dark Comedies*, p. 13. From *The Fragments of the Works of Heraclitus of Ephesus*, trans. G. T. W. Patrick (Baltimore: University of Maryland Press, 1889), p. 86.
7. Fitzgerald, Introduction to *Everything That Rises Must Converge*, p. xii.
8. Marie Louise von Franz, *Shadow and Evil in Fairy Tales*, p. 40.
9. Harding, *Woman's Mysteries*, p. 192.
10. Ibid., p. 194.
11. Edward Edinger, *Ego and Archetype*, p. 245. From C. G. Jung, *Collected Works*, 14, p. 307.
12. Harding, *Woman's Mysteries*, p. 205.
13. Franz, *Shadow and Evil in Fairy Tales*, p. 173.
14. Mircea Eliade, *Patterns in Comparative Religion*, pp. 14ff.

Chapter 6

1. *The Letters of Jean Rhys*, p. 157.
2. C. G. Jung, *Collected Works*, 14, p. 417.
3. Marie Louise von Franz, *Individuation in Fairy Tales*, p. 120. See Martha Harrell's "The Hidden Self: A Study in the Development of the Feminine Psyche."
4. *Letters*, p. 232. To Diana Athill, Aug. 16, 1963.
5. Marie Louise von Franz, *Shadow and Evil in Fairy Tales*, p. 258.
6. Esther Harding, *The I and the Not I*, p. 39.
7. Edward Edinger, *Ego and Archetype*, p. 4.
8. Edward Edinger, "An Outline of Analytical Psychology," p. 9.
9. Juana Elbein dos Santos, "Resistance et cohesion de groupe," pp. 123–24.
10. Esther Harding, *Psychic Energy*, p. 165.

Chapter 7

1. June Singer, *Androgyny*, p. 11. From Pierre Teilhard de Chardin, *The Prayer of the Universe*, p. 143.
2. Singer, p. 33. From Mircea Eliade, *Mephistopheles and the Androgyne*, p. 100.
3. Jean Shinoda Bolen, *Goddesses in Everywoman*, p. 74.
4. Nathalie Sarraute, *L'ère du soupçon*, pp. 6–9.
5. Ibid.
6. Micheline Tison Braun, *Nathalie Sarraute ou la recherche de l'authenticité*, pp. 11–12.
7. Bettina L. Knapp, *Off-Stage Voices*, p. 173.
8. Gershom G. Scholem, *Major Trends in Jewish Mysticism*, pp. 75–76; pp. 217ff.
9. Ibid., pp. 217ff.
10. Nathalie Sarraute, *Between Life and Death* (translation), p. 1; *Entre la vie et la mort*, p. 7.
11. Valerie Minogue, *Nathalie Sarraute and the War of the Words*, p. 150. See Gretchen Besser, *Nathalie Sarraute*.
12. C. G. Jung, *Collected Works*, "Analytical Psychology," p. 192.
13. Barbara Hannah, *Encounters with the Soul: Active Imagination*, p. 1. Introduction by Marie Louise von Franz.
14. Braun, 225.
15. Ibid., p. 223.

Chapter 8

1. Pa Chin, *Family*, pp. vii–xxvi.
2. Laurence G. Thompson, *Chinese Religion: An Introduction*, p. 5.
3. *The Sayings of Confucius*, p. 21.
4. Thompson, p. 39.
5. *Confucius: The Analects*, p. 13.
6. Thompson, p. 5.
7. Marie Louise von Franz, *Creation Myths*, p. 197.
8. C. G. Jung, *Collected Works*, 8, p. 213.
9. Franz, *Creation Myths*, p. 7. From C. G. Jung, *Collected Works*, 6, pp. 552–53.
10. C. G. Jung, *Collected Works*, 10, p. 498.
11. C. G. Jung, *Dream Analysis*, p. 416.
12. Thompson, p. 6.
13. Ibid., p. 10.
14. Ibid., p. 27.
15. Charles Ponce, *The Nature of the I Ching*, p. 8.
16. Thompson, p. 35.
17. C. G. Jung, *Collected Works*, 11, p. 600.
18. C. A. S. Williams, *Chinese Symbolism and Art Motives*, p. 135.
19. Ibid.
20. C. G. Jung, *Collected Works*, 14, p. 52.
21. Marie Louise von Franz, *Shadow and Evil in Fairy Tales*, p. 5.
22. Williams, p. 233; *Sources of Chinese Tradition*, 1, p. 175.
23. *The Sayings of Confucius*, p. 27.
24. Thompson, p. 37.
25. Geoffrey Parrinder, *Sex in the World Religions*, p. 85.
26. Ibid.
27. Richard Wilhelm, *Lectures on the I Ching*, p. 145.
28. *Confucius: The Analects*, p. 25; Parrinder, p. 90.
29. Parrinder, p. 90. From *The Book of Rites*.
30. Ibid., p. 91.
31. Ibid., p. 92.
32. Marion Woodman, *Addiction to Perfection*, p. 20.
33. Bani Shorter, "The Concealed Body Language of Anorexia Nervosa," pp. 1–27.
34. *The Sayings of Confucius*, p. 43.
35. Marie Louise von Franz, *The Feminine in Fairytales*, 2, p. 20.
36. Thompson, p. 39.
37. Wilhelm, *Lectures on the I Ching*, p. 4.
38. Liliane Frey-Rohn, "Evil from the Psychological Point of View," in *Evil*, p. 36.
39. *The Sayings of Confucius*, p. 76.

Chapter 9

1. Pallas Athena, the Greek goddess of wisdom, was born from Zeus's forehead.
2. Hayao Kawai, "The Figure of the Sun Goddess in Japanese Mythology."
3. Sokyo Ono, *Shinto: The Kami Way*, p. 42.
4. Esther Harding, *Psychic Energy*, p. 163.
5. *Sources of Japanese Tradition*, 1, p. 177.
6. Yolande Jacobi, *Complex Archetype Symbol in the Psychology of C. G. Jung*, p. 36.
7. Fumiko Enchi, *Masks*, p. 3.
8. Michael Czaja, *Gods of Myth: Stone Phallicism in Japanese Folk Religion*, p. 187.
9. Associations may be made with the Tantric Shakti; the Sumerian Innaga; the Babylonian Ishtar; the Canaanite Ashtart. See Merlin Stone, *Ancient Mirrors of Womanhood*.

10. C. G. Jung, *Collected Works*, 16, p. 179.
11. William K. Bunce, *Religions in Japan*, p. 103.
12. Mircea Eliade, *Patterns in Comparative Religion*, p. 399.
13. Esther Harding, *The Way of All Women*, p. 58.
14. Ibid., p. 185.
15. Czaja, p. 208.
16. Murray Stein, "A Polarity in Conscience: Solar and Lunar Aspects," p. 26.
17. Kawai, p. 76.
18. C. G. Jung, *Collected Works*, 7, p. 222.
19. Ibid., 4, p. 130.
20. Ibid., 3, p. 40.
21. Czaja, p. 210.

Chapter 10

1. Mircea Eliade, *Rites and Symbols of Initiation*, p. ix.
2. Mircea Eliade, *Yoga*, p. 247.
3. Merlin Stone, *Ancient Mirrors of Womanhood*, p. 16.
4. Eliade, *Yoga*, p. 133.
5. *The Bhagavad Gita*, 2, p. 29.
6. Manisha Roy, *Bengali Woman*, p. 41.
7. *Sources of Indian Tradition*, 1, pp. 211–19.
8. Heinrich Zimmer, *Philosophies of India*, pp. 41, 44.
9. Heinrich Zimmer, *Myths and Symbols in Indian Art and Civilization*, p. 127.
10. Ibid., p. 215.
11. Stone, p. 23.
12. W. J. Wilkins, *Hindu Mythology*, pp. 21–29.
13. *Sources of Indian Tradition*, 1, pp. 7–8.
14. C. G. Jung, *Collected Works*, 8, pp. 29–30.
15. Ann Belford Ulanov, *Receiving Woman*, pp. 18–19.
16. *The Bhagavad Gita*, pp. 10–11.

Bibliography

Allen, Rupert C. *Psyche and Symbol in the Theatre of Federico García Lorca*. Austin: University of Texas Press, 1974.

Austin, Allan E. *Elizabeth Bowen*. New York: Twayne Publishers, 1971.

Baynes, H. G. *Mythology of the Soul*. Baltimore: Williams and Wilkins, 1940.

Besser, Gretchen Rous. *Nathalie Sarraute*. Boston: Twayne Publishers, 1979.

The Bhagavad Gita. Translated by Geoffrey Parrinder. New York: E. P. Dutton and Co., 1975.

Bolen, Jean Shinoda. *Goddesses in Everywoman*. San Francisco: Harper and Row, 1948.

Bowen, Elizabeth. *The Death of the Heart*. New York: Alfred A. Knopf, 1966.

Braun, Micheline Tison. *Nathalie Sarraute ou la recherche de l'authenticité*. Paris: Gallimard, 1971.

Bray, Frank Chapin. *University Dictionary of Mythology*. New York: Thomas Y. Crowell Co., 1964.

Bunce, William K. *Religions in Japan*. Tokyo: Charles E. Tuttle Co., 1970.

Castillejo, Irene Claremont de. *Knowing Woman*. New York: G. P. Putnam's, 1973.

Confucius: The Analects. Translated by D. C. Lau. New York: Penguin Books, 1979.

Cowan, Lyn. *Masochism: A Jungian View*. Thalwil, Switzerland: Spring Publications, 1982.

Czaja, Michael. *Gods of Myth: Stone Phallicism in Japanese Folk Religion*. Tokyo: Weatherhill, 1974.

Davidson, H. R. Ellis. *Scandinavian Mythology*. New York: Paul Hamlyn, 1969.

Debusigne, Birgitte. "Karen Blixen's Literary Technique in *Out of Africa*." Nice: Faculte des lettres et sciences humaines de l'Université de Nice, mai 1985. Unpublished.

Desai, Anita. *Fire on the Mountain*. New York: Penguin Books, 1981.

Dinesen, Isak. *Winter's Tales*. New York: Vintage Books, 1970.

Douglas, Claire. "Analytical Psychology and the Feminine: A Historical and Critical Analysis." Thesis, Saybrook Institute, Oct. 1984.

Duran, Manuel, ed. *Lorca: A Collection of Critical Essays*. Englewood Cliffs: Prentice-Hall, 1962.

Edinger, Edward. "An Outline of Analytical Psychology." *Quadrant* 1 (1968).

———. *Ego and Archetype*. New York: G. P. Putnam's, 1972.

———. *Melville's Moby-Dick*. New York: A New Directions Book, 1978.

Eliade, Mircea. *Rites and Symbols of Initiation*. New York: Harper Torchbooks, 1965.

———. *Yoga*. Princeton: Princeton University Press, 1973.

———. *Patterns in Comparative Religion*. New York: New American Library, 1974.

Enchi, Fumiko. *Masks*. Translated by Juliet Winters Carpenter. New York: Random House, 1983.

Ferguson, George. *Signs and Symbols in Christian Art*. London: Oxford University Press, 1973.

Franz, Marie Louise von. *Apuleius' Golden Ass*. New York: Spring Publications, 1970.

———. *Creation Myths*. Zurich: Spring Publications, 1972.

———. *The Feminine in Fairytales*. New York: Spring Publications, 1972.

———. *Number and Time*. Translated by Andrea Dykes. Evanston: Northwestern University Press, 1974.

———. *Shadow and Evil in Fairy Tales*. Zurich: Spring Publications, 1974.

———. *Individuation in Fairy Tales*. Zurich: Spring Publications, 1977.

Frey-Rohn, Liliane. "Evil from the Psychological Point of View." In *Evil*, edited by the Jung Institute Curatorium. Evanston: Northwestern University Press, 1967.

Ginzburg, Natalia. *All Our Yesterdays*. Translated by Angus Davidson. Exeter, England: Carcanet Press, 1985.

Glendinning, Victoria. *Elizabeth Bowen*. New York: Alfred A. Knopf, 1978.

Goldenberg, Naomi. *Changing of the Gods*. Boston: Beacon Press, 1979.

Graham-Campbell, James, and Dafydd Kidd. *The Vikings*. New York: Metropolitan Museum of Art, 1980.

Hannah, Barbara. *Encounters with the Soul: Active Imagination*. Santa Monica, California: Sigo Press, 1981.

Harding, Esther. *The Parental Image*. New York: G. P. Putnam's, 1965.

———. *The Way of All Women*. New York: Harper Colophon Books, 1965.

———. *Woman's Mysteries*. New York: G. P. Putnam's, 1971.

———. *The I and the Not I*. Princeton: Princeton University Press, 1973.

———. *Psychic Energy*. Princeton: Princeton University Press, 1973.

Harrell, Martha. "The Hidden Self: A Study in the Development of the Feminine Psyche." Thesis, C. G. Jung Training Institute, New York City, 1983.

Jacobi, Yolande. *Complex Archetype Symbol in the Psychology of C. G. Jung*. Princeton: Princeton University Press, 1957.

Jacoby, Mario. *Longing for Paradise*. Boston: Sigo Press, 1985.

Jung, C. G. *Collected Works*. Vol. 1–20. Princeton: Princeton University Press, 1957–79.

———. *The Visions Seminars*. Vol. 2. Zurich: Spring Publications, 1976.

———. *Dream Analysis*. Princeton: Princeton University Press, 1984.

Jung, C. G., and C. Kerenyi. *Essays on a Science of Mythology*. Princeton: Princeton University Press, 1969.

Jung, Emma. *Animus and Anima*. Zurich: Spring Publications, 1972.

Kawai, Hayao. "The Figure of the Sun Goddess in Japanese Mythology." Unpublished thesis presented at the Jung Institute, Zurich, December 1964.

Kirksey, Barbara. "Hestia: A Background of Psychological Focusing." In *Facing the Gods*, edited by James Hillman. Irving, Texas: Spring Publications, 1980.

Kluger, Rivkah Scharf. *Satan in the Old Testament*. Translated by Hildegard Nagel. Evanston: Northwestern University Press, 1967.

Knapp, Bettina L. *Off-Stage Voices*. Troy, New York: The Whitston Press, 1975.

———. *Theatre and Alchemy*. Detroit: Wayne State University Press, 1980.

———. *A Jungian Approach to Literature*. Carbondale: Southern Illinois University Press, 1984.

———. *Archetype, Architecture, and the Writer*. Bloomington: Indiana University Press, 1986.

Lauter, Estella, and Carol S. Rupprecht, eds. *Feminist Archetypal Theory*. Knoxville: University of Tennessee Press, 1985.

The Letters of Jean Rhys. Selected and edited by Francis Wyndham and Diana Melly. New York: Viking, 1984.

Londre, Felicia Hardison. *Federico García Lorca*. New York: F. Ungar Pub. Co., 1984.

Lorca, Federico García. *Tragedies*. Translated by James Graham-Lujan and Richard L. O'Connell. New York: A New Directions Book, 1955.

Meier, C. A. *The Unconscious in Its Empirical Manifestations: Creative Effects of the Unconscious*. Translated by Eugene Rolf. Boston: Sigo Press, 1984.

Minogue, Valerie. *Nathalie Sarraute and the War of the Words*. Edinburgh: Edinburgh University Press, 1981.

Neumann, Erich. *The Great Mother*. New York: Pantheon Books, 1955.

———. *Depth Psychology and a New Ethic*. New York: G. P. Putnam's, 1969.

———. *The Child*. New York: G. P. Putnam's, 1973.

The New Columbia Encyclopedia. New York: Columbia University Press, 1975.

New Larousse Encyclopedia of Mythology. Translated by Richard Aldington and Delano Ames. Hong Kong: Hamlyn House, 1959.

Ochs, Carol. *Behind the Sex of God*. Boston: Beacon Press, 1977.

O'Connor, Flannery. *Everything That Rises Must Converge*. Introduction by Robert Fitzgerald. New York: Farrar, Straus and Giroux, 1985.

Ono, Sokyo. *Shinto: The Kami Way*. Tokyo: Charles E. Tuttle, 1963.

Pa Chin. *Family*. New York: Anchor Books, 1972.

Parrinder, Geoffrey. *Sex in the World Religions*. New York: Oxford University Press, 1980.

Ponce, Charles. *The Nature of the I Ching*. New York: Award Books, 1970.

Pratt, Annis. *Archetypal Patterns in Women's Fiction*. Bloomington: Indiana University Press, 1981.

Rhys, Jean. *Wide Sargasso Sea*. New York: W. W. Norton and Co., 1982.

Roy, Manisha. *Bengali Woman*. Chicago: University of Chicago Press, 1975.

Santos, Juana Elbein dos. "Resistance et cohesion de groupe." *Archives de sciences sociales des religions* (janvier-mars 1979).

Sarraute, Nathalie. *L'ère du soupçon*. Paris: Gallimard, 1956.

———. *Entre la vie et la mort*. Paris: Gallimard, 1968.

———. *Between Life and Death*. Translated by Maria Jolas. New York: George Braziller, 1969.

The Sayings of Confucius. Translated by James R. Ware. New York: A Mentor Book, 1955.

Schloss, Carol. *Flannery O'Connor's Dark Comedies*. Baton Rouge: Louisiana State University Press, 1980.

Scholem, Gershom G. *Major Trends in Jewish Mysticism*. New York: Schocken Books, 1965.

Shorter, Bani. "The Concealed Body Language of Anorexia Nervosa." Lecture at the 8th International Congress for Analytical Psychology, San Francisco, Sept. 1980.

Singer, June. *Androgyny*. New York: Anchor Press/Doubleday, 1976.

Sources of Chinese Tradition. Vol. 1. Compiled by Wm. Theodore de Bary, Wing-Tsit Chan, Burton Watson. Vol. 2. Compiled by Wm. Theodore de Bary, Wing-Tsit Chan, Chester Tan. New York: Columbia University Press, 1960 and 1964.

Sources of Indian Tradition. Vol. 1. Edited by Wm. Theodore de Bary. Compiled by A. L. Basham, R. N. Dandekar, Peter Hardy, V. Raghavan, R. Weiler. Vol. 2. Edited by Theodore de Bary. Compiled by Stephen Hay and I. H. Qureshi. New York: Columbia University Press, 1958.

Sources of Japanese Tradition. Vol. 1. Edited by Wm. Theodore de Bary. Compiled by Ryusaku Tsunoda, Wm. Theodore de Bary, Donald Keene. New York: Columbia University Press, 1963.

Stein, Murray. "A Polarity in Conscience: Solar and Lunar Aspects." Diploma thesis, C. G. Jung Institute, Zurich, 1973.

Stewart, Harold, ed. and trans. *A Net of Fireflies*. Tokyo: Charles E. Tuttle Co., 1960.

Stone, Merlin. *Ancient Mirrors of Womanhood*. Vol. 2. New York: Sibylline Books, 1979.

Thompson, Laurence G. *Chinese Religion: An Introduction*. Belmont, California: Dickenson Publishing Co., 1969.

Ulanov, Ann Belford. *Receiving Woman*. Philadelphia: The Westminster Press, 1981.

Werner, Marina. *Alone of All Her Sex*. New York: Alfred A. Knopf, 1976.

Wilhelm, Richard. *The Secret of the Golden Flower*. New York: Harcourt, Brace and World, 1969.

———. *Lectures on the I Ching*. Princeton: Princeton University Press, 1979.

Wilkins, W. J. *Hindu Mythology*. Bombay: Rupa and Co., 1981.

Williams, C. A. S. *Chinese Symbolism and Art Motives*. New York: The Julian Press, 1960.

Woodman, Marion. *Addiction to Perfection*. Toronto: Inner City Books, 1982.

———. *The Pregnant Virgin*. Toronto: Inner City Books, 1985.

Zimmer, Heinrich. *Myths and Symbols in Indian Art and Civilization*. Princeton: Princeton University Press, 1974.

———. *Philosophies of India*. Princeton: Princeton University Press, 1974.

Index